PRACTICAL CT TECHNOLOGY AND TECHNIQUES

Practical CT Technology and Techniques

Lincoln L. Berland, M.D.

Associate Professor of Radiology
Chief, Body Computed Tomography and Sonography
University of Alabama at Birmingham
Birmingham, Alabama

Raven Press New York

Raven Press, 1185 Avenue of the Americas, New York, New York 10036

Made in the United States of America
9 8 7 6 5 4 3 2 1

Library of Congress Cataloging-in-Publication Data

Berland, Lincoln L.
Practical CT.

Includes bibliographies and index.
1. Tomography—Technique—Handbooks, manuals, etc.
2. Diagnosis, Radioscopic—Technique—Handbooks, manuals, etc. I. Title. [DNLM: 1. Tomography, X-Ray Computed—methods. WN 160 B514p]
RC78.7.T6B46 1986 616.07′572 86-19947
ISBN 0-88167-261-0

The material contained in this volume was submitted as previously unpublished material, except in the instances in which credit has been given to the source from which some of the illustrative material was derived.

Great care has been taken to maintain the accuracy of the information contained in the volume. However, Raven Press cannot be held responsible for errors or for any consequences arising from the use of the information contained herein.

To Nancy, Matthew, and Nicole,
my supportive and patient family

Preface

As the first word of the title of this text suggests, its primary objective is to present computed tomographic (CT) technology and techniques in a practical form. Although these topics are often discussed from a technical perspective, my purpose is to blend the physicists' and engineers' science and technology of creating machines with the radiologists' art of creating images. As a radiologist with an interest in the physical aspects of imaging, and having trained during the period of rapid evolution of CT, I have tried to learn to sort relevant from irrelevant technical material. In this book, I have tried to communicate this sense of relevance clearly, in a form digestible even to those with a distaste for such topics.

As these goals indicate, this text is intended for both the radiologist performing CT and the radiologist-in-training. Although the section on examination technique protocols in Part 2 excludes examination protocols for the head and spine and for pediatric CT, there is much in both parts that is relevant to neuroradiologists and pediatric radiologists.

Of further use to the radiology resident is the discussion of several principles of X-ray physics and technology that apply to both CT and general radiography. Such topics as the modulation transfer function (MTF), magnification, and the X-ray tube are often feared by the resident who has little technical background or aptitude. Therefore, these concepts are discussed in nonmathematical terms with the intent of creating a comfortable familiarity, leading, I hope, to a willingness to learn more about and to use these ideas to improve examination quality.

Chapters 1 through 10 are structured to provide an understanding of both the principles of CT and of the usefulness of these principles. Other material in these chapters is required as a background for understanding further concepts, to provide a more complete discussion, and to answer the questions of those who simply are curious about the mechanisms and process of image generation. Chapters 11 and 12 are designed both to be read through and to be used as a reference for recognizing, understanding, and correcting image artifacts and mechanical malfunctions. Chapter 13 is addressed to individuals trying to decide which model of scanner to buy and what options to purchase.

Part 2 is an expansion of a commonly used form of cookbook "technique manual" for specific CT examinations excluding the head and spine, and examinations of children. To make this portion of the book applicable to many different scanners, institutions, and personal preferences, I have used a descriptive outline format, including ranges of suggested values and the rationales supporting various technique selections.

Among the difficult tasks in constructing this book was writing it to apply to the multitude of scanners in current use and to various radiologic practice situations, creating a balanced view of the strengths and weaknesses of those scanners that are still commercially available (many with which I have had no personal experience), and avoiding material that is likely to become quickly obsolete. To achieve this, I established contact with all the current manufacturers of CT scanners worldwide, all of whom were cooperative and helpful and are cited in the acknowledgments. I have also included illustrations provided by manufacturers and have mentioned many of the features that the manufacturers themselves believe are unique or particularly advantageous about their own units.

However, the requirements of general applicability and timeliness have necessarily prevented inclusion of much of the information that applies to any particular scanner. Discussions in the text that refer to technical factors for one scanner are drawn from personal experience and are intended only to illustrate broader principles.

The last and most difficult burden was the pursuit of accuracy. Partly because of its youth and commercial importance, CT is beset by an incomplete standardization of terminology and a relative dearth of written information directed to the radiologist. Additionally, having completed my formal technical education at the undergraduate level, I required the extensive assistance and extreme patience of Gary T. Barnes, Ph.D., Professor of Radiology and Chief, Division of Radiological Physics, University of Alabama at Birmingham. Despite these precautions, those who are technically astute or who have a particular interest or more experience with certain areas discussed may detect inaccuracies or omissions. I hope and believe that these are few in number and minor in importance.

As CT "high technology" evolves to higher technology, the need to completely understand CT equipment and examination techniques and to appreciate its vast and growing capabilities grows in importance. I hope that this work helps fill the need for the broader appreciation of this potential.

Acknowledgments

There were two prerequisites to my undertaking the writing of this book. The first and most crucial was the willingness of Gary T. Barnes, Ph.D., Professor of Radiology and Chief, Division of Radiological Physics, University of Alabama at Birmingham, to support and assist me. During numerous sessions, Dr. Barnes patiently led me through a more complete understanding of the complex technical issues that affect CT examination quality. He was of the greatest possible assistance and also provided invaluable comments from reviews of several versions of the manuscript.

This second necessary element was the Apple Macintosh computer. I certainly would not have attempted such an undertaking without being able to interact freely with the manuscript during drafting, revision, and reorganization. Also, all of the line drawings not supplied by CT manufacturers were generated on the Macintosh using MacPaint by Apple, ClickArt Effects from T/Maker Graphics, and ThunderScan by Thunderware, Inc. I hope the reader will find that the use of this word processing equipment and graphics capability has helped lead to clarity and good organization.

I also thank others who provided many helpful suggestions after reviewing all or parts of the manuscript, including Robert J. Stanley, M.D., Robert E. Koehler, M.D., and A. V. Lakshminarayanan, Ph.D. I also gratefully acknowledge those who have taught me the most about clinical body CT scanning, and who have provided invaluable support and direction, including Robert J. Stanley, M.D., Thomas L. Lawson, M.D., and W. Dennis Foley, M.D.

During the preparation of this manuscript, I established contact with representatives of each of the current manufacturers of CT equipment. All were helpful and open in revealing technical specifications and details about their instruments. Thus, I would like to thank A. Robert Sohval, Ph.D., CT Product Manager, Elscint, Inc.; Patricia Brigman, Manager, CT Product Planning, General Electric Company; Cynthia L. Haugland, Marketing Product Manager, Imatron, Inc.; Walter E. Cullen, CT Technical Marketing Manager, Philips Medical Systems; Roger N. Phillips, CT Marketing Manager, Picker Corporation; Diane Poles, CT Product Specialist, Siemens Medical Systems, Inc.; Mardi Sawyer, CT Product Specialist, Thomson-CGR Medical Corporation; and Don Karle, Product Manager, CT, Toshiba Medical Systems.

Over several years, many others also taught me the principles that provided a basis for understanding the concepts discussed in this book. Unfortunately, the engineers, physicists, marketing and sales specialists, and radiologist colleagues are too numerous to mention individually. This background provided the basis for my interest in this topic and awareness of its great importance and underemphasis.

I also thank Anthony F. Zagar for his expert preparation of prints for the illustrations and Gail Stewart for her invaluable assistance in manuscript preparation.

Contents

Part 1
Practical CT Technology

1

Introduction to the Technological Principles of CT

In conventional radiography, three-dimensional objects are viewed in two dimensions. That is, the complex shape, internal structure, and anatomic relationships of organs are reduced to a flat film. In contrast, cross-sectional techniques exclude confusing superimposed structures from the image, displaying only two physical dimensions on the two-dimensional film. Conventional X-ray tomography is similar to sonography and computed tomography in this way, but conventional tomography blurs superimposed slices (Fig. 1-1) (1), whereas the newer methods simply do not include the information from these slices at all (Fig. 1-2).

However, each slice on a CT scan does have a specific thickness, usually 8 to 10 mm for body scanning, and this is the source of troublesome artifacts, which will be discussed later. The third dimension of length is restored to the examination by scanning levels in succession and viewing them sequentially.

Another advantage of CT is its high sensitivity to small differences in X-ray attenuation. This is partly accomplished by avoiding the imaging of superimposed structures, which is also termed *structural noise* (2). CT also displays slight attenuation differences well because of the high percentage of photons detected, and because the contribution of nonuseful scattered X-rays is reduced. In conventional radiography, scattered photons carrying no useful information cause a significant percentage of film darkening, which decreases contrast (see Chapter 10, p. 134) (4). In CT, scatter is reduced by collimating the beam near the X-ray source and in some cases beyond the patient, and by filtering the transmitted beam at the detector assembly by the shape and nature of the detectors and the spacers between each detector elements (3). For example, one system uses a grid fixed to the detector array to suppress scattered radiation. Others have long, slender detectors which help to perform this function in a similar manner to a grid. Still other units depend primarily on an air gap (Fig. 1-3) to reduce the contribution of scatter. The effectiveness of suppressing scatter varies greatly among scanners and seriously affects image quality.

The most important disadvantages of CT compared to conventional radiography are lower spatial resolution and long exposure times. Spatial resolution is determined by specific measurements made with test objects

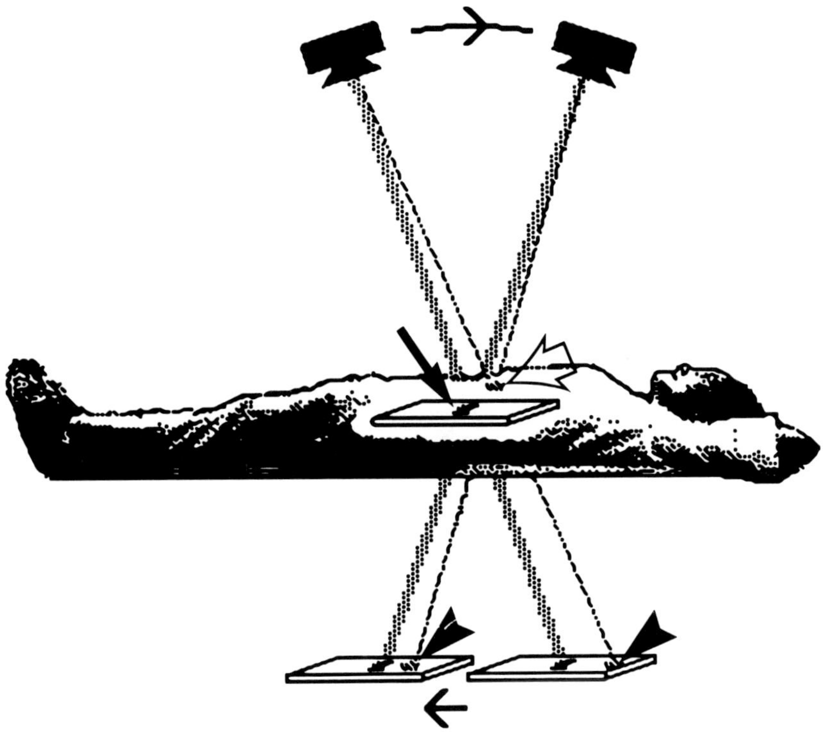

FIG. 1–1. Patient undergoing conventional tomography. Motion of the tube and the X-ray film is coordinated so that a structure within the selected plane of section (long arrow) is projected on the same point on the film throughout the exposure. A structure (open arrow) outside the selected plane of section is projected on different parts of the film (arrowheads) during the exposure so that it is blurred on the image.

in which rows of small holes are embedded. A spatial resolution of 1 mm indicates the ability to visually separate adjacent structures only 1 mm apart within such an object. The best spatial resolution currently available with CT is about 0.35 mm, versus 0.25 mm or better with conventional radiography. However, this spatial resolution value for CT is somewhat deceiving because such high resolution is not routinely achieved. Also, spatial resolution should be distinguished from the ability to perceive clinically relevant detail, which is dependent on but not the same as spatial resolution (see Chapter 8, p. 89). For example, structures such as gas bubbles or surgical staples may be visible even though smaller than the rated spatial resolution if they are quite different in density from their surroundings, whereas a larger structure may be invisible if it is similar in density to its environment. Also, the location of small objects relative to the position of the pixel (picture element; see chapter 5, pp. 49) in which they may be seen may affect visualization (5). That is, if a tiny object falls on the border between two

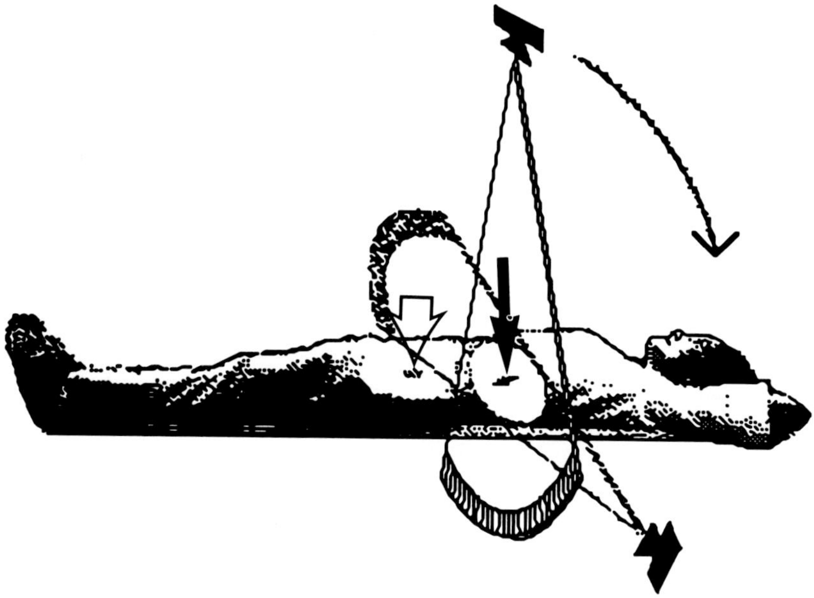

FIG. 1–2. Patient undergoing computed tomography. With CT, only structures (long straight arrow) within the selected plane of section are exposed to X-rays. There is no superimposition or blurring of structures (open arrow) outside the plane of section.

pixels, its density may be averaged between the adjacent pixels and the object will be invisible, whereas if it falls squarely within a pixel it might be seen.

In some systems, particularly older ones, the ability to perceive clinically relevant detail is limited by the method chosen to display the image. That is, between 256 and 512 rows and columns of pixels are shown, which may limit depiction of detail to less than that inherent within the original data before computer calculations. When in addition the thickness of the slice is being considered, the term *voxel,* or volume element, is used. For routine scanning techniques, this usually means that each pixel represents a block of tissue (voxel) measuring about 1 × 1 × 10 mm. Thus we cannot often expect to see structures smaller than that unless they are quite different in attenuation from their surroundings (see Chapter 5, pp. 45, 47). In most currently available systems, display is well matched to resolution, and detail is limited only by the X-ray geometry rather than by the method chosen for display. Nevertheless, the diagnostic handicap of lower spatial resolution than we are accustomed to with conventional radiography is usually overcome by the advantage of eliminating the superimposition of adjacent anatomic structures (eliminating structural noise).

Long exposure time is a serious problem that has been addressed by every CT manufacturer. Early body scanners acquired data for 2½ min to obtain

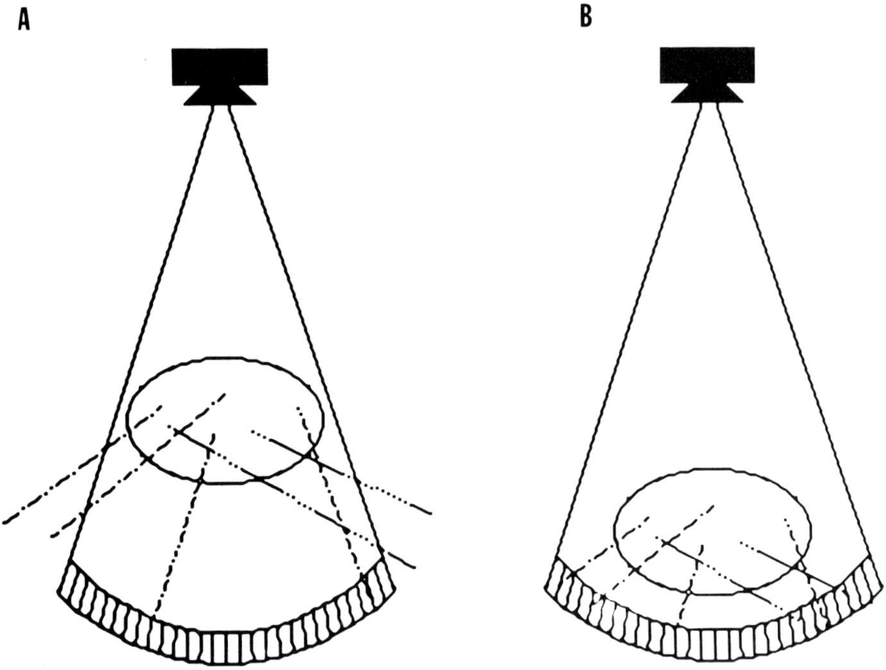

FIG. 1–3. Effect of an air gap on scattered radiation striking the X-ray detectors. **A**. The detectors are placed at a distance from the patient, and much scattered radiation passes to the sides of the detectors. **B**. The detector is closer to the patient, and more of the scattered X-rays strike the detector array.

a single picture. Contemporary scanners typically take from 50 msec to 5 sec to acquire data for one scan, exposing the patient to a fraction of the X-ray dose formerly required and producing an image considerably better than what was once considered miraculous. However, there are still limitations with scanning times even in the range of 1 to 10 sec (see Chapter 5, p. 59). Patient breathing and motion, bowel motion, pulsating blood vessels, and the beating heart may all contribute to nondiagnostic images or examinations, even with the best scanners. Subsecond scanning may help solve some of these problems, but the fundamental physical limitations of CT will persist, as will be outlined in later chapters.

REFERENCES

1. Coulam, C. M., Erickson, J. J., and Gibbs, S. J. (1981): Image and equipment considerations in conventional tomography. In: *The Physical Basis of Medical Imaging,* edited by C. M. Coulam, J. J. Erickson, F. D. Rollo, and A. E. James, pp. 123–140. Appleton-Century-Crofts, New York.
2. Hanson, K. M. (1981): Noise and contrast discrimination in computed tomography. In:

Radiology of the Skull and Brain: Technical Aspects of Computed Tomography, edited by T. H. Newton and D. G. Potts, pp. 3941–3955. C. V. Mosby, St. Louis.

3. Joseph, P. M. (1981): Artifacts in computed tomography. In: *Radiology of the Skull and Brain: Technical Aspects of Computed Tomography,* edited by T. H. Newton and D. G. Potts, pp. 3956–3992. C. V. Mosby, St. Louis.
4. Meredith, W. J., and Massey, J. B. (1977): Diagnostic radiology: the effects and control of scattered radiation. In: *Fundamental Physics of Radiology,* 3rd edition, Chapter XX, pp. 244–263. Year Book Medical Publishers, Chicago.
5. Zatz, L. M. (1981): Basic principles of computed tomography scanning. In: *Radiology of the Skull and Brain: Technical Aspects of Computed Tomography,* edited by T. H. Newton and D. G. Potts, pp. 3853–3876. C. V. Mosby, St. Louis.

2

Basic Technological Aspects of CT Scanners

This chapter highlights 11 basic aspects of CT scanners: CT "generations" and design; the X-ray source; detectors; magnification; the focal spot; detector aperture; collmation; calibration; table shape and material; table weight limitations, height adjustment, and ability to increment in small steps; and gantry aperture and structure. The discussion of these will help lead to a better understanding of the differences between scanners and provide a foundation for understanding selectable factors that affect image quality.

CT GENERATIONS AND DESIGN

The term *generation* as used to label types of CT equipment has been at times considered a status symbol by those possessing units of a later generation. The generation terminology was coined by one of the major CT manufacturers to help market its new X-ray geometry design. Competitors cleverly one-upped them, the terminology has stuck, and the significance of CT generations continues to be misunderstood. The generation number of a scanner simply refers to its fundamental tube-detector structure and not to the many other factors that together contribute to the quality of its images. Each design has its peculiar advantages and deficiencies, which must be weighed against each other. **It is the manner in which a manufacturer compensates for design deficiencies and exploits its strengths that determines the relative value of the machine** (15).

A first-generation system is one in which a thin, tubular X-ray beam is passed linearly over the patient, with a single detector mechanically following the X-ray source on the far side of the patient. After a single pass, the tube and detector are rotated a small increment, such as 1°, and the process is repeated until a 180° arc is covered. This is termed a *translate-rotate scanner.* The original CT scanner manufactured by the now-defunct EMI medical division used this geometry, but first-generation machines are no longer built and will not be discussed further.

A second-generation instrument uses a pie-shaped or fan beam of X-rays, but also passes linearly across the patient before rotating. Elscint was the last manufacturer to pursue this technology, taking it to a remarkable degree of sophistication, but they have now also abandoned development of second-generation instruments. Thus this type of geometry will also not be discussed further.

A major advance was the invention of the rotate-rotate or rotate-only scanner, in which the tube and the detector array both pass in a circle around the patient (Fig. 2-1). This is the third generation and is used by Elscint, General Electric, Philips, Siemens, Thomson-CGR, and Toshiba.

The fourth generation uses a rotating tube, but the detector array is fixed in position in a full 360° (Fig. 2-2). This may also be termed a *rotate-only scanner* or *rotate-stationary*. This basic fourth-generation design is presently used only by Picker.

A fifth design uses a nutating detector ring. In this configuration, a 360° ring of detectors is placed inside the ring of travel of the X-ray tube, unlike in the standard fourth-generation instrument in which the tube is placed within the fixed detector array. The detector array must angle out of the path of the X-ray tube as the tube revolves around the patient. This motion is

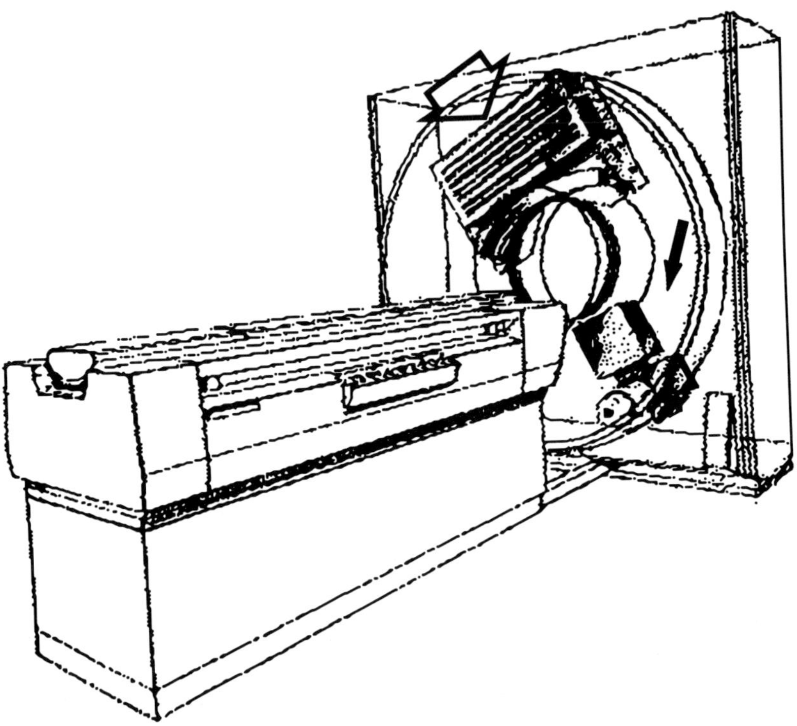

FIG. 2–1. Transparent illustration of a third-generation scanner. The tube and collimator (arrow) and the detector array with its accompanying data acquisition system (open arrow) all travel simultaneously in a circular motion around the patient. (After a diagram courtesy of General Electric Company, Medical Systems.)

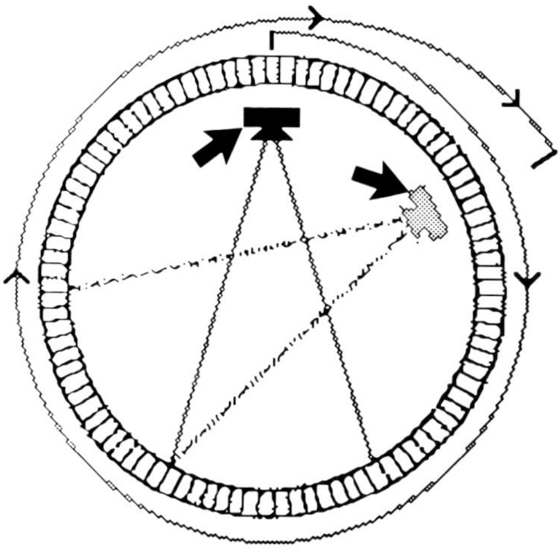

FIG. 2–2. A fourth-generation scanner. The tube (arrows) producing a fan beam of X-rays moves in a circular motion around the patient as indicated by the circular line with arrowheads. The detector array is fixed in a stationary ring around the patient.

termed *nutation,* a term derived from astronomy to describe the wobble in the orbit of some celestial bodies. This is similar to the type of motion seen by a spinning coin as it slows to come to rest on a flat surface (Fig. 2-3). This geometry resembles that of the fourth-generation design because of its 360° detector ring, and is now employed only by Toshiba, although it was originally used by EMI.

A sixth scanner configuration is also commercially available. In this design, the X-ray source is a large electron gun with a massive anode target oriented in a semicircular ring around the patient (Fig. 2-4). Thus neither the "tube" nor the detectors move, and scans are obtained in as short a time as 50 msec. Although X-ray photon fluence is limited at this speed, multiple slices may be obtained simultaneously because there are two rings of detectors. (Photon fluence is the number of photons striking a unit area, or, in this context, the total number of photons contributing to an image. The term *flux,* with which the reader may be more familiar, is the rate at which photons strike an area *per unit time.*) Scans of 360° or greater are not possible, and some slices are slightly angled off axial because of the detector ring configuration. This design also has much in common with the fourth-generation design because of its fixed detectors. This scanner, produced by Imatron, was originally designed as a cardiac scanning device but has now been adapted to general-purpose scanning.

Another type of CT device of prototypical design has been in operation at the Mayo Clinic in Rochester, Minnesota. This unit is called the dynamic spatial reconstructor (DSR) and is a very large unit with numerous simultaneously operating X-ray tubes. Such a unit is not likely to be reproduced elsewhere because of its great expense and size. Because most scanners in use today are third- or fourth-generation units, these will be discussed in greatest detail in this text.

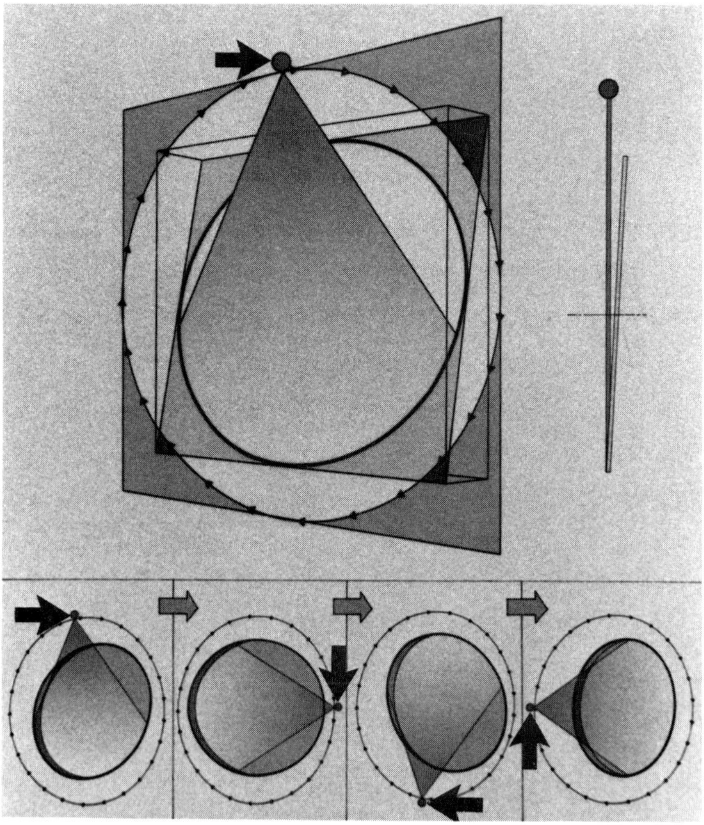

FIG. 2–3. The nutating ring scanner. The tube moves in the ring defined by the small arrowheads. The 360° ring of detectors is angled out of the path of the tube. This is also illustrated in profile with the tube shown traveling in a vertical plane and the detector ring slightly angled. The configuration of the system in various tube positions (black arrows) is shown at the bottom. (Diagram courtesy of Toshiba Medical Systems.)

X-RAY SOURCE

There are several important aspects of the X-ray source of a CT scanner. First, most CT tubes are modified from a design based on a standard rotating-anode angiographic X-ray tube. Tubes are put under enormous stress in many CT departments. Whereas angiographic tubes are called upon for series of exposures about two to five times during a procedure, CT scanners may perform 30 or more exposures per patient for 15 to 25 examinations per day at high tube output. Even the best tubes may last only a few months under these conditions. The life of a tube depends on its design and whether it is being consistently operated near maximum output. The tubes of one of our units have averaged as few as 11,000 scans before failure, whereas we have had the tube of another system last for 140,000 slices.

Milliampere-seconds (mAs) is a measure of X-ray output from the tube and is directly proportional to radiation exposure to the patient if all other factors remain constant. The mAs is also proportional to tube heating, but not in a direct linear relationship. To calculate the mAs, one must know whether the tube operates by emitting pulses of X-rays or by continuously emitting X-rays. For example, compare a scanner using a scan time of 2 sec,

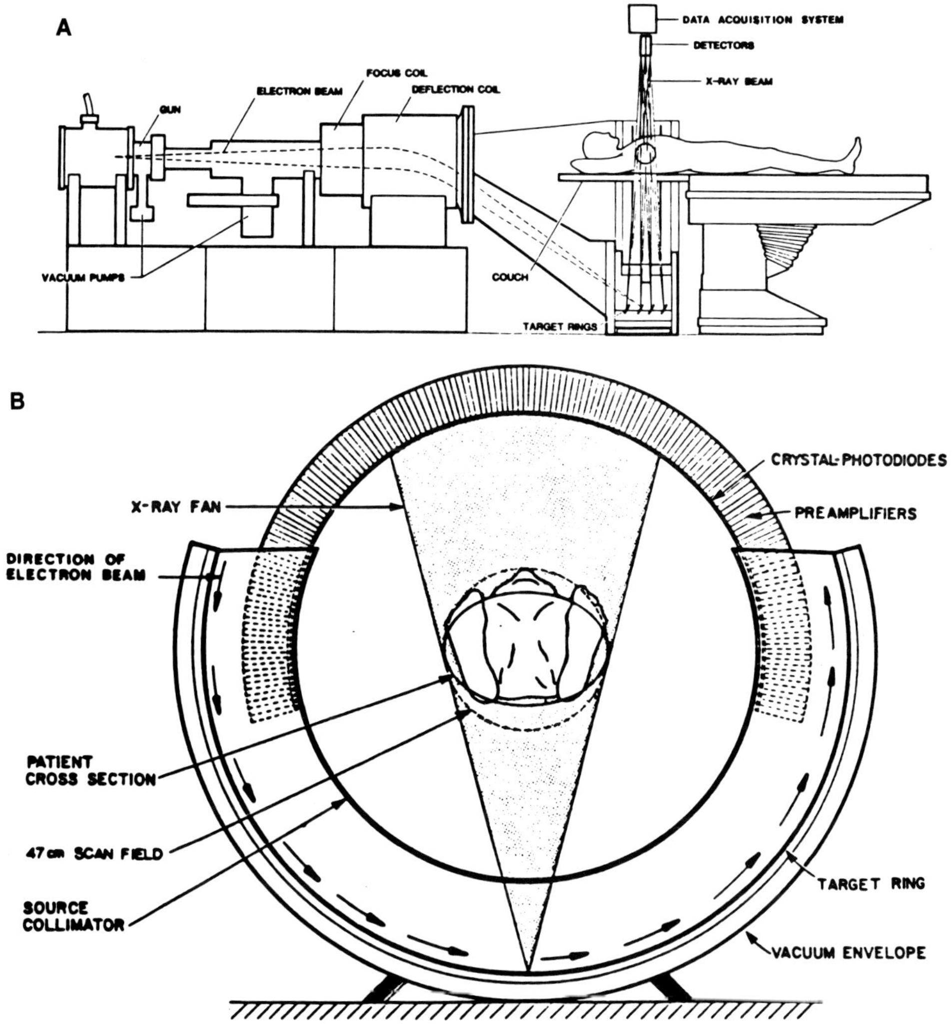

FIG. 2–4. The Imatron scanner. **A**. Profile view showing the deflected electron beam striking multiple targets to achieve multiple slices simultaneously. However, the slices are slightly angled off true axial, and the patient couch is tilted rather than the gantry as with other CT units to achieve greater deviation from axial angulation. **B**. End-on view showing fixed semicircular X-ray targets and detector arrays. (Diagrams courtesy of Imatron, Inc.)

during which the X-ray tube is on continuously, with scanner using a pulsed tube with a scan time of 4.8 sec, during which X-rays are on for 1.2 sec. In the first case, the milliamperage (mA) is multiplied by scan time to obtain the mAs, whereas for the second case the mA is multiplied by the number of pulses and the duration of each pulse, or by the total time (1.2 sec) of X-ray exposure.

Calculations of mAs are further complicated because the length of each pulse may be adjustable, as well as the number of pulses. For example, pulse widths such as 1.1, 2.2, and 3.3 msec per pulse may be chosen. Then, for a scan of 9.6 sec with 576 pulses at a pulse length of 3.3 msec, using an mA setting of 320, the mAs is $3.3 \times 10^{-3} \times 576 \times 320$, or about 608.

The reasons for using pulsed or continuous-output tubes are related to cost as well as to technical performance. The factors affecting these business decisions are complex but involve scanning speed, the quality of the amplifiers, the speed of the data acquisition system (DAS), and stress on the tube components.

All X-ray sources for CT and conventional radiography are polychromatic, emitting X-rays over a broad spectrum of energies. This is particularly important in CT because CT detector systems convert received X-rays into a single numerical data entry without evaluating the relative contribution of the number of photons (photon fluence) and the energy of each photon (measured in kiloelectron Volts, keV). Lower energy components of the beam are preferentially absorbed in the patient, leaving the transmitted beam with photons of higher average keV (8,11,13,14). Thus the greater the amount and density of the tissue, the higher the average energy of the transmitted beam. This higher average energy is interpreted as higher intensity, and therefore lower attenuation. This phenomenon is termed *beam hardening* and is discussed further in Chapter 8, p. 93 (Fig. 2-5).

Beam hardening may be alleviated somewhat by filtering the X-ray beam with a substance such as graphite, aluminum, or Teflon as the beam leaves the tube. This has the effect of narrowing the X-ray spectrum before it is affected by the patient. X-rays are then attenuated in the patient, and standard computed corrections are made for beam hardening. These corrections are imperfect and are affected by numerous factors including the position of dense structures within the field; the presence of contrast material, which affects the overall tissue density; and the immediate surroundings of a structure of interest. When beam hardening corrections are applied to a patient who deviates too far from average size, artifacts are worsened.

Most types of artifacts (e.g., streaks, density changes, interpetrous artifact) have multiple physical causes, and most physical sources of artifacts (e.g., beam hardening, motion) have several different types of effects on images. Therefore, when acting to minimize an artifact, one should realize that one may often lessen the artifact without eliminating it.

In the case of beam hardening, the multiple effects include a cupping artifact (see Chapter 11, p. 153), a low-density streak between or adjacent to

A

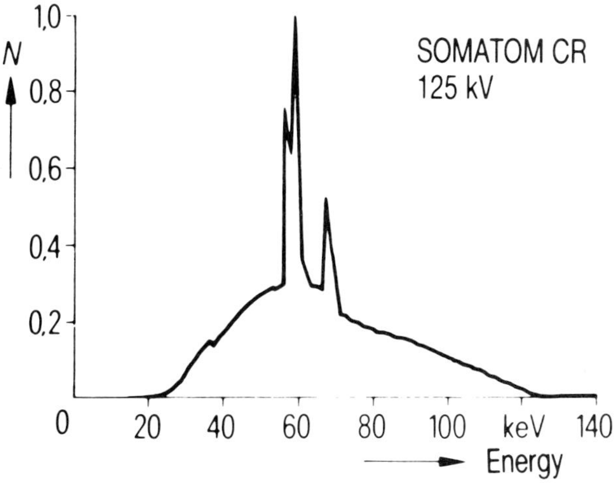

B

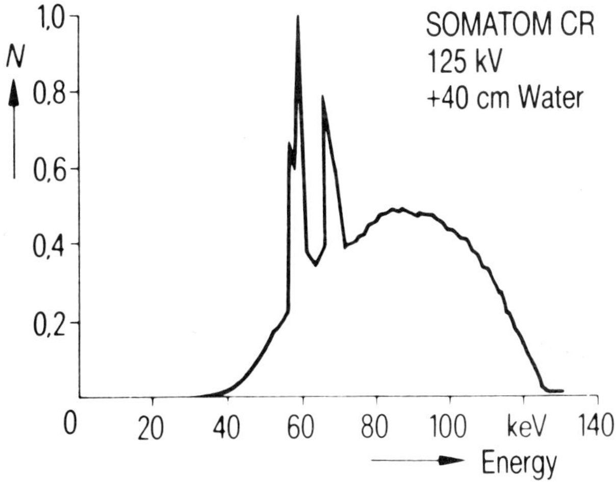

FIG. 2–5. **A**. Profile of the polychromatic spectrum of an unattenuated 125-kVp beam. The spikes represent characteristic radiation related to the nature of the metal target within the tube. The vertical axis represents the relative photon intensity, with the peak normalized to a value of 1.0. **B**. Spectrum of a 125-kVp beam attenuated by 40 cm of water. The average keV of the noncharacteristic radiation has shifted from about 55 to about 85. The curve is higher than in **A** because this represents relative rather than absolute intensity. The actual photon intensity is lower. (Diagrams courtesy of Siemens Medical Systems, Inc.)

high-density structures, or a general CT attenuation number shift. The streak type of beam hardening artifacts is particularly noticeable near dense areas such as the petrous ridges, the femoral heads, or the ribs, although, as mentioned, other types of artifacts contribute to the degraded image quality in these areas.

DETECTORS

One important difference among scanners lies in the number, size, and type of detectors used. A detector is a single element of the group of detectors (detector array) found in a machine. The characteristics of the detector and the detector array are different. For example, the sensitivity of a detector to incoming X-rays may be nearly 100%, whereas if one also considers the space between the detectors and their shape (the features of the array), the sensitivity of the detector array may fall to 90% or less. These characteristics of the array help determine the spatial and contrast resolution (contrast resolution will be discussed below) of the instrument. Other important elements include scatter suppression, the form of the convolution filter (also termed the *kernel*), and the sophistication of the beam hardening corrections. Detectors are among the more expensive components of a scanner, and although more is usually better, more detectors make the unit more expensive.

Currently used detectors are either hollow chambers filled with pressurized xenon (10) or solid-state crystals (5,6) of various compositions. The solid-state detectors absorb nearly 100% of photons incident upon them, versus about 60% to 93% for gas detectors, depending on their size and degree of pressurization. Thus, the significant advantage of solid-state detectors is their increased photon capture and therefore the improved statistical quality of the image. However, other features of the geometry strongly affect the spatial resolution and the statistical smoothness of the image (7), and the composition of the solid-state detectors must be carefully selected and controlled. Some varieties of solid-state detectors produce a brief, persistent flash of scintillation known as afterglow (1,8), and the persistence of light must be taken into account and subtracted when using the raw data for image reconstruction.

Despite the difference in sensitivity, xenon is still used in some currently marketed systems for several reasons including cost and technical considerations. The research and development costs for changing detector technology are great. Also, gas detectors are somewhat easier to calibrate against one another because the detectors share a high-pressure chamber. There has been a trend to convert to using solid-state detectors because of their higher photon capture efficiency, although xenon remains a valuable and reliable detector material.

Although an oversimplification, it is generally true that, for any specific system, greater detector efficiency leads to better contrast resolution, and greater numbers of detectors lead to higher spatial resolution. However, there is more to consider than just the number of detectors when assessing the limits of spatial resolution. The geometrical features of the tube-patient-detector axis determining spatial resolution include the magnification factor, the focal spot size, the effective detector aperture size when projected back to the patient, and even the way the image is reconstructed from the raw data.

Another important characteristic of the detector array and the associated DAS is its dynamic range. A detector may receive either very low photon intensities (e.g., if the beam passes through metal) or high photon intensities (e.g., if the beam passes through air during a high-mA scan). A system that more accurately records the received intensities at the ends of the scale has a wider *dynamic range.* Systems with a lower dynamic range may create more image artifacts through areas such as the shoulders and hips because the dense bone too severely attentuates the beam; this effect is termed *photon starvation.* Some scanners may signal an operator who has selected an inappropriately low or high technique by indicating an "underrange" or "overrange," respectively. Although this factor has a significant effect on image quality, its influence on the image may be difficult for a nontechnician to understand because so many factors affect the image. This is one reason why a potential CT customer may be better advised to evaluate more closely the quality of a unit's images than the printed technical specifications.

MAGNIFICATION

Magnification in CT has a different meaning from standard magnification in radiography, because with CT there is not necessarily any image magnification. With conventional radiography the patient is placed in contact with the film cassette, and the resulting image is nearly the same size as the body part examined. With conventional magnification such as is used in angiography and skeletal radiography, the patient is usually removed a specified distance from the film, the tube is moved closer to the patient, and the resulting image is enlarged and the spatial resolution improved as long as the focal spot is sufficiently small (3). With CT, the patient is always removed a specified distance from the detectors and the tube, and the computer is programmed to accommodate for the magnification and to produce accurate scale factors. However, some units may be able to select the magnification factor by moving the tube and detector array relative to the center of the scanning field (Fig. 2-6).

FOCAL SPOT

The focal spot is another important factor in resolution. With conventional radiography, larger focal spots permit higher X-ray output but limit spatial resolution. The limits of spatial resolution become more apparent as

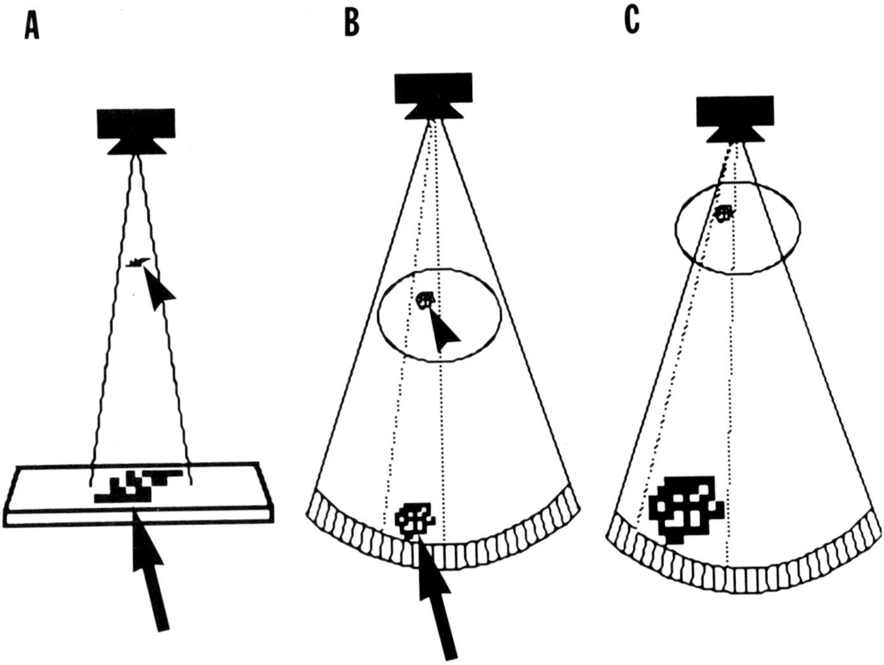

FIG. 2–6. Conventional and computed tomographic radiographic magnification. **A**. In simple radiographic magnification the image (arrow) projected on a film is larger than the actual object (arrowhead). If the focal spot is sufficiently small, such magnification techniques improve spatial resolution. The magnification factor is determined by dividing the tube-detector distance by the tube-object distance. **B**. In a computed tomographic system, the image (arrow) projected on the detector array is also larger than the actual object (arrowhead). However, the computer automatically calculates appropriate scale factors, and the structures are represented on the image at their appropriate size. The radiographic magnification factor is determined in the same way as with a conventional system. **C**. If the tube is moved closer to the patient, with the same tube-detector distance, then the image projected on the detector array encompasses a large number of detectors and the magnification factor is increased. Provided the focal spot is sufficiently small, this improves spatial resolution. Again, because the tube-object-detector distance is known, appropriate scale factors are calculated and displayed. However, the area of the body encompassed by the X-ray beam (the scanned field of view) is smaller in this configuration, and the X-ray dose to the patient for a specific tube output is increased.

the magnification factor is increased. When a focal spot is far away from an object, it appears to that object as a point source and projects a sharp shadow. As the focal spot approaches the object, it appears larger and projects a slightly blurred shadow as illustrated in Fig. 2-7. The same blurring effect occurs as the film is moved farther away from the object. This is why high-magnification systems, which place the tube close the patient and the film far away, require fine focal spots to minimize this blurring (3). These same facts of physics apply to CT. As the magnification factor is increased, the focal spot size becomes more crucial with current CT systems.

DETECTOR APERTURE

The limits of spatial resolution are partly defined by the angular arc of the exposed portion of the X-ray detector when projected back toward the focal spot to the patient. This is the effective detector aperture (7). That is, if you draw lines from the tube focal spot to the two edges of a single detector element, the distance between the two lines as they pass through the patient helps determine the spatial resolution (Fig. 2-8).

The effective detector aperture is affected by the actual detector aperture, the tube-object distance, and the object-detector distance. A manufacturer's choice of generation or geometrical design strongly affects the decisions that lead to determining the effective detector aperture. For example, a fourth-generation system using 1,200 detectors in a fixed ring of 360° has fewer detectors per degree of arc than a third-generation system using 600 detectors in a 30° arc that rotates with the tube. The larger size of these detectors is compensated for by increasing the magnification factor and by overlap-

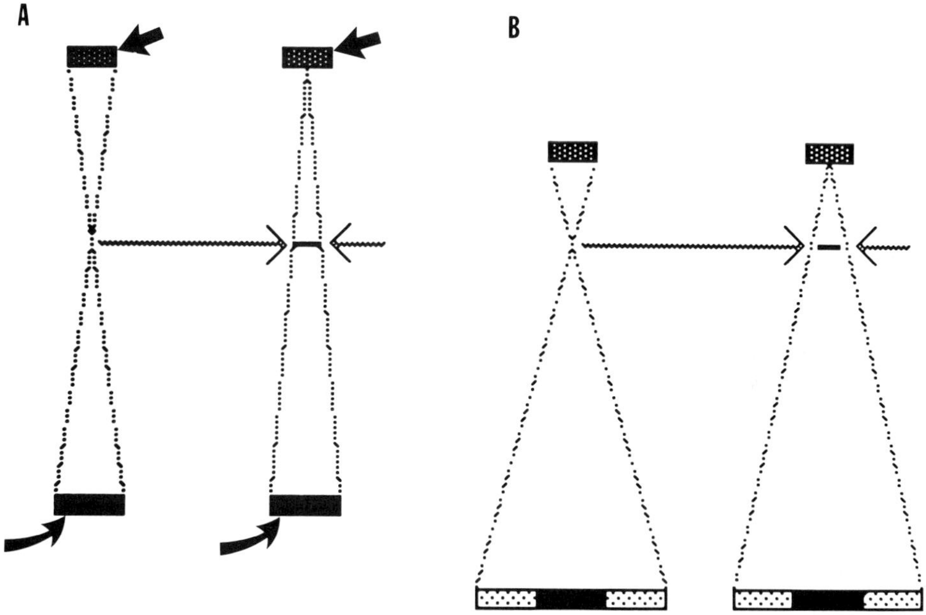

FIG. 2–7. Importance of focal spot size on spatial resolution. **A**. With standard geometry, the edges of the focal spot (short arrows) are projected onto a portion of the detector (curved arrows) through the center of the field of view (long thin arrows). Therefore, the size of the focal spot is related to the size of an object projected onto the detector array. A larger focal spot will create more blurring of the edges of a structure. **B**. If the same focal spot-detector distance is maintained but the focal spot is moved closer to the center of the field of view (arrows), then the image of the focal spot projected on the detector array is larger. This introduces more blur into the image, which may be compensated for by decreasing the size of the focal spot for this new tube-object-detector geometry.

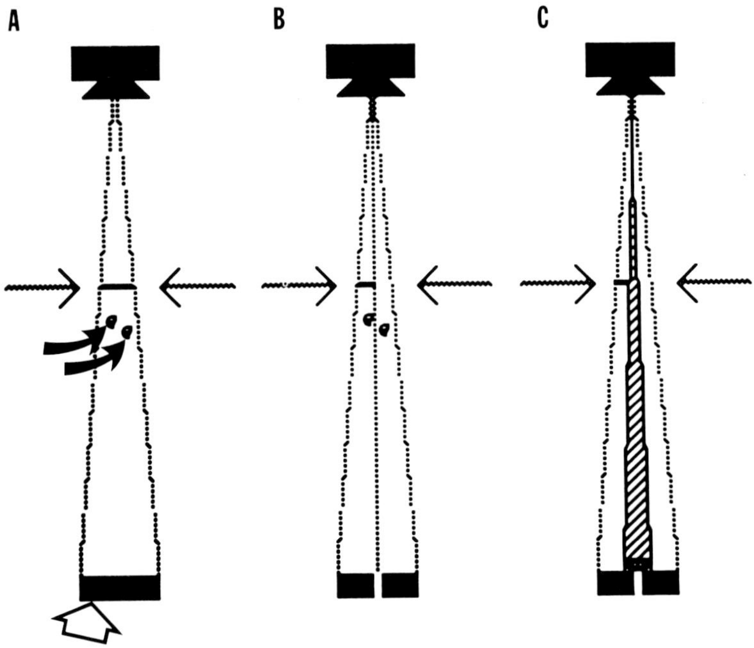

FIG. 2–8. Effect of detector width on spatial resolution. Long thin arrows indicate the center of the field of view. **A**. The beam is projected from the tube to a single detector (open arrow). Two small objects (curved arrows) are encompassed within the beam and thus cannot be discriminated or resolved from one another. The width of the line at the center of the field of view represents the size of the detector projected back to that point and is known as the effective detector aperture. **B**. If the single detector is divided into two detectors, then the small objects may now be within separate beams or rays and may be resolved from one another. The effective detector aperture is decreased to one-half its original value. **C**. If the detectors are further unchanged in size, but a pin is placed blocking the peripheral portions of each detector, then the effective detector aperture may be further reduced. However, a portion of the beam irradiating the patient is then wasted, and the tube output may have to be increased to compensate for the decreased number of photons reaching the detector array. This technique is used by some current fourth-generation scanners to provide high spatial resolution for special applications.

ping readings to varying degrees (2). That is, as the tube travels around the patient, more than one sample may be obtained for each detector. However, the effective detector aperture is still an important limiting factor. Newer fourth-generation equipment has improved effective detector aperture by increasing the number of detectors and decreasing their width.

If the number of detectors is held constant in a fourth-generation scanner, but part of each detector is masked, detector efficiency will decrease, and part of the X-ray beam passing through the patient is wasted; thus contrast resolution also decreases, but spatial resolution will increase (see Fig. 2-9).

If the width of the detectors in a third-generation scanner were narrowed, with all other factors unchanged, spatial resolution would increase. However, the number of detectors must then increase to span the entire patient. Another technique for increasing spatial resolution in a third-generation scanner is to keep the actual detector aperture constant but increase the magnification factor by constructing the tube closer to the gantry center and the detector array farther away, while also increasing the number of detectors used to span the patient (see Fig. 2-6). This approach has been taken by at least one manufacturer.

If the tube is moved closer to the patient and the detectors remain fixed or move away from the patient, then X-ray exposure to the patient is increased per mAs, but spatial resolution is improved because the magnification factor is increased. In Fig. 2-10, which illustrates effective detector aperture, drawing lines between the focal spot and the detector edges shows that the distance between the lines decreases where they pass through the patient as the tube is moved closer to the patient or the detectors are moved away. One trade-off in such a system is that, as the tube is moved closer, a smaller field of view is realized because of the fixed arc of the detector array.

The location of an object within the field of view may also influence how well it is seen. Spatial resolution is fairly uniform throughout the scanned field but does diminish somewhat in the periphery of the field, because of

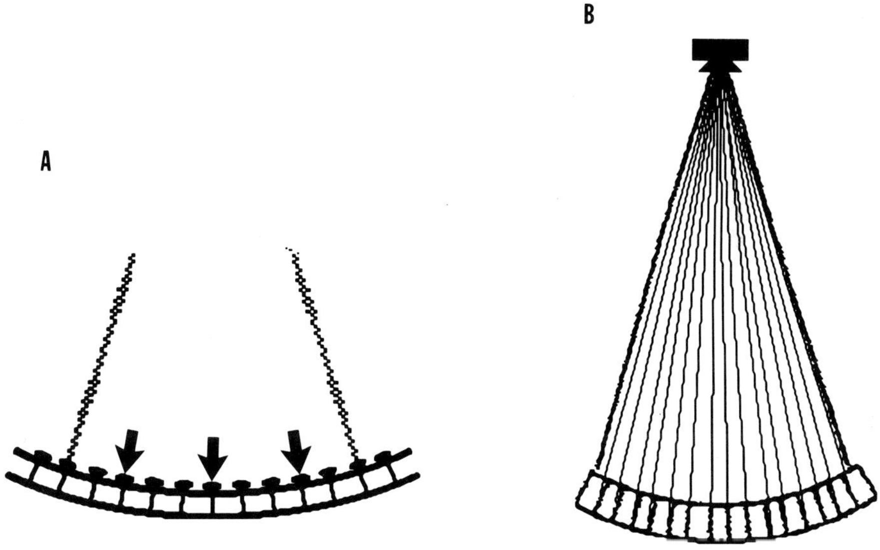

FIG. 2–9. Fourth-generation detector geometry. **A**. Part of a fourth-generation detector array with pins (arrows) shielding the detectors. This is known as an aperture grid. **B**. A fourth-generation tube-detector array showing a deviation from optimal geometry at the periphery of the fan beam. Because the detector interspaces are focused on the center of the circle, rather than the tube focal spot as with a third-generation scanner, some additional portion of the beam is wasted.

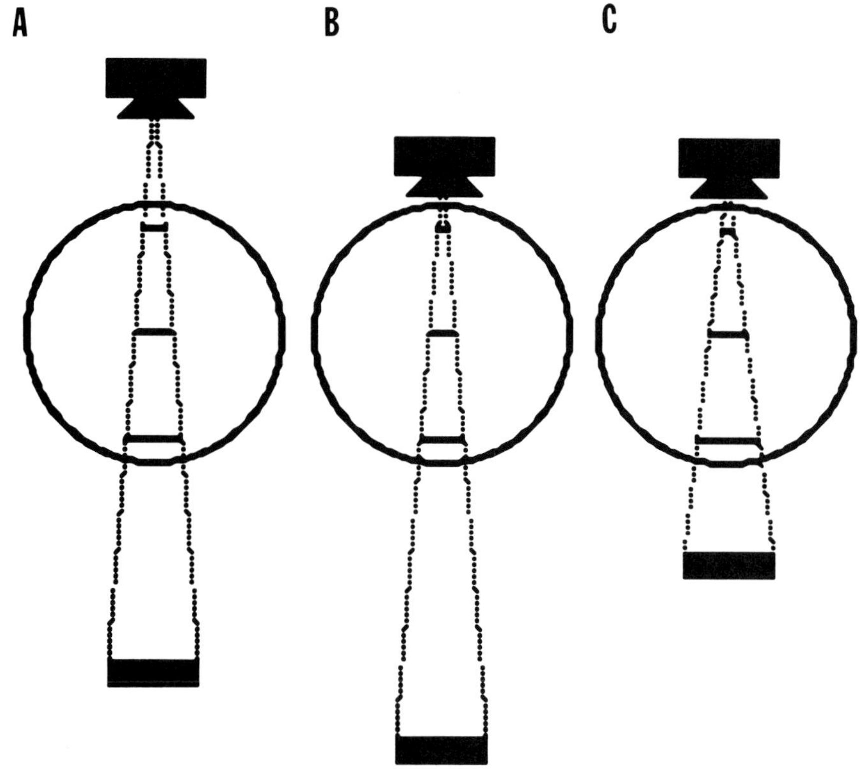

FIG. 2–10. Various tube-object-detector geometries illustrating their effect on projections of detector size at various points within the field of view. **A**. As illustrated in Fig. 2–8, the effective detector aperture may be measured at the center of the field of view. However, projections of the detector size at various points within the field of view vary because of the divergence of the X-ray beam. For a long tube-detector distance and a moderate tube-object distance, there is relatively little difference between projections of detector size at various points within the field. **B**. For the same tube-detector distance, but a shorter tube-object distance, there is a more marked difference between the projected detector sizes in the near and far fields. **C**. For a short tube-detector distance and a short tube-object distance, there is an even more marked difference between the projected detector sizes in the near and far fields. The inconsistency in projected detector size and effective detector aperture in various parts of the field affects image quality in various parts of the field. Because of differences in tube-object-detector distances and detector sizes, as well as other sampling factors, image quality at the periphery of the field of view may vary considerably among scanners and not be reflected in quoted specifications.

the use of the fan beam in modern scanners. A point near the patient's skin will "see" a relatively small effective detector aperture when the tube is on the same side as the point in question. However, when the tube is on the opposite side of the patient, the effective aperture is significantly larger (see Fig. 2-10). This inconsistency affects image quality in the periphery of the patient, where this effect is most marked, but the visual effect is usually very subtle.

Therefore, when attempting to assess the potential spatial resolution of a scanner, knowing the number of detectors alone has little meaning. One must know the position within the field that is being considered, the usable detector size, sampling rates, focal spot size choices, tube-object and object-detector distances, the angle of the arc occupied by the detectors, and other factors. It is clear that the complexity of this issue limits our ability as non-technicians to evaluate a unit's image quality on the basis of specifications such as effective detector aperture and the number of detectors. This type of information may be useful to the CT customer only to permit a comparison of the different units offered by a single manufacturer using essentially similar designs. Such detailed specifications are of considerably less value for comparing units with fundamentally different structures. The test of image quality must be in the image, although finding comparable images to compare may be quite difficult. This will be discussed further.

COLLIMATION

Scattered radiation affects image quality as well as radiation dose to the patient and to those in the room during scanning. One of the advantages of CT scanners is that radiation scattered into the detectors is minimized by fine slit collimation of from 1 to 10 mm in the axial direction (2), eliminating most of the radiographic scatter that occurs on conventional radiography. This improves the contrast resolution of CT compared to conventional radiography, because with conventional radiography much of the film darkening is caused by scattered radiation, which contains no usable information (9). Grids between the patient and the film are used to suppress scattered radiation with plain filming, but most such grids are less effective than the methods used for CT.

The technique of fine beam collimation has even been applied to other conventional forms of radiography because of its potential to reduce patient exposure and increase contrast resolution. In fact, the scanogram or scan projection radiograph obtained from the CT for localization has some technical advantages over the plain film partly because of this reason, as will be discussed below. However, scanograms are usually diagnostically poor because spatial resolution is limited by detector size and spacing, and the images are usually spatially filtered, which enhances edges (4) and thereby distorts some anatomic features (see Chapter 3, p. 33).

Scatter remains a problem in the transverse dimension (8) and is managed by collimation in some form at the detector assembly or by use of an air gap (see Fig. 1-3). Xenon detectors in third-generation instruments are long and slender, thus acting to some degree as grids (Fig. 2-11). In other third-generation units using solid-state detectors, grids adjacent to the detectors are used. A beam-shaping filter, which reduces the amount of radiation passing through the peripheral thinner parts of the subject, reduces the contribution

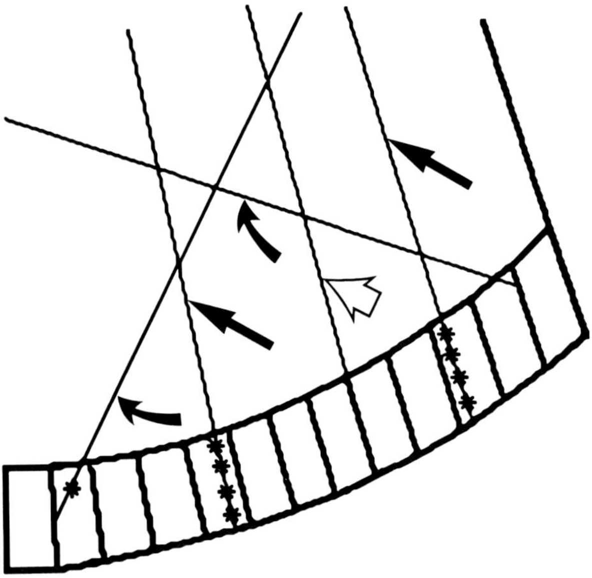

FIG. 2–11. Portion of a third-generation detector array. Boxes represent xenon chamber detectors. Most rays in the primary beam (long arrows) are detected because of interaction with the detector material. Some rays (open arrow) are absorbed in the detector interspaces and are not detected. This mostly accounts for the difference in sensitivity between the detector elements and the detector array. X-rays scattered out of the direction of the primary beam (curved arrows) either go unabsorbed or produce a smaller response within the detector because the entire detector material is not traversed.

of scatter to the image. The diminished number of photons decreases the number available for scattering.

CALIBRATION, GAIN, OFFSET, AND REFERENCE CORRECTIONS

One of the features affecting image quality is the need for calibration to ensure a uniformly accurate representation of CT numbers throughout the field of view. Some scanners require time-consuming and/or frequent calibration. Often this calibration must be done on each selected combination of factors. That is, if only one of the factors is changed while all others remain the same, an entire new calibration procedure must be performed for this new combination. Because of the number of selectable factors, the combinations are very numerous. This is one reason that scan factors are limited in some scanners to preprogrammed sets. Therefore, the type and complexity of the calibration procedure and the consequent flexibility of selecting scan variables are factors that salespeople may not freely discuss with potential customers and are difficult to assess. It is worthwhile to pursue answers about the nature of calibration procedures, the time required to perform them, and how often they should be done. Calibration may be done with phantoms simulating water density and/or with air. Because the water-simulating phantom or air is entirely uniform, the computer can compensate for artifactual alterations in response caused by detector or electronic inconsistencies. This calibration procedure is done at differing intervals depending on the scanner. Some require routine calibration every 1 or 2 weeks, others suggest brief calibrations every 2 hr, and still others need lengthy calibration after tube replacement. Recalibration may also be performed whenever difficulties are encountered that might be related to calibration (such as rings).

Imperfections in amplifiers require offset and gain corrections. Amplifiers produce a small signal even when no X-rays are reaching the detectors. This type of electronic background is termed *offset.* Also, for various reasons, the amplifiers receiving signals from each detector may amplify the detector response to a specific photon intensity by a slightly different degree from channel to channel. The degree of amplification is termed *gain,* and these slight differences can be corrected for.

Slight variations in X-ray output from moment to moment are monitored by reference detectors receiving unattenuated X-rays. In third-generation designs, the reference detectors may be fixed at the extreme ends of the detector array, or the unattenuated beam may be sampled prior to reaching the patient. In fourth-generation designs and their variants, the same detectors used for imaging sequentially serve as reference channels as the beam sweeps around the patient.

PATIENT TABLE OR COUCH

Most currently available scanners use a patient support table with a cantilever design created from a carbon fiber material. This material is strong but low in X-ray density and must be designed to handle huge forces caused by the leverage placed on the table and supporting structure (see Fig. 2-1). One end of the table is unsupported as the patient is placed within the gantry aperture. This is similar to standing on the end of a diving board, but the board must not bend or break! Thus the weight limits indicated by the manufacturer should be considered when deciding whether to scan an obese patient. We sometimes decline scanning patients who exceed the weight limits even if they can fit the scanning aperture because table damage can lead to lengthy downtime and be expensive to repair. Somc companics have voided service contracts when rated weight limits are exceeded, leaving the radiology group or the hospital financially liable.

Table material and shape can affect examination quality. Naturally, tables must be nonmetallic to avoid beam attenuation and artifacts, but their shape must also be specifically designed to avoid creating other artifacts. Some of the older scanners used a table design that often led to artifactual streaks through the patient (Fig. 2-12), radiating from sharp interfaces between structures of markedly differing density such as table and air (the edge gradient effect is discussed in Chapter 11, p. 149). This effect was enhanced by the smaller number of views (view sampling error or view aliasing is discussed in Chapter 5, p. 59) and fewer samples in older scanners. These streaks cannot be eliminated, but their location within the scanning field can be predominantly directed away from the patient with proper table shape (Fig. 2-13), and their prominence can be minimized by increasing the number of views or samples. Because artifacts are also caused by solid material within the scanning gantry but outside the field of reconstruction, the table should be shaped properly and be small enough so that it can be included within the scanned field of view (see Chapter 5, p. 45) without occupying too much of the field. However, it is not necessary to include the table within the displayed field of view.

Scanning for radiation therapy planning requires a flat tabletop to simulate the conditions of therapy. If the tabletop itself is not already flat, the flat surface is created with specially designed cushions. However, some cushions are bulky and may cause more artifacts. These should be used only for radia-

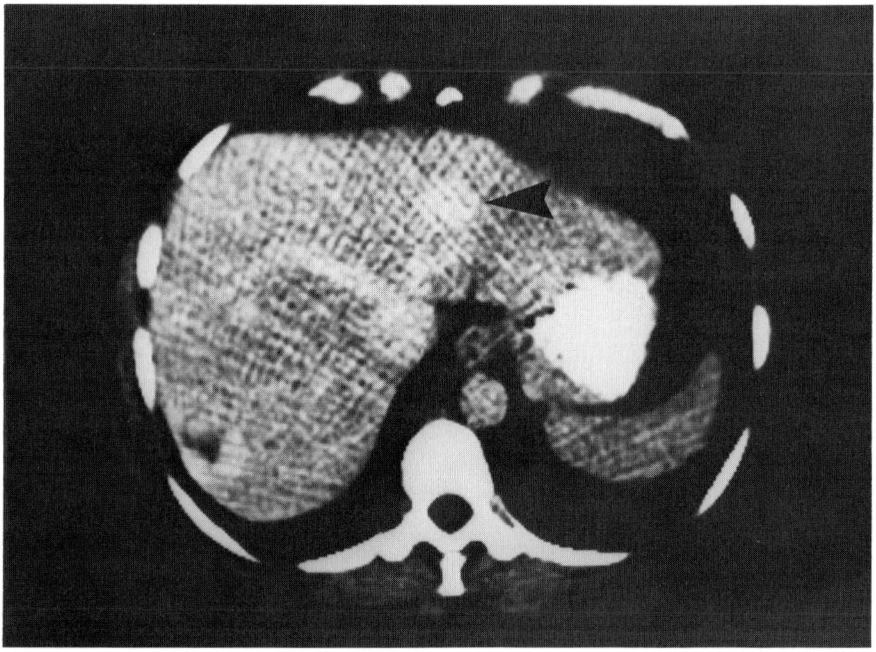

FIG. 2–12. Scan degraded by aliasing streaks crossing through the body, radiating from the edges of the patient couch. The streaks are partly a result of table design and were made more prominent by degenerating couch material, which caused high spatial frequency interfaces within the table. They could be considerably diminished on this scanner by using a large number of detector samples to diminish the aliasing effect. Incidentally seen is a hepatic hemangioma (arrowhead), with a second located in the posterior right lobe.

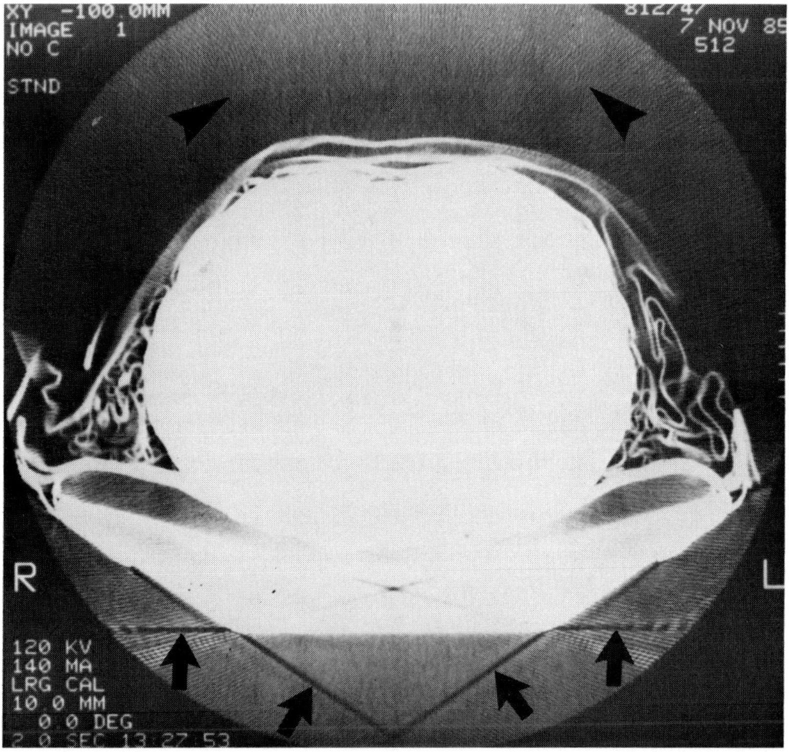

FIG. 2–13. Edge gradient effect on the patient couch. At certain window width and window level settings, streaks are easily seen (arrows) radiating from the flat surfaces between the table and the air. The table shape is designed to transmit these streaks outside the patient field of view. Fine aliasing streaks (arrowheads) are still seen, as on the previous image, but they are much less apparent because of the table redesign and the much larger number of data samples obtained.

tion therapy planning. Other accessories are usually available for special purposes such as coronal head or body scanning.

TABLE HEIGHT AND INCREMENTATION

Table height adjustment may be important for ease of patient handling. For example, some tables may not be able to descend as low as some patient transports may be able to elevate, making transfer difficult for disabled patients. The minimum table height for different scanners varies between 30 and 80 cm from the floor.

Accuracy of table incrementation (movement along the patient axis) is crucial to obtaining fine detail scans of such areas as the temporal bone. Tables should be able to increment accurately in 1-mm steps or less. They should also be able to increment quickly so that scans can be taken in rapid sequence with table incrementation. The time required to move the table between scans (the interscan delay) for rapid-sequence (dynamic) scanning is under 2 sec for most scanners.

GANTRY

The circular opening in the gantry housing that accepts the patient is termed the *gantry aperture.* It varies in diameter from about 54 to 85 cm from scanner to scanner. The gantry aperture size is important for obese patients, who may be within weight limits for the table but not fit into the gantry of the smaller CT units. Small gantry size may also limit the capacity of the scanner to perform unusual types of examinations. For example, direct coronal or sagittal scanning of the head may be precluded in some patients on CT scanners with small gantry apertures. Also, direct sagittal and coronal body imaging and longitudinal and oblique extremity imaging have been shown to be valuable with some scanners (12) but are not feasible with others. However, interest in such maneuvers has not been high, and unusual planes of section can be routinely obtained with magnetic resonance imaging.

Gantry aperture size also affects patient comfort. Small apertures force patients whose abdomen or chest is being scanned to raise their arms to an uncomfortable position; this would not be necessary with a larger gantry opening. Having the plane of X-rays close to the front (table support side) of the gantry also promotes patient comfort and permits scans needing unusual positioning.

Gantry angulation is another feature of scanning that is important for specialized applications, particularly spine and head scanning. The entire assembly housing the tube and detector array may be moved in either direction to a maximum angle of between 15° and 30°, depending on the scanner. For those doing many of these types of examinations, the extra few degrees offered by some scanners may lead to significantly better examinations.

One often-overlooked effect of gantry angulation is a slightly increased overlapping of slices, with a resulting increase in radiation dosage to the patient. At 25° of angulation, a 10-mm slice intersects almost 12 mm of the table, yet the table incrementation does not increase to accommodate for this.

As an alternative or adjunct to gantry angulation, some scanners have tables that may slant off the horizontal plane. Other units also provide the capacity to swivel the table from side to side to accommodate unusual positioning for specialized examinations.

REFERENCES

1. Coulam, C. M., and Erickson, J. J. (1981): Equipment considerations in computed tomography. In: *The Physical Basis of Medical Imaging,* edited by C. M. Coulam, J. J. Erickson, F. D. Rollo, and A. E. James, pp. 213–229. Appleton-Century-Crofts, New York.
2. Coulam, C. M., and Erickson, J. J. (1981): Image considerations in computed tomography. In: *The Physical Basis of Medical Imaging,* edited by C. M. Coulam, J. J. Erickson, F. D. Rollo, and A. E. James, pp. 189–211. Appleton-Century-Crofts, New York.
3. Erickson, J. J., and Coulam, C. M. (1981): Production of X-rays. In: *The Physical Basis of Medical Imaging,* edited by C. M. Coulam, J. J. Erickson, F. D. Rollo, and A. E. James, pp. 37–45. Appleton-Century-Crofts, New York.
4. Foley, W. D., and DiBianca, F. A. (1981): Computed radiography. In: *Radiology of the Skull and Brain: Technical Aspects of Computed Tomography,* edited by T. H. Newton and D. G. Potts, pp. 4312–4325. C. V. Mosby, St. Louis.
5. Freundlich, D., and Zaklad, H. (1981): Detector systems: Section II. Scintillation crystal-photomultiplier tube detectors. In: *Radiology of the Skull and Brain: Technical Aspects of Computed Tomography,* edited by T. H. Newton and D. G. Potts, pp. 4104–4112. C. V. Mosby, St. Louis.
6. Haque, P. (1981): Detector systems: Section IV. Scintillation crystal-photodiode array detectors. In: *Radiology of the Skull and Brain Technical Aspects of Computed Tomography,* edited by T. H. Newton and D. G. Potts, pp. 4127–4132. C. V. Mosby, St. Louis.
7. Haque, P., and Stanley, J. H. (1981): Detector systems: Section I. Basic principles of computed tomography detectors. In: *Radiology of the Skull and Brain: Technical Aspects of Computed Tomography,* edited by T. H. Newton and D. G. Potts, pp. 4097–4103. C. V. Mosby, St. Louis.
8. Joseph, P. M. (1981): Artifacts in computed tomography. In *Radiology of the Skull and Brain: Technical Aspects of Computed Tomography,* edited by T. H. Newton and D. G. Potts, pp. 3956–3992. C. V. Mosby, St. Louis.
9. Meredith, W. J., and Massey, J. B. (1977): Diagnostic radiology: The effects and control of scattered radiation. In: *Fundamental Physics of Radiology,* 3rd edition, Chapter XX, pp. 244–263. PSG Publishing, Littleton, MA.
10. Peschmann, K. R. (1981): Detector systems: Section III. Xenon gas ionization detectors. In: *Radiology of the Skull and Brain: Technical Aspects of Computed Tomography,* edited by T. H. Newton and D. G. Potts, pp. 4112–4126. C. V. Mosby, St. Louis.
11. Rao, P. S., and Alfidi, R. J. (1981): The environmental density artifact: A beam-hardening effect in computed tomography. *Radiology,* 141:223–227.
12. van Waes, P. F. G. M., and Zonneveld, F. W. (1982): Patient positioning for direct coronal computed tomography of the entire body. *Radiology,* 142:531–532.
13. Young S. W., Muller, H. H., and Marshall, W. H. (1983): Computed tomography: Beam hardening and environmental density artifact *Radiology,* 148:279–283.
14. Zatz, L. M. (1981): Basic principles of computed tomography scanning. In: *Radiology of the Skull and Brain: Technical Aspects of Computed Tomography,* edited by T. H. Newton and D. G. Potts, pp. 3853–3876. C. V. Mosby, St. Louis.
15. Zatz, L. M. (1981): General overview of computed tomography instrumentation. In: *Radiology of the Skull and Brain: Technical Aspects of Computed Tomography,* edited by T. H. Newton and D. G. Potts, pp. 4025–4057. C. V. Mosby, St. Louis.

3

Scan Projection Radiography

The scan projection radiograph produced by the CT scanner goes by several names, including scanogram, ScoutView™, pilot scan, Topogram™, Scanoscope™, Surview™, radiographic mode, and localizer image. The term *scanogram* is used in this text to refer to all of these systems. The scanogram is analogous to a plain film and has as its primary purpose the prescription of the location or registration of scans, using the same device as is used for scanning. This eliminates the need to use conventional plain film localizer images prior to scanning as was done with early CT scanners. Lines indicating the locations of slices to be scanned or that have already been scanned can be superimposed on the scanogram (Fig. 3-1) (2).

For an ordinary CT scan slice, the X-ray tube is rotated around the patient while the patient couch remains stationary. However, during a scanogram, the tube remains stationary while the couch is moved smoothly through the gantry aperture (Fig. 3-2). The position of the tube determines the projection of the image. PA, AP, lateral, and oblique images are possible. The image is reconstructed from a series of thin slit pictures taken in sequence as the patient passes through the beam. The length of the scanogram is determined by the length of time the X-ray tube is on and the speed of table movement, which varies considerably from scanner to scanner.

Some units provide choices of resolution for their scanograms. A standard scanogram is obtained by exposing a series of 1.0- or 1.5-mm sections arranged contiguously and then reconstructing the data in a format analogous to a plain film (see Fig. 3-1). However, if slices of 1.0- or 1.5-mm thickness are obtained every 0.5 or 0.75 mm, then the data from the overlapped slices can be averaged, and scanograms of technically better resolution in the axial or longitudinal direction result, although it is usually difficult to appreciate any difference visually.

ADVANTAGES OF THE SCANOGRAM

The scanogram has limited spatial resolution and requires a long exposure time compared to conventional radiography, but other features give it a competitive advantage over plain film imaging. Taking a succession of thin slit scans and using the collimated detectors minimizes the contribution of scattered X-rays to the image (see Chapter 2, p. 23) (2). With plain films, scatter accounts for a significant percentage of film darkening and serves only to decrease contrast. Therefore, this effective suppression of scatter permits lower doses of X-rays to be used. Also, the digitization of the image allows computer manipulation of image quality. Computerized image manipulation and scatter suppression permit wider exposure latitude. Repeat exposures need not be done when a film is too dark or light, in contrast to conventional radiography. As with the CT scan slices, differences in X-ray exposure affect the graininess or noise in the image rather than its brightness.

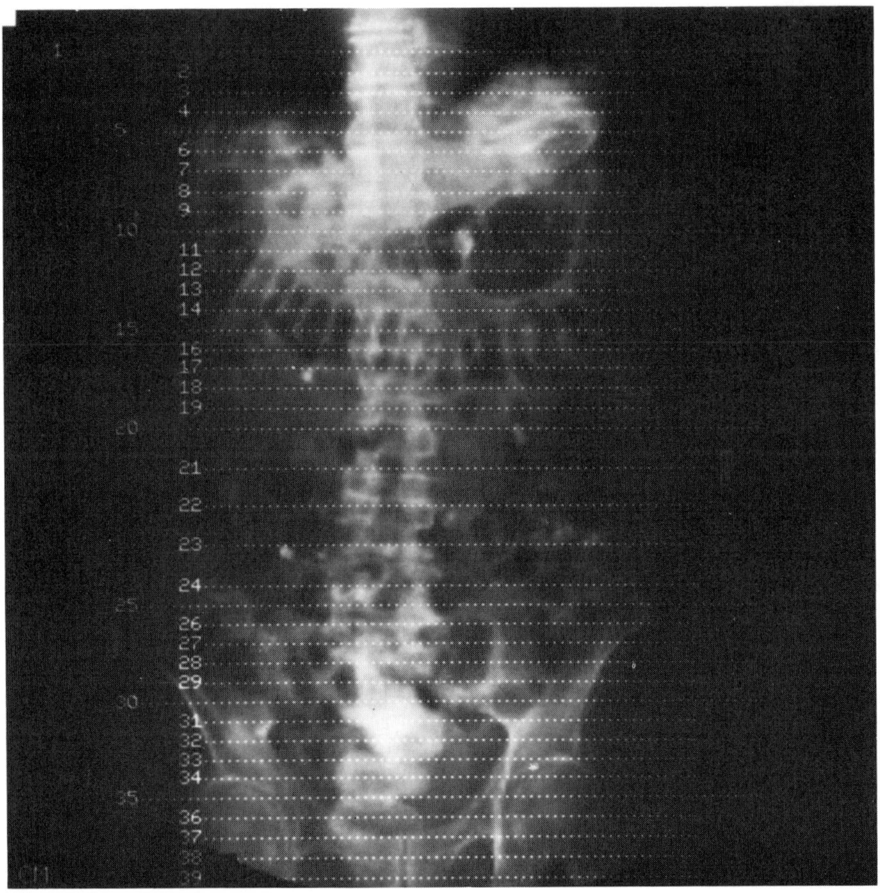

FIG. 3–1. Scanogram with slice level annotation. Each level scanned is associated with a number, which represents the slice number taken in chronological sequence. We film images both with and without slice annotation because the annotations tend to obscure some subtle anatomic features that may be required for localization. Limited spatial detail results from the large detector size compared to plain X-ray film silver grain "detectors."

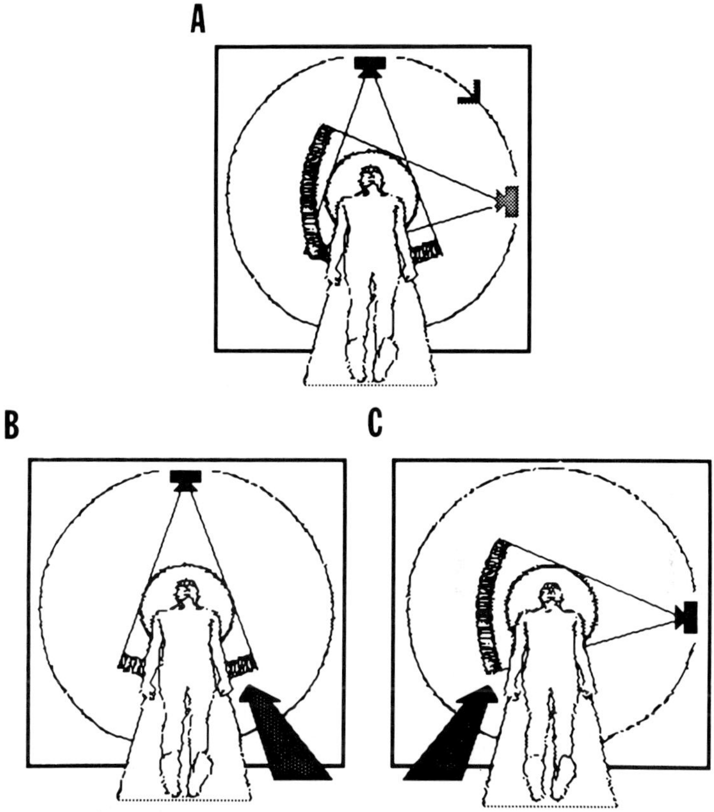

FIG. 3–2. Difference in method of data acquisition between a CT slice and a scanogram. **A**. For a CT slice, the tube and the detector array rotate around the patient, who lies on a stationary table. **B**. For a scanogram, the tube and the detector array remain fixed in position while the patient couch moves. This is an AP projection; however, a variety of projections may be obtained. **C**. Lateral scanogram projection. (After diagrams courtesy General Electric Company, Medical Systems.)

IMAGE PROCESSING

The quality of the image can be manipulated by making it darker or lighter or by changing contrast as is done with CT slices, but also by spatially filtering the image. Spatial filtering is a process by which the value of each pixel is weighted based on the differences in density between adjacent pixels (1,5). These differences correspond to the spatial frequency, which reflects the sharpness of the density difference between a point and its surroundings (see Chapter 8, p. 89). For example, the edge between bone and soft tissue has a high spatial frequency whereas the border of a liver metastasis has a low frequency.

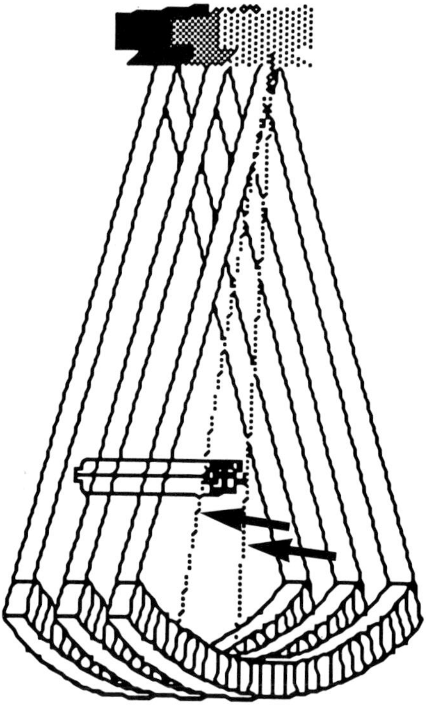

FIG. 3–3. Differences in magnification in the lateral and axial dimensions. Because of the relatively short tube-detector distance, moderate radiographic magnification of structures occurs, with greater magnification in those structures closer to the X-ray tube. This effect is illustrated by the diverging lines (arrows) encompassing a hypothetical structure. In contrast, because of the nature of the table motion, there is no magnification effect in the longitudinal direction.

Scans can be adjusted to emphasize or suppress certain spatial frequencies. High pass and low-pass filters selectively filter out low and high spatial frequencies, respectively (3). For example, a high-pass filter passes through or emphasizes the high spatial frequencies (for example, enhancing edges) while suppressing the low frequencies (see Chapter 7, p. 79). The process of spatial filtration is performed on both scanograms and slices and is applied to the data received directly from the detectors before reconstruction of the scanogram or slice image. However, the purposes and the nature of the spatial filters chosen for these two applications differ.

A more complete explanation of spatial filtration is offered in the preceding section. However, one way of conceptualizing spatial filtering is as a method for modifying the attenuation value of a specific pixel by using information from surrounding tissue. The attenuation of the adjacent tissue is averaged and weighted to affect the attenuation value of the central pixel. This technique may be used, for example, to enhance or soften edges.

FIG. 3–4. Use of a program to annotate the location of lesions from CT slices to scanograms. **A**. CT slice in which a lesion (in this case a metastasis from breast carcinoma) is marked by a box. Adjacent slices in which the mass is seen were also marked with boxes defining the AP and lateral boundaries of the area. **B**. Frontal scanogram outlining the margins of the area as indicated by the boxes placed on the CT slices.

A

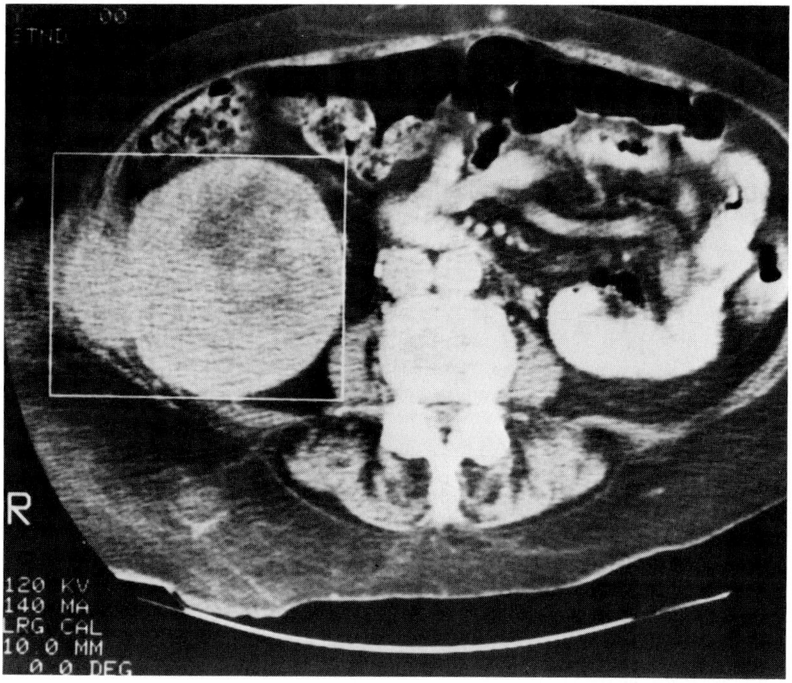

B

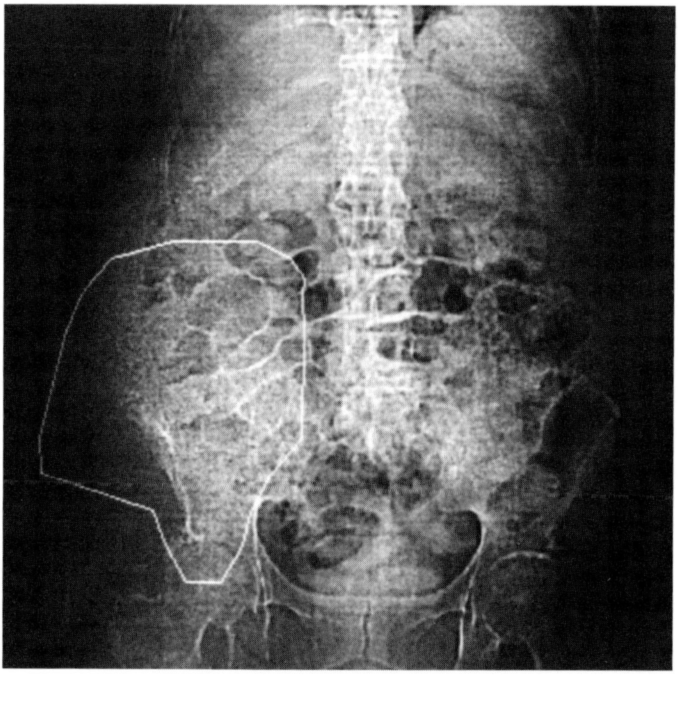

If there are differences in attenuation between adjacent points in space, as one sees at organ boundaries, then these differences can be increased by applying an arithmetic weighting to increase the value of the already higher reading and decrease the value of the lower one, thereby enhancing the edge. This effect produces in some scanograms an image in which bone, organ, and skin lines appear outlined or traced.

Most manufacturers design a spatial filter that creates a scanogram with wide latitude and enhanced edges, so that the entire range of tissue interfaces and densities can be seen at a single set of window width and window level settings. That is, the gradual variations in density from point to point (low spatial frequency data) are suppressed while the abrupt changes (high spatial frequency data) such as edges are enhanced, even if these abrupt changes are relatively small in degree. For example, a change in an arbitrary pixel value from 1 unit to 5 units between adjacent pixels might be enhanced, while a change from 1 unit to 10 units occurring gradually over 5 adjacent pixels might be suppressed.

SCANOGRAM RESOLUTION

Usually the narrowest collimator in the cephalocaudad direction is used for the scanogram. This factor limits the resolution in this plane. The resolution in the transverse plane is limited by the detector width, detector-to-detector spacing, and tube-detector geometry. This puts most fixed detector ring (fourth-generation) scanners at a disadvantage relative to most rotate-only (third-generation) scanners because most fourth-generation scanners have a wider detector-to-detector spacing than their third-generation counterparts. For example, a fourth-generation system using 1,200 detectors distributed over 360° has 3.3 detectors per degree of arc, whereas a third-generation scanner using 730 detectors over a 46° arc has about 16 detectors per degree. This difference is somewhat alleviated by the greater magnification factors on most fourth-generation scanners and their variants. Thus, the quality of the scanogram is seriously affected by these specifications, and this, in turn, influences the spatial filtering that is employed by the manufacturer.

The quality of the scanogram is clinically important because it may be difficult to localize a vertebral level or biopsy needle accurately with a poor scanogram. Also, when searching for small masses or lung nodules, a good scanogram is crucial because the plain film may not correspond well to the scanogram, which is obtained with the patient supine rather than upright as for the plain film. If plain films are not available, one may have to depend on the scanogram to differentiate such structures as small surgical staples or clips from abnormal calcifications; this is more difficult with a low-resolution scanogram.

Another factor affecting interpretations from scanograms is radiographic magnification (2). In plain film systems, tube-object distances are long. This minimizes the effect of magnifying the superficial and deep portions of the body part differently. With CT, the tube-object distance is short and fixed. Although the scale of magnification of the image is compensated for in the computer, differential magnification of structures located closest to and farthest from the tube can be striking. Therefore, findings such as cardiomegaly must be suggested cautiously, not only because of magnification but also because of the supine positioning. However, this effect of differentially magnifying organs occurs only in the transverse plane. There is no geometrical magnification along the patient's long axis because there is no divergence of the beam in this dimension (Fig. 3-3).

SCANOGRAM ANNOTATION

More sophisticated annotation than slice level alone is possible on the scanogram. Areas marked on the CT slices may be translated to the scanograms automatically. This is primarily useful for designing radiation therapy ports (Fig. 3-4; see Chapter 9, p. 111) (4). The tumor outlined on the CT slices can be encompassed by ports outlined by radiopaque catheters placed on the patient's skin. The study cited above indicated that this program led to changing 77% of treatment plans. This feature should also help surgeons better plan surgical approaches.

REFERENCES

1. Blumenfeld, S. M., and Glover, G. (1981): Spatial resolution in computed tomography. In: *Radiology of the Skull and Brain: Technical Aspects of Computed Tomography,* edited by T. H. Newton and D. G. Potts, pp. 3918–3940. C. V. Mosby, St. Louis.
2. Foley, W. D., and DiBianca, F. A. (1981): Computed radiography. In: *Radiology of the Skull and Brain: Technical Aspects of Computed Tomography,* edited by T. H. Newton and D. G. Potts, pp. 4312–4325. C. V. Mosby, St. Louis.
3. Fu, T. Y., and Hayworth, M. (1986): The digital image: Its structure, storage, and transmission. In: *The Computer in Radiology,* edited by T. B. Hunter, pp. 94–120. Aspen Systems, Rockville, MD.
4. Shuman, W. P., Griffin, B. R., Yoshy, C. S., Listerud, J. A., Mack, L. A., Rowberg, A. H., and Moss, A. A. (1985): The impact of CT correlate scoutview images on radiation therapy planning. *AJR,* 145:633–638.
5. Zatz, L. M. (1981): Basic principles of computed tomography scanning. In: *Radiology of the Skull and Brain: Technical Aspects of Computed Tomography,* edited by T. H. Newton and D. G. Potts, pp. 3853–3876. C. V. Mosby, St. Louis.

4

Radiation

Radiation protection measures for CT scanners are often misunderstood because of the dissimilarities to cônventional X-ray techniques. However, the similarities outweigh the differences, and ordinary radiation precautions should be taken. Stray and leakage radiation from CT scanners is usually low, and the patterns of stray radiation differ from those of ordinary X-ray systems because of the complex moving geometry of the X-ray source.

In this chapter, three features of radiation exposure will be considered; (a) radiation to portions of the patient within the scan slice, (b) radiation to parts of the patient not being scanned, and (c) radiation to individuals standing in the examining room to inject contrast material or monitor the patient.

RADIATION DOSE TO THE PATIENT

The radiation dose to a patient undergoing a CT study is within the range of many other diagnostic examinations and much less than for some specialized studies such as angiograms. However, under certain circumstances the patient dose may be surprisingly high, even exceeding 70 rads skin dose (3). Even this figure may be deceivingly low because dose does not decrease approximately exponentially with depth, as discussed below. The conditions leading to higher doses include multiple scans at a single level or use of older scanners with poorly optimized geometry, tubes, and electronics. Dose also increases for high-resolution scans with long scan times, high mAs settings, or geometrical modifications such as moving the tube closer to the patient, as is done in third-generation scanners. The use of pins (aperture grids) to decrease detector apertures in fourth-generation scanners requires increasing mAs and therefore radiation dose to compensate for the decreased absorption of photons by the detector array. Thin slices may also elevate the dose because of the need to increase tube output to suppress noise. Slight divergence of the beam out of the plane of the slice causes immediately adjacent tissue to be irradiated. Therefore, contiguous slices cause an increase in the dose of 20% to 40% (3). Overlapping slices also increase the dose.

The following are typical skin doses for a commonly available scanner using the manufaturer's recommended mAs and kVp settings with the scanner properly calibrated for testing:

Abdomen, 10 mm contiguous	2 to 4.5 rads
Abdomen, 5 mm contiguous	2 to 6.5 rads
Head	2 to 3 rads
Scanogram	0.05 to 0.1 rad

These figures will vary somewhat from scanner to scanner and with different technique factor selections. Every manufacturer publishes radiation dose values for its equipment, which should be reviewed. Radiation exposure should also be periodically tested.

As noted above, the skin dose figure can be misleading because the total tissue dose with CT is actually greater than with plain radiography (2,7). With conventional radiography, dose decreases approximately exponentially with tissue penetration. By contrast, in a CT scan of the head, the absorbed dose may be more nearly uniform throughout the entire head. With body scans, the dose in the center of the patient may be on the order of about one-third of the skin dose.

One should view marketing claims regarding radiation dose to the patient skeptically. Although a manufacturer may claim that patients on their scanners are exposed to only modest levels of radiation, special conditions may require increasing the X-ray dose to satisfy advertised resolution specifications, such as the need to use aperture grids as mentioned above and illustrated in Fig. 2-9. Also, solid-state detector arrays absorb almost 100% of all radiation reaching them, versus 60% to 80% for gas detectors. Therefore solid-state systems can help reduce patient radiation dose. However, the ability to modify dose also depends on other features.

Patient radiation exposure may vary greatly from scanner to scanner. Therefore it is worthwhile to have figures available for one's own scanners so that if questions arise regarding the radiation of a fetus, for example, they can be answered without guessing or doing time-consuming testing. The references at the end of this chapter discuss this important issue in much greater depth.

STRAY RADIATION

The dose to parts of the patient not directly irradiated and to individuals in the scanning room is quite small and results from scattering from within the patient, limitations in complete collimation of the beam, and radiation leakage directly from the X-ray tube (7). Figures for stray and leakage radiation from newer model scanners varies from about 1.5 to 5 mrads per scan at 1 meter from the scanner center at standard scan techniques (about 400 mAs, 140 kVp, with a body phantom in place). The radiation value depends on the scanner, the tube output, and the presence of scattering material (such as a patient) within the gantry. However, the values vary by about a factor of three from scanner to scanner, and one should be aware of the performance of one's own machine. Dose varies strongly with distance from the scanner. The area of highest dose falls roughly in the shape of a dumbbell emanating from the ring of tube rotation (Fig. 4-1). The minimum dose to a person standing in the room is received in the plane of the scanner gantry outside the gantry aperture because most of the radiation in this plane is collimated, shielded, or absorbed in the patient and the detectors.

The inverse square law applies to point sources of radiation of any kind. However, CT scanners do not approximate point sources because of colli-

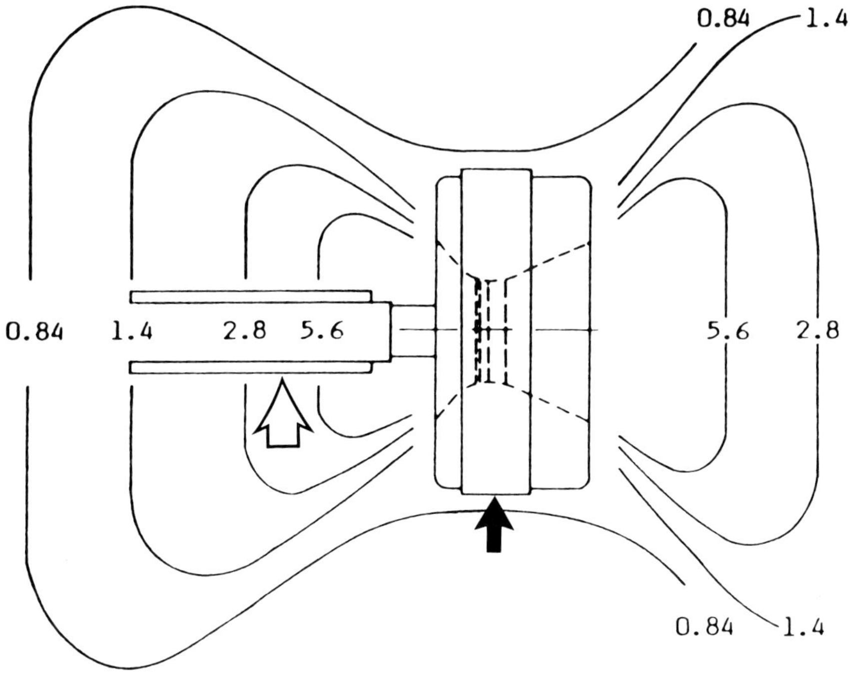

FIG. 4–1. Radiation emissions from a CT scanner. The scanner is viewed from above, with the gantry (arrow) and table (open arrow) indicated. The lines are isodose lines for radiation emissions including leakage and scatter from a body phantom. The greatest emissions occur immediately adjacent to the patient. Virtually no radiation is emitted in the plane of X-rays because of absorption in the detectors and gantry material. The numbers represent millirads per exposure for a 1,600-mAs scan, which is 4 to 6 times higher than an ordinary abdominal scan. The "5.6" line is at about 1 meter from isocenter. Thus the usual dose per scan to a person standing next to this scanner at this point, using average abdominal technique, is about 1 to 1.4 millirads. Figures for various scanners may vary by a factor of three or higher. (Diagram courtesy of General Electric Company, Medical Systems.)

mation and the circular motion of the tube assembly. Therefore, near a CT scanner, dose decreases less with distance than dictated by the inverse square law. However, at greater distances the scanner more closely resembles a point source, and the inverse square rule is better approximated. A radiological physicist should periodically measure radiation leakage.

RADIATION PROTECTION RULES

Despite the differences between fluoroscopy and CT, the usual rules regarding distance, time, and shielding apply as well as the principles regarding position relative to the scanner (5,6). Thus, dose may be minimized to other persons in the room by having them stand as far from the scanner and the patient as is feasible. The person injecting contrast is effectively protected by standing at arm's length and using an additional length of extension tubing. Time of exposure can be minimized by stepping out of the room as soon as the injection is completed. Standard lead aprons or movable lead shields reduce exposure to negligible levels. We routinely use all of these measures, including a lead apron as well as a shield, as a precaution if the person injecting must step away from the shield to aid the patient while scanning is proceeding. Shields are the most effective and preferred method of reducing exposure.

If attention to radiation precautions is poor, it is possible to exceed allowed personnel exposure limits, as occurred in our institution when one of our residents routinely reclined against the scanner gantry only 30 to 40 cm from the circle of tube travel while performing injections during his one month on the CT service. This dose was recorded by a badge outside of his lead apron at the neck. With proper precautions of distance, shielding, and time, it is possible to register virtually no radiation dose to an individual who regularly performs dynamic scanning as described above.

Several methods may be used for dynamic scanning (1), as discussed more fully in Chapters 6 and 14. One method uses a 2-min hand injection of contrast, with scanning started 45 to 60 sec later (4). Therefore, the person injecting is in the room for 60 to 75 sec after scanning begins and thus may be present for four to six scans. An alternative is to use a power injector, which we now often use. A third technique involves hanging a bottle of contrast material and pressurizing it with injected air, thereby also eliminating the need for someone to be present in the room during scanning (8).

REFERENCES

1. Burgener, F. A., and Hamlin, D. J. (1983): Contrast enhancement of hepatic tumors in CT: Comparison between bolus and infusion techniques. *AJR,* 140:291–295.

2. Chopp, M., Ewald, L., and Hartson, M. (1981): The contribution of internal scatter radiation dose during CT scan of the head. *Neuroradiology,* 22:145–150.
3. Coulam, C. M., and Erickson, J. J. (1981): Equipment considerations in computed tomography. In: *The Physical Basis of Medical Imaging,* edited by C. M. Coulam, J. J. Erickson, F. D. Rollo, and A. E. James, pp. 213–229. Appleton-Century-Crofts, New York.
4. Foley, W. D., Berland, L. L., Lawson, T. L., Smith, D. F., and Thorsen, M. K. (1983): Contrast enhancement technique for dynamic hepatic computed tomographic scanning. *Radiology,* 147:797–803.
5. Meredith, W. J., and Massey, J. B. (1977): Radiation protection: General principles and materials. In: *Fundamental Physics of Radiology,* 3rd edition, Chapter XLIII, pp. 629–642. Year Book Medical Publishers, Chicago.
6. Pagel, J. (1981): Radiation protection in diagnostic radiology. In: *The Physical Basis of Medical Imaging,* edited by C. M. Coulam, J. J. Erickson, F. D. Rollo, and A. E, James, pp. 303–327. Appleton-Century-Crofts, New York.
7. Pentlow, K. S. (1981): Dosimetry in computed tomography. In: *Radiology of the Skull and Brain: Technical Aspects of Computed Tomography,* edited by T. H. Newton and D. G. Potts, pp. 4228–4258. C. V. Mosby, St. Louis.
8. Zelenik, M. E., Mathis, J. M., and McDaniel, E. C. (1984): An infusion system for improved vascular opacification during CT. *Radiology* 152:816.

5

Selectable Scan Factors: Routine Scanning

Scanners offer differing degrees of flexibility in selecting scan factors. Each factor affects image quality, and the proper selection of certain factors is crucial to specialized applications. These scan factors include (a) scanned field of view, (b) reconstructed field of view, (c) matrix size, (d) slice thickness, (e) scan time and rotational arc of tube travel, (f) X-ray tube output (mAs and kVp), and (g) focal spot size and tube geometry. On some scanners factors are selected independently, whereas other units allow only factory preprogrammed or user-programmable sets of image factors supposedly optimized for various applications or patients of differing body habitus.

Nonstandardized nomenclature seriously confuses technique factor selection and equipment purchases by making comparisons of scanners more difficult. Sometimes companies are restricted from using the same terms for similar hardware and software items because of copyright limitations. However, the nomenclature may also serve to hide a scanner's limitations. Terminology may also be coined to attempt to make the terms simple enough so "even a radiologist could understand them."

These efforts often make the system harder to understand. One example is the use of the term *pulse width code* to indicate the length of a pulse of X-rays. A pulse width code of 1 indicates a 1.1-msec pulse. A code of 2 is 2.2 msec and 3 is 3.3 msec. Another example is one manufacturer's use of the terms *regular, precision,* and *high precision.* These refer to a combination of focal spot size, modified geometry, and the number of views obtained. A third company uses the term *scan time* to refer not to actual scan time, but as a code indicating the speed with which the tube travels in a circle around the patient during the scan. That is, a "scan time" of 2 may indicate an actual scan time of from approximately 2 to 4 sec depending on whether a tube rotation of 220°, 360°, or 398° is chosen. These idiosyncrasies can often be sorted out only by carefully reading the manuals and specifications or by consulting knowledgeable service or technical personnel.

SCANNED FIELD OF VIEW

In most scanners, two categories of field-of-view choices may be selected: (a) the scanned field of view and (b) the reconstructed or displayed field of view. The scanned field of view refers to the size of the field within the gantry aperture, from which data are used for reconstruction. If a small patient is being scanned, then no useful information is received by the detectors in the periphery of the detector array, and the computer is instructed to ignore these values to streamline reconstruction.

A term that may be applied to the choice of scanned field size is *body calibration.* This differs from the types of calibration for field uniformity mentioned in Chapter 2, p. 24. For example, a "small" body calibration may refer to a 25-cm scanned field of view, "medium" to a 35-cm field, and "large" to a 48-cm field. Each of these selections involves different computed corrections for beam hardening and scatter based on anticipated body size.

The presence of tissue outside the scanned field diminishes the accuracy of CT attenuation numbers and may introduce shading artifacts to the edges of the picture (Fig. 5-1). Streaks may also occur, although the severity of these artifacts varies from scanner to scanner. These shading and streak artifacts are termed *out-of-field artifacts* and occur because the reconstruction process depends on attenuation information from all of the tissue in the field. This information is unavailable if the values from some of the detectors receiving an attenuated beam are ignored for reconstruction. Also, in some scanners, the detectors at the extreme ends of the array serve as ongo-

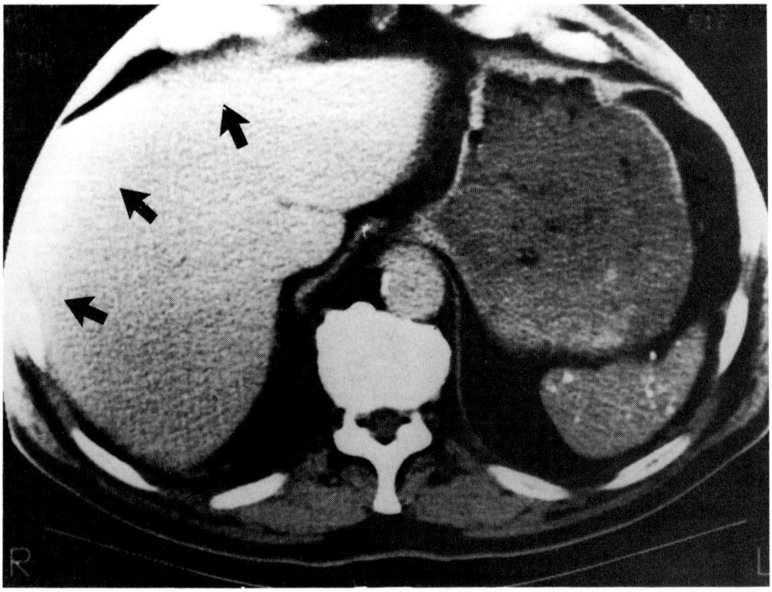

FIG. 5–1. Use of an inappropriately small scanned field of view on a third-generation scanner. Because data from outside the scanned field-of-view are ignored, shading artifacts occur at the periphery of the image (arrows). A small portion of the patient's anatomy is not displayed, and the CT attenuation numbers are inaccurate.

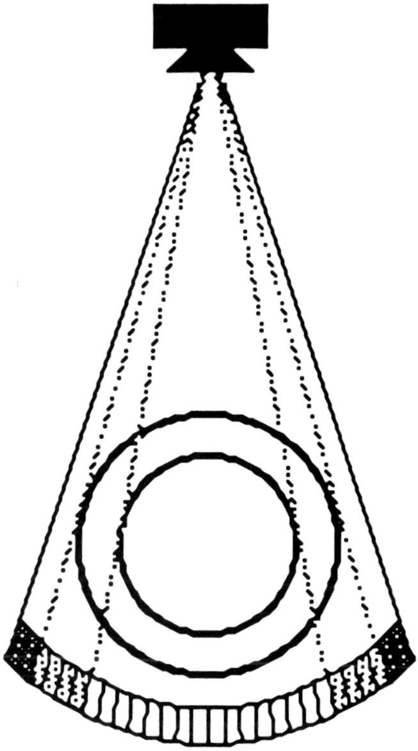

FIG. 5–2. Different field-of-view choices. In the larger field-of-view circle, only a small number of detectors are available at the periphery of the field of view to receive unattenuated X-rays for detector calibration. When the smaller field of view is selected, no useful information is received in the lightly shaded detectors. In some scanners, to streamline the reconstruction process, the data from these peripheral, nonreference detectors are deleted from the computation process.

ing reference channels for moment-to-moment variations in X-ray output (Fig. 5-2), as discussed in Chapter 2, p. 24. If these detectors are obstructed by a large patient, then corrections will be inaccurate.

Optimizing the scanned field of view also affects the image resolution in third-generation scanners that decrease the tube-object distance for high-resolution scans. This decreases the effective detector aperture and therefore improves the spatial resolution, but decreases the scanned field of view (see Fig. 2-6).

DISPLAYED FIELD OF VIEW

Properly selecting the scanned field of view is important primarily to minimize artifacts, but properly selecting the displaying field of view is important to optimize lesion detectability. Therefore, scanners permit a second type of field-of-view selection: the displayed field of view. This field size determines the size of the image on the monitor and hard copy (film) and, along with matrix size, determines the limits of perceived detail.

The displayed or reconstructed field of view is the area (usually circular for bodies or oval for heads) selected for display on the monitor (Fig. 5-3). When a selection for the scanned field is also required, the displayed field may be equal to or smaller than the scanned field, but never larger. The displayed field may be at the center of the scanned field or may be off-center. Examples of the need for off-center fields are temporal bone studies and evaluation of one limb when both are scanned.

Many technologists are prone to select too large a field of view, thus creating smaller images than optimal. They do this because positioning the patient within the exact center of the scanning ring is then less crucial and because visualizing the entire body contour is more aesthetically pleasing. However, this practice usually diminishes diagnostic information.

There are two reasons why selecting too large a displayed field of view is disadvantageous. First, when the displayed field is too large, the size of the body region being examined within the image is reduced. This impairs the perceptibility of detail by decreasing the size of the image on the viewer's retina (5). Second, in addition to the problem of trying to interpret small pictures, the actual displayed detail is diminished because the body is displayed on fewer pixels. Therefore, the amount of tissue occupied by each pixel is greater (see Fig. 5-3). Theoretically, objects on the order of the size of one pixel (ordinarily 0.5 to 1.5 mm) might not be resolved with the smaller image, whereas they might be seen with the larger image.

On the other hand, selecting too small a field of view may delete the display of an important part of the body if abnormalities are near the skin. Although light localizers are routinely used to aid in positioning, poor centering may still occur, particularly with large patients, or the patient may move after being properly positioned. Off-center positioning is more

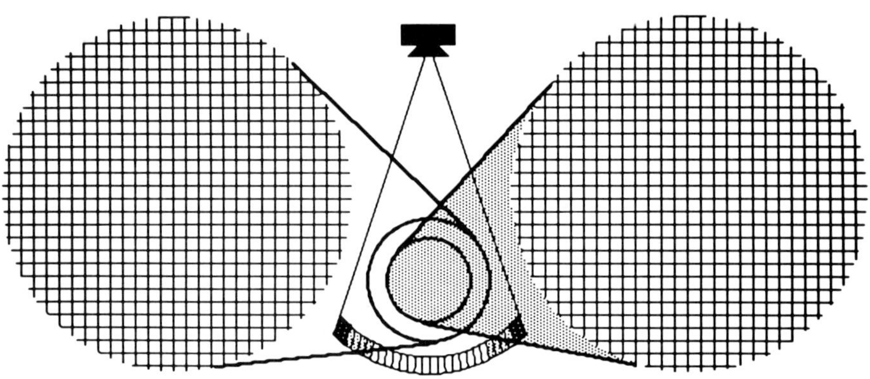

FIG. 5–3. Effects of different field-of-view choices on the matrix. Despite differences in the size of the displayed field of view selected, both fields may still be displayed with the same number of pixels. With the smaller field-of-view choice, a smaller amount of tissue is represented by each pixel. The resulting representation of tissue on the screen will therefore be larger. Thus, a smaller field-of-view selection leads to a smaller amount of tissue per pixel, a higher spatial resolution, and a larger image of the selected tissue on the monitor.

obvious on a small pixel size because one side of the patient may be cut off while the other is well within the field. Usually, the best compromise is to select a scanned field that includes the lateral body contours and use a displayed field for the area of interest only (Fig. 5-4). This optimizes resolution and minimizes artifacts.

Most units permit more than one reconstruction to be performed on a slice. If the raw data representing the actual numerical attenuation values obtained from each detector are saved, a new image may be reconstructed to display a new field, which may be of any size up to the scanned field of view. Units vary in their options for this type of operation. For example, some scanners require an indication of the intention to perform these secondary reconstructions even before the scan is performed.

MATRIX AND PIXEL SIZES

In some older or less expensive systems, the information in the image is "display limited." That is, more information is present in the raw data than can be shown in the matrix. The reasons for using smaller display matrices are the markedly reduced requirements for memory and the faster speed of reconstruction. It is also expensive to produce monitors satisfactory for displaying large matrices. The discrepancy between resolution limits in the raw data and display capacity is handled in many systems by providing a second chance to reconstruct the raw data on a smaller displayed field of view as mentioned above. This "target," "zoom," or "ReView™" reconstruction is different from simple image magnification, which will be discussed later. However, the newer, top-of-the-line systems use a standard 512 matrix in which the display much more closely approaches the theoretical limits of resolution than could the 256 and 320 matrices. Thus the need for secondary reconstructions may be reduced.

Note that when discussing "smaller" and "larger" matrices we are referring only to the number of pixels in the matrix, not the physical size of the image or monitor, the scanned or displayed field of view, or the amount of tissue displayed in each pixel. These concepts must be considered separately to understand this somewhat confusing topic.

As an example, a system with a 320 × 320 pixel matrix and a 35-cm field of view has a 1.1-mm pixel size, whereas the same matrix with a 45-cm field of view has a 1.3-mm pixel. If the 320 × 320 matrix is expanded to a 512 × 512 matrix, then the pixel size decreases to 0.69 mm and 0.81 mm for the same field-of-view choices, respectively, thus providing the basis for displaying improved detail. Again, this designation of pixel size does not refer to the size of the point on the monitor, but rather to the amount of tissue represented by each pixel.

Commonly used matrix sizes are 256 × 256, 320 × 320, 360 × 360, and

A

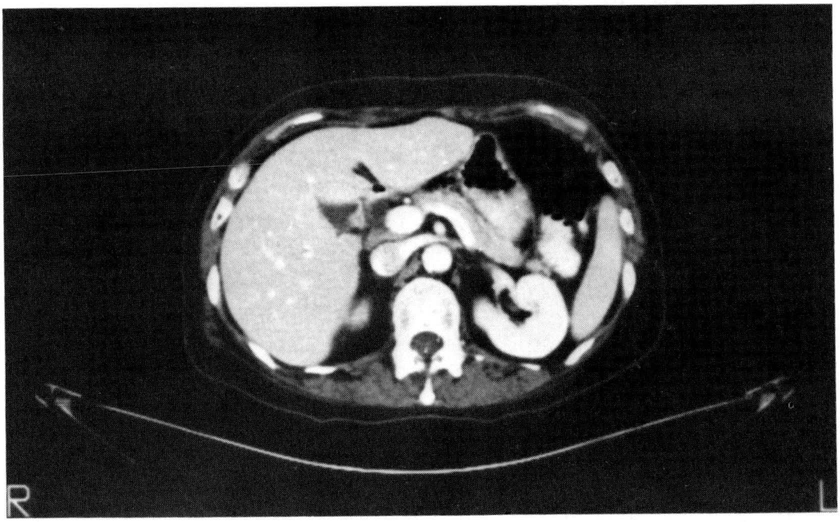

FIG. 5–4. Effects of various displayed and scanned field-of-view choices. **A**. Scan reconstructed on too large a displayed field of view. The image is small within the center of the displayed field, making appreciation of detail more difficult, increasing the amount of tissue represented per pixel, thus decreasing spatial resolution, and wasting the space around the patient. **B**. Scan in another patient demonstrating an appropriate selection of field of view but improper patient positioning. No shading artifacts are introduced to the edge of the image as in Fig. 5–1 because the scanned field of view was large enough to encompass the patient whereas the displayed field of view deletes the left portion of the patient's image. If a larger displayed field of view had been selected, the poor positioning would have been less apparent. **C**. A field of view that is appropriate under most conditions may not be appropriate for every patient. In this case, a subcutaneous abscess (arrow) was partly obscured by the selection of too small a displayed field of view for this patient.

512 × 512 pixels. Some systems provide only one of these, whereas others permit two or three. A circular-field 256 matrix uses over 51,000 pixels. A circular 512 matrix has about four times as many, with almost 206,000 pixels. This comparison alone strikingly indicates the much more demanding computer requirements of the larger matrix scanners. However, many other more complex and time-consuming calculations occur in the newer, high-resolution scanners. It is only because of advances in technology and design that image reconstruction times have decreased rather than increased with the newer scanners. Nevertheless, for any one scanner, increasing matrix size increases reconstruction time. However, the differences in reconstruction time between the 512 and 256 matrices are not on the order of the 4:1 ratio just mentioned, because some of the reconstruction time is occupied by calibration and correction programs, which must be done regardless of matrix size.

As reconstruction time decreases for smaller matrices, so does the ability to perceive detail. Using a 256 matrix routinely for viewing body scans may lead to interpretive uncertainties and errors that do not occur with a larger matrix. However, it is possible to achieve the same resolution with a 256

B

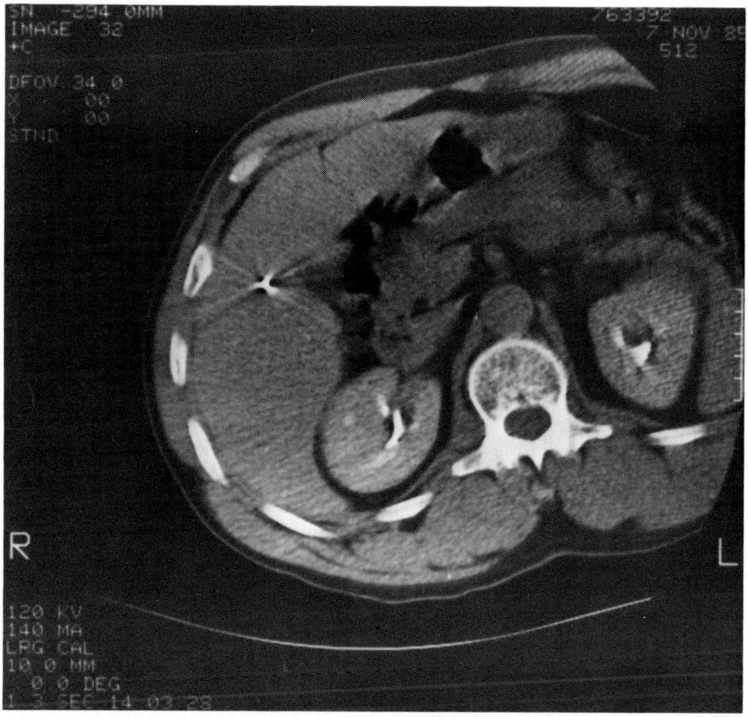
IMAGE 32
DFOV 34.0
STND
763392
7 NOV 85
512
R
L
120 KV
140 MA
LRG CAL
10.0 MM
0.0 DEG
1.3 SEC 14:03:28

C

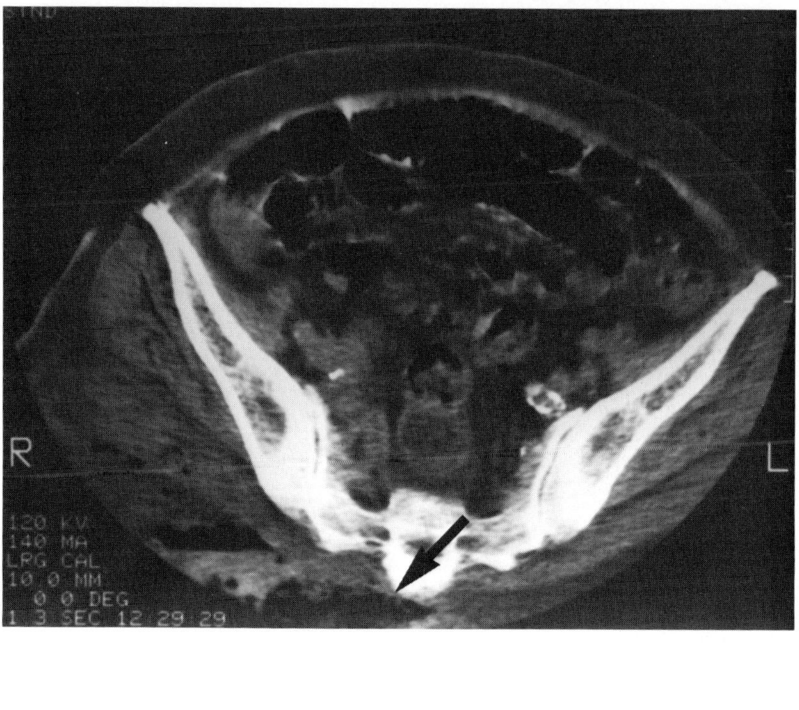
R
L
120 KV
140 MA
LRG CAL
10.0 MM
0.0 DEG
1.3 SEC 12:29:29

matrix and a 512 matrix if the displayed field of view is limited to half the diameter on the smaller matrix, because the amount of tissue represented by each pixel is the same in both situations. Thus matrix size is only one of the several determinants of resolution.

Some older systems employed a 512 matrix system for display, while reconstructing only to a smaller matrix. These are not of equivalent quality to true 512 matrix images because data calculated for a smaller matrix are expanded to fill more pixels. However, if each pixel were simply magnified, the edges of the pixels would be visible and the image would appear "boxy" (Fig. 5-5). Thus these expanded pixels are smoothed to a larger matrix by a process called interpolation, in which adjacent pixel values are averaged. This process is also used for magnifying small fields within images originally reconstructed to large matrices.

A system using a 512 matrix may offer the smaller matrices to provide faster image reconstruction, but then only display the image on the center 256 × 256 or 320 × 320 pixels of the 512 display, thus creating a tiny image. However, these smaller matrix images may then be interpolated to the larger matrix to make the image size comparable.

One application for a small matrix option is pediatric imaging, where pixel size on a small matrix may approach the theoretical limits of resolution. Also, scans done just to localize biopsy needles or organ boundaries may not require high resolution, and the faster reconstruction of the smaller matrices improves efficiency. In practice, one matrix is usually selected for a specific application. On our scanners, we prefer the 512 matrix for full-

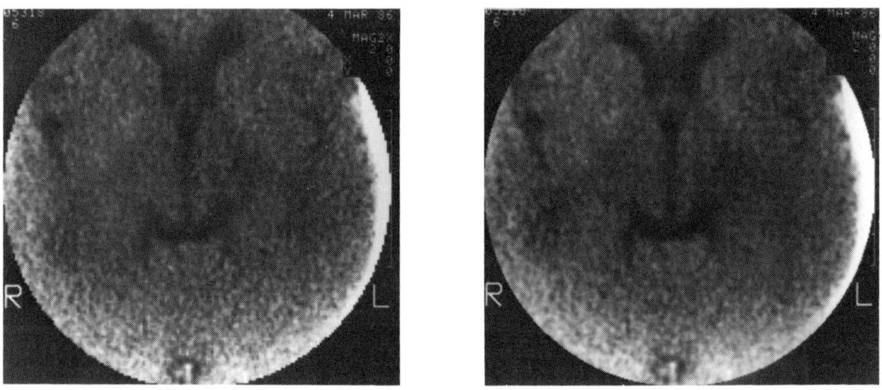

FIG. 5-5. Effects of interpolation. **A**. This image was produced by magnifying each pixel by a factor of two. The edges of the pixels are apparent, giving the image a noisy or "boxy" appearance. **B**. This image illustrates the influence of interpolation in which the sharp edges between the magnified pixels are averaged and therefore smoothed.

body scanning. Although the 320 matrix is often a reasonable alternative, we believe that the 256 matrix is diagnostically inferior or unacceptable.

SLICE THICKNESS

Slice thickness strongly affects perceived detail because of the effect of volume averaging of structures with complex shapes. The pixel represents only two of the three dimensions observed on a CT scan. The third is depth, which is determined by slice thickness. The combination of pixel size and slice thickness is represented by the voxel, or volume element. Thus, for example, changing slice thickness from 10 mm to 5 mm changes voxel size by a factor of two, and improves resolution.

However, the disadvantages of using thin slices are formidable. To scan the same area as with 10-mm slices, 5-mm slices require twice as many scans and twice the reconstruction time, filming time, and tube wear, and thus greater cost. Nevertheless, thin-slice technique is valuable for several applications, particularly for areas with complex anatomy and intrinsically high subject contrast such as the temporal bones and orbits. For body scanning, thin slices may be used despite low subject contrast in such areas as the larynx (2), parathyroids (9), and biliary system.

Although using the thinner slice diminishes the problem of the averaging of tissues within thicker slices, thin-slice images are degraded by noise if tube output is unchanged, because the X-ray collimator creates thinner slices by shielding part of the X-ray beam. The detector is unchanged (Fig. 5-6). Therefore, for a given tube X-ray output, about one-half the number of photons are received in the detectors for a 5-mm slice as for a 10-mm slice. This increases the level of "quantum noise" (7), a statistical phenomenon seen in any system that uses photons or quanta to produce an image. As the number of photons contributing to the image decreases, the appearance of statistical noise increases. This is the same phenomenon that is seen with "fast" X-ray or photographic film, which is more sensitive to the X-ray or light photons. Each photon is responsible for relatively more exposure than with slower films, and the film reaches a satisfactory level of density more quickly, but the resulting image is more "grainy" or "noisy."

To compensate for increased noise in thin-section CT, tube output is usually moderately increased. However, tube output does not necessarily need to be doubled because minimizing the effect of volume averaging with the thin slice improves clinical detail. This improved detail partly compensates for the noise. Also, the relationship between photon fluence and perceived image quality is not linear (Figs. 5-7, 5-8) (6,10). That is, if X-ray photon fluence is doubled, the subjective impression of image quality is not necessarily doubled. There is a threshold beyond which less additional information is gained.

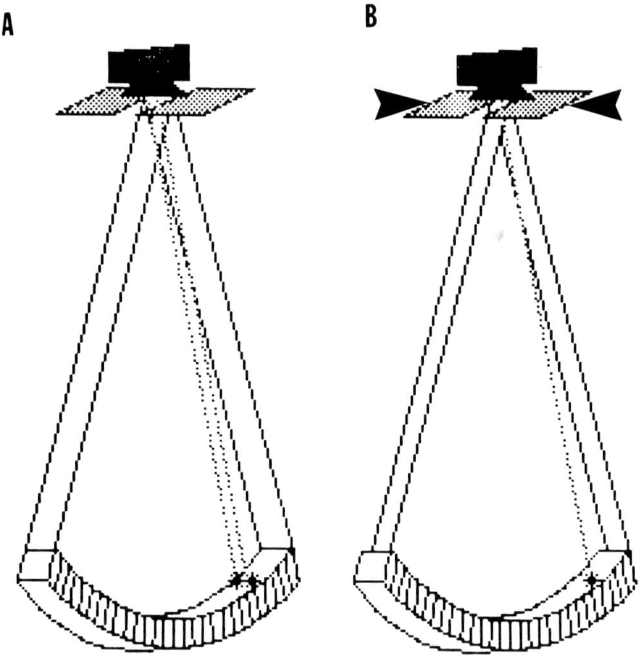

FIG. 5–6. Effect of thinner slices on photon absorption. **A**. Rays striking a single detector at a standard slice thickness. **B**. The beam collimators (arrowheads) are moved closer together, narrowing the beam and decreasing the number of photons that may strike the detector array. Therefore, X-ray tube output may have to be increased somewhat to compensate for the decreased number of photons used to compose an image.

With our newer scanners, we usually use tube output settings for both standard and thin slices that are slightly lower than the manufacturers' recommendations. This has led to a greater ability to perform extended dynamic scans and has extended the life of our X-ray tubes without seriously diminishing our image quality.

X-ray dose changes are also related to intrinsic subject contrast. For example, temporal bones must be scanned with thin (1.0 or 1.5 mm) slices because the clinically relevant anatomic detail is considerably smaller than the standard 1 × 1 × 10 mm voxel. However, this is also an area of high subject contrast and therefore small pixel-to-pixel density differences or noise within these areas may not interfere with interpretation because of the great inherent differences in density among the tissues being studied. Therefore, if one decreases the slice thickness from 10 to 1.5 mm, one need not compensate by increasing tube output by a factor of 10 to 1.5, or 6.7 (Fig. 5-9).

We routinely use 10-mm slices for body scanning. However, slices of 3 to

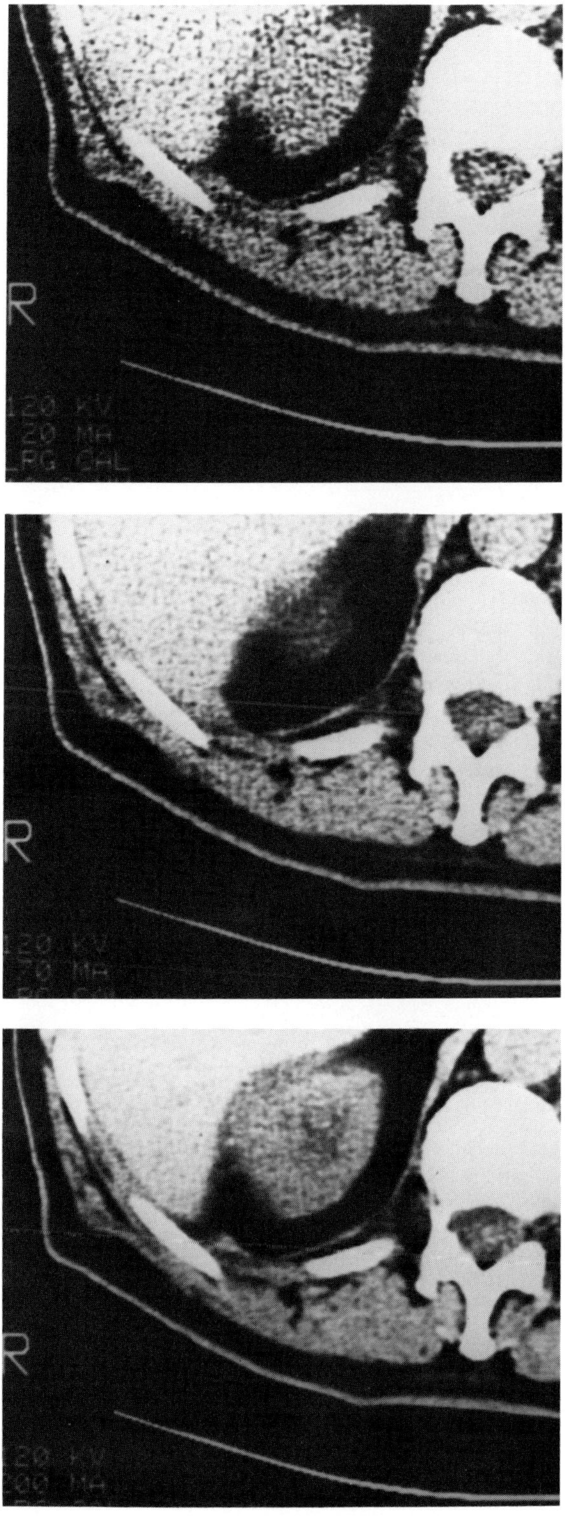

A

B

C

FIG. 5–7. Influence of increasing mAs on image noise. **A** was done with 40-mAs technique, **B** with 140 mAs, and **C** with 400 mAs. There is a more marked difference in image quality between **A** and **B** than between **B** and **C**. Therefore, increasing the mAs beyond an approximate threshold level may cause a diminishing improvement in scan quality.

A B

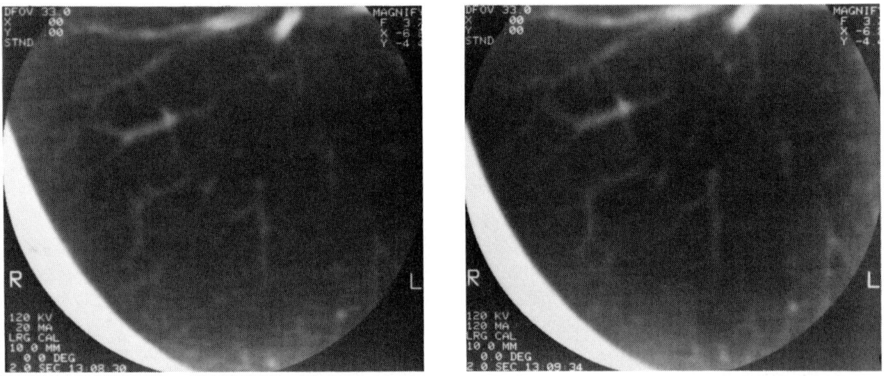

FIG. 5–8. Images of the lung taken at markedly different mAs. **A** was done with 40 mAs and **B** with 240 mAs. Despite this marked difference in tube output, there is very little difference in image quality because there is an inherently large subject contrast between lung tissue and vessels. Because these images are viewed at a wide window, the displayed contrast of the image noise is suppressed.

A

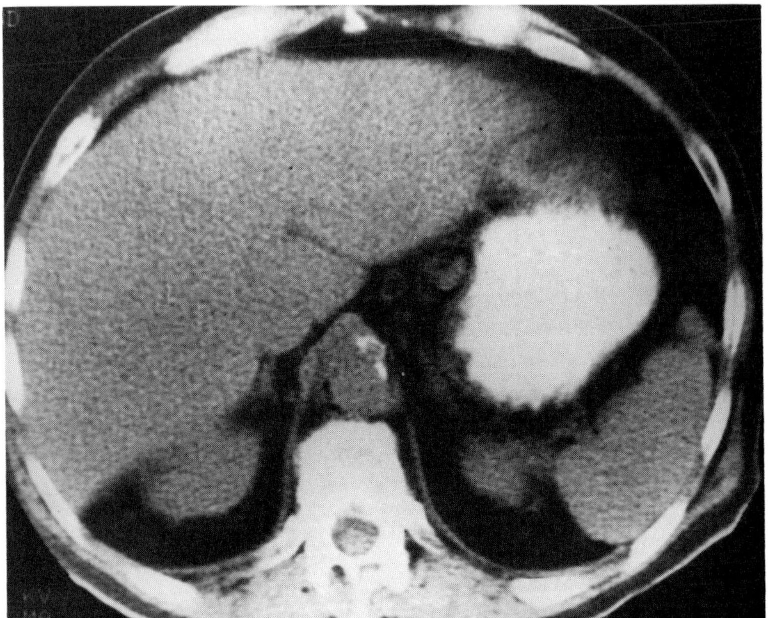

FIG. 5–9. Influence of thin slices and changing mAs on image quality. **A.** A 10-mm slice of the abdomen done at 280 mAs. This is a standard abdominal technique. **B.** A 3-mm slice done at the same level with the same mAs. Spatial detail is improved, with better definition of smaller vascular structures and nodes in the gastrohepatic ligament area (arrow), but quantum noise is increased because of the thinness of the slice at the same mAs. **C.** A 3-mm slice

B

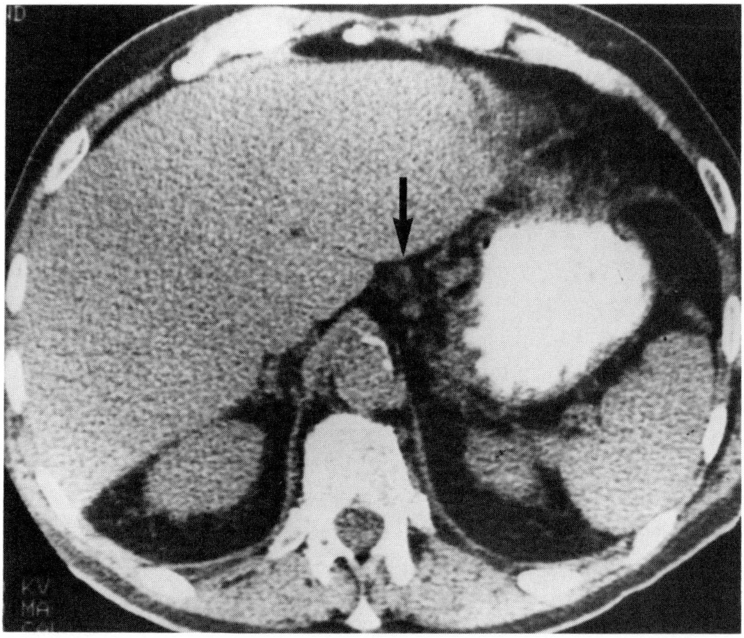

C

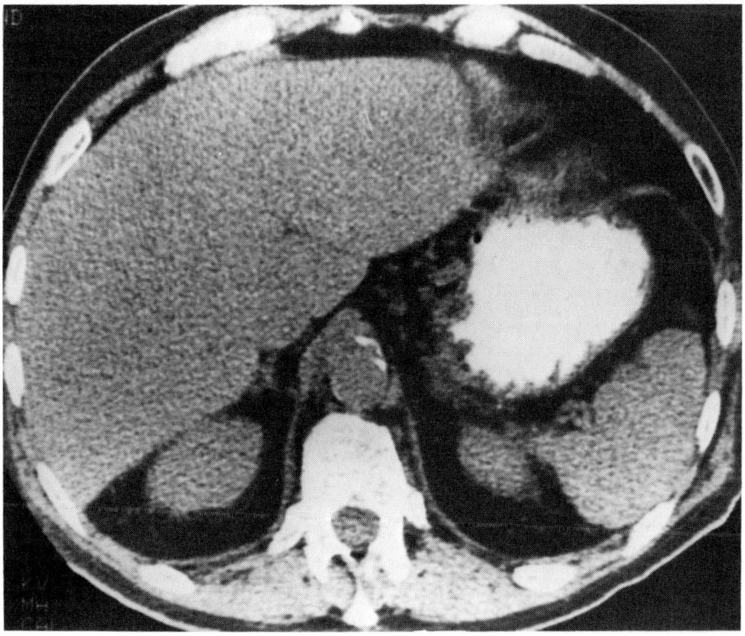

at the same level with 400 mAs. The increase in mAs has decreased the quantum noise compared to the 280-mAs image, and the improved spatial detail is retained. This leads to an overall improvement in diagnostic image quality compared to the 10-mm slice despite a slightly increased level of noise compared to the thicker slice.

6 mm are commonly used to display complex anatomy in the pancreas, porta hepatis, pulmonary hila, neck, bones such as hips and feet, and the head. Slices of 1 to 2 mm thick are reserved for areas of intrinsically high contrast such as the temporal bones.

We will define and discuss window widths and levels in Chapter 10, but it is relevant to allude to them at this point (10). For example, lung and bone have intrinsically high contrast (density differences) and are usually viewed at wide window settings. Small differences in density may not be discriminated in an image viewed at a wide window. However, scans of whole body regions including high-contrast areas such as lung and bone also usually include areas with low subject contrast. Therefore, scans of many areas are usually done at a relatively high X-ray output to provide diagnostic information about areas of both low and high subject contrast within the same slice. For example, scans of the chest include lung, which, if present alone within the slice, could be scanned at low radiation dose because of its high intrinsic contrast. However, such scans also include the mediastinum, which has a low subject contrast and thus must be scanned at a higher radiation dose to give satisfactory diagnostic information (Fig. 5-10). Another example is scans of the head to examine the temporal bone, which include the high-contrast temporal bone and low-contrast brain. However, if one wishes only to study the high-contrast areas, such the lung and the temporal bone in these examples, then lower X-ray output and/or thinner slices may be used.

An alternative to contiguous thin-slice scanning is noncontiguous thin-slice scanning: for example, 5-mm slices at 10-mm intervals. This option retains the advantage of higher resolution while eliminating the disadvantage of greater time and expense. This solution is clearly not applicable to some examinations where skipping 5-mm sections may lead to missing small lesions or detailed anatomy. Also, it may not be possible to perform coronal or sagittal reformations of images if this approach is used.

Another commonly used approach is overlapping of slices, for example, 5-mm slices at 3-mm intervals. This is done to improve the appreciaton of the continuity of fine detail, while avoiding the use of photon-poorer thinner slices. Overlapping slices are particularly useful for multiplanar or three-dimensional reformations. Slice-to-slice discontinuities are smoothed by the averaging created with overlapping areas. One disadvantage of using overlapping slices is an increased radiation dose.

The approach in our institution is to virtually always do thin slices in a contiguous, nonoverlapping manner. The rationale for this policy is that if sufficient detail is required to warrant thin slices, then examining the entire area rather than only half of it is probably indicated, and overlapped slices do not provide as great detail, although they increase the dose. However, this type of selection depends on the quality of the scanner and the specific application.

A

B

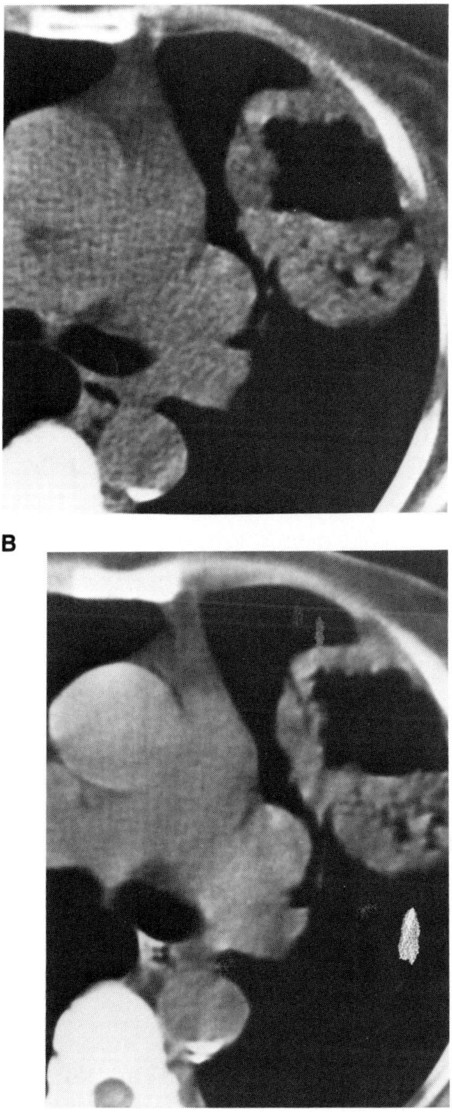

FIG. 5–10. Portions of the same slices as in Fig. 5–8, filmed at soft-tissue settings. The difference in mAs between the 40-mAs scan (**A**) and the 240-mAs scan (**B**) is more apparent when filmed at soft-tissue settings than at lung settings. Therefore, tube output may have to be increased somewhat to obtain satisfactory diagnostic information in both high and low subject contrast areas within the same slice.

SCAN TIME, SAMPLING, AND ROTATIONAL ARC

Scan times have decreased by orders of magnitude since the earliest scanners. Scans formerly requiring 4½ min may now take less than 1 sec. This has been accomplished by advances in all aspects of CT technology including the patient support table, gantry, tube, detectors, and computers. However, this section will be concerned not with these advances, but rather with the significance of using various scan speed options on any specific scanner. Every scanner offers multiple scan speeds because the most rapid speed possible is not advantageous for every application. Faster scan speeds may too severely limit X-ray photon fluence or data sampling.

The maximum rate of X-ray output is indicated by the maximum milliampereage (mA), which is a measure of the electrical current across the X-ray tube. The specifics of selecting mA will be discussed later, but the maximum mA achievable with modern X-ray tubes is one of the significant limitations to building machines with even faster scan speeds. For any machine, the mAs can be selected by changing the mA (tube output per unit time), by changing the speed at which the X-ray tube (for a fourth-generation scanner) or tube-detector system (for a third-generation system) travels around the patient, or by changing the length of the arc through which the tube or tube-detector system travels (Fig. 5-11). Typical choices for scan arc are about 220° and 360° for most third-generation scanners and an additional choice of 400° for most fourth-generation scanners and their variants. Scan times may vary on a modern conventional scanner from about 1 to 10 sec. Choices for scan angle also significantly affect other aspects of image quality, and the effect of scan angle choices is also quite different between third- and fourth-generation units, as will be discussed below.

Longer scan times may be preferable for areas that may easily be held motionless, such as the head and the spine. When scan times (exposure time in seconds) are lengthened and tube output (mA) is reduced while the product of the two (mAs) is held constant, somewhat less stress is put on the X-ray tube. The greatest stress occurs when the tube is operated consistently near the maximum mA allowable.

With conventional radiography, motion causes edges to blur because they project onto different parts of the film during different parts of the exposure. With CT, motion causes artifacts because when the body is viewed from different perspectives at different times during the scan, the received data are inconsistent. Therefore, theoretically, shortening scan time does not always reduce motion artifact. This is partly explainable by considering the intermittent nature of motion. If, for example, a segment of bowel moves only for 2 sec out of 10 and a 2-sec scan is done, then motion may occur throughout the scan and will create artifacts. If a 10-sec scan were done on the same segment, motion would be occurring during only one-fifth of the scan, and the artifact would be reduced because there would be fewer inconsistent data.

Nevertheless, empirically, shorter scan times usually diminish motion artifacts and minimize the effects of intrinsic motion in such organs as the heart and the bowel. Also, children and uncooperative patients are better scanned with short scan times. Fast scanning also usually helps to improve patient comfort. Several scanners are now capable of producing consistently good images with 3-sec scans or less, and this may be taken as the standard by which units should be compared.

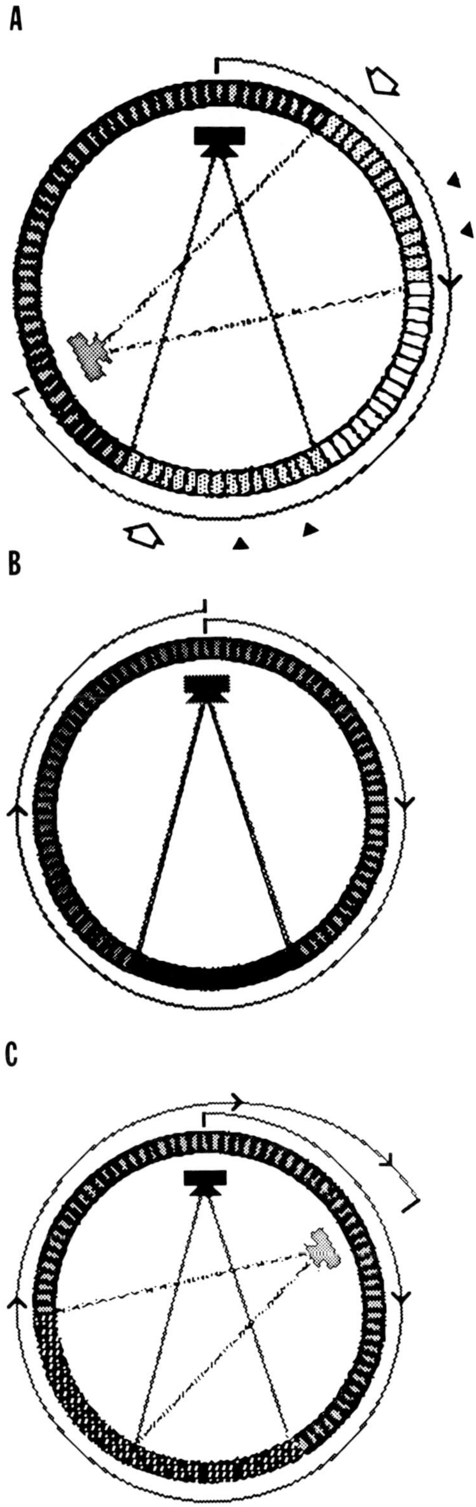

FIG. 5–11. Varying arcs of tube rotation for a fourth-generation scanner. **A**. Half scan. Tube rotation as indicated by the outer arrow is 180° plus the approximate arc of the fan beam. The detectors that are more lightly shaded are sampled for a smaller number of rays than those that are more heavily shaded. For example, the detectors indicated by the arrowheads receive X-rays from only a part of the fan beam. The detectors indicated by the open arrows receive X-rays from most but not all of the fan beam, whereas the remainder of the heavily shaded detectors receive X-rays from the entire span of the fan beam. **B**. Full scan. The tube starts and ends at the same point. The detectors exposed at the start and stop points receive some X-rays from the beginning and near the end of the scan. **C**. Overscan. A full scan plus an additional rotation equivalent to the approximate angular arc of the fan beam. Every detector now receives rays from contiguous points in time throughout the full arc of the fan beam, unlike in **B**, in which some detectors receive some information from the beginning and some information from the end of the scan only.

Data sampling is the other important factor affecting scan time selection. A minimum number of samples is usually required to create an image free of noticeable sampling artifacts (aliasing) (8), although this number varies from one application and one scanner to the next. The number of samples or views is determined by the nature of the unit, the scan angle, and the scan time.

The issue of aliasing highlights a significant difference between third- and fourth-generation machines. Understanding this topic first requires a clear comprehension of the terms *ray* and *view*. The entire set of data samples that is used to reconstruct a CT image is composed of the information from thousands of rays. A ray is a single line of X-rays from the tube to a single detector at a single moment in time. A view or projection is a set of rays. A view may be thought of as similar to a view of an eye or a camera. That is, one can "view" a scene from a particular vantage point. If one wishes to obtain more information about an object or landscape, one moves to a different position to obtain a different "view." Therefore, with a CT scanner, a view is the set of rays from a particular vantage point or angle. For a third-generation scanner the vantage point is the X-ray tube at a particular moment in time. For a fourth-generation scanner, the vantage point is a detector element. This is discussed more fully below.

There are two components of sampling: angular sampling and ray sampling. Angular sampling is determined by the angular distance between each view obtained during the scan (Fig. 5-12). Ray sampling is determined by the angle between each pair of rays within a view. The difference between rays and views in various scanners is also discussed in Chapter 7, p. 77.

In a third-generation scanner, a view is a projection of rays on the detector array. More views are obtained by moving the tube-detector assembly a smaller angle before taking more samples. Thus the number of views can be and often is variable, but the number of rays per view is fixed by the assembly geometry. Therefore, the angular sampling or number of different views is variable, but ordinarily the ray sampling is fixed. However, a clever development by Elscint increases the ray sampling for a third-generation system by rapidly switching between two focal spots as the tube travels around the patient (Fig. 5-13).

With a third-generation system, the successive views are composed of data from the detector as it moves incrementally around the patient. Every view is captured in one instant as the tube-detector array moves around the patient. Thus views may be averaged with one another, but the data composing one view represent data from only a single moment. The number of views is modified by changing the number of times the detectors are sampled.

By contrast, on a fourth-generation scanner, a view is the set of rays received by a single detector. Therefore, the number of views is fixed at a maximum by the number of detectors, but the tube may be moved in

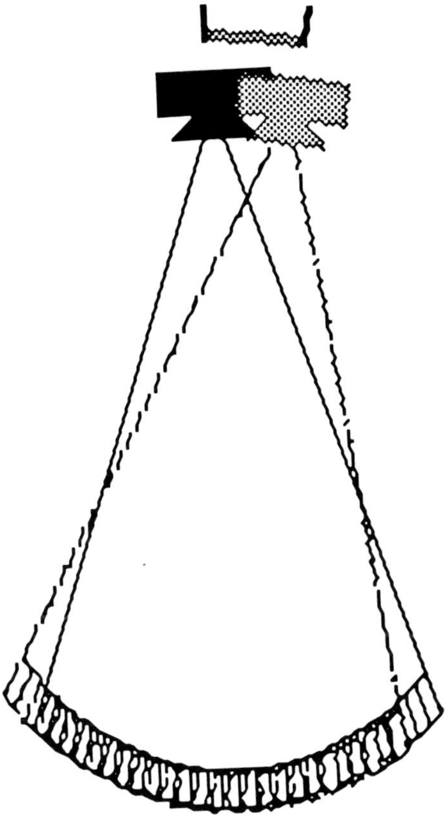

FIG. 5–12. Angular sampling for a third-generation scanner. The tube-detector assembly is moved through a small angle for successive views. For a third-generation scanner, the smaller the angle between samples, the greater the number of views. For a fourth-generation scanner, angular sampling is fixed by the geometry of the fixed detectors, but ray sampling may be varied.

shorter increments to obtain more rays per view. Thus, the angular sampling is fixed, whereas the ray sampling is variable. The greater the number of detectors for a specific arc, the greater the number of rays and the greater the potential spatial resolution.

For a fourth-generation scanner, because the detector array is fixed in space, views are constructed from sequential rays striking single detectors as the fan beam passes the detectors (Fig. 5-14). Each view is then constructed from data obtained over a short period of time rather than in a single moment as with third-generation scanners. Furthermore, detectors (responsible for individual views) receiving X-rays only near the beginning and the end of each scan contain the most inconsistent data because of motion during the scan. The rays from these "tainted" views may then be averaged or "feathered" by weighting factors with data from the views taken at the tube position 180° apart as described above (see Chapter 7, p. 77).

The Nyquist theorem (1) relates the sampling frequency to the inherent spatial frequencies (Fig. 5-15), which were mentioned earlier regarding scanograms. The theorem states that sampling must be done at least twice the

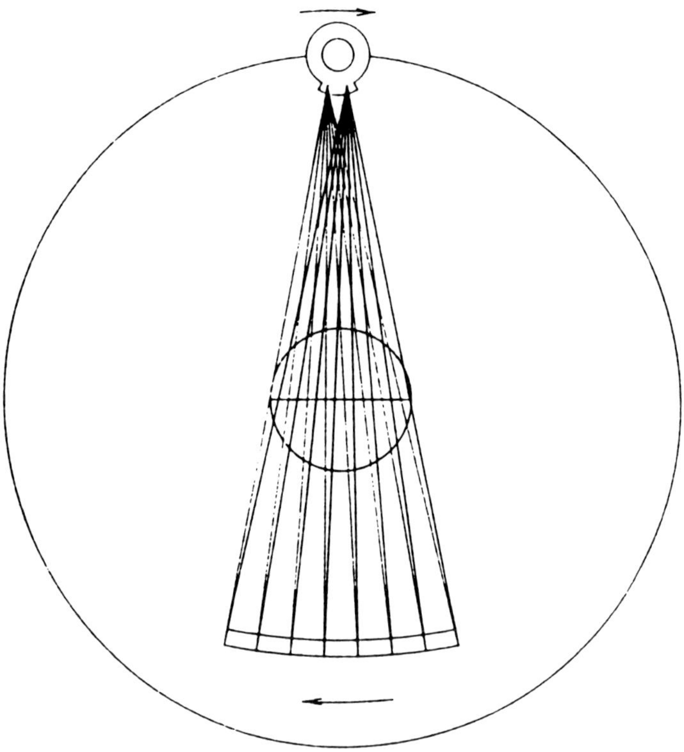

FIG. 5–13. Use of the dynamic focal spot to increase ray sampling on a third-generation scanner. The X-ray source is electronically switched rapidly between two positions. This extra perspective effectively increases the number of rays per view without increasing the number of detectors. (Diagram courtesy of Elscint, Inc.)

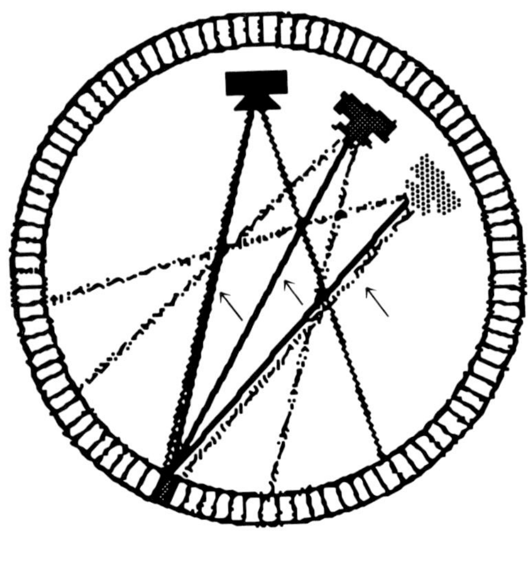

FIG. 5–14. Nature of views on a fourth-generation scanner. For this type of scanner, a view is composed of a set of rays (arrows) from various parts of the fan angle as the tube passes by, in contrast to a third-generation view, which is acquired at a single instant in time.

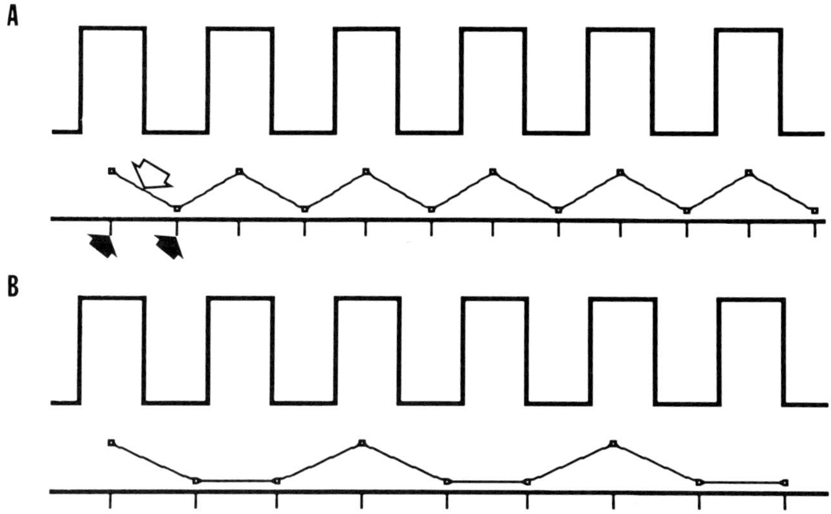

FIG. 5–15. Illustration of the Nyquist theorem with regard to the required sampling frequency for various spatial frequencies. **A**. The square wave represents an actual object with a spatial frequency as illustrated. The hatch marks (black arrows) on the horizontal line at the bottom indicate points at which the object is viewed or sampled. The response curve (open arrow) is also indicated. When the object is sampled often enough so that there is one sample for each peak and trough of the wave, the response curve has the appropriate frequency. However, samples are still not obtained often enough to represent the true shape of the curve. **B**. If samples are taken less often, the interpreted frequency (response curve) is lower than the true spatial frequency. Therefore, the interpreted spatial frequency is an "alias" of the true spatial frequency.

spatial frequency of the object scanned. Thus a sample should be taken at least as often as each peak and trough of the wave defining the frequency. If a lesser sampling rate is used, then only occasional peaks and troughs may be seen, which will lead to the interpretation of a lower frequency that is not really present (an alias frequency). This means further that for a specific sampling rate, the only frequencies that are accurately detectable are ones less than half of that rate. A corollary is that at least two samples should be obtained per beam width (the width of the component of the fan beam composing a ray). When sampling is insufficient, streak artifacts may emanate from objects with higher spatial frequencies than are accurately readable, such as bone edges or gas-soft tissue interfaces in bowel. When these streaks are fine and regular, they may contribute to what appears to be noise in the image. This is particularly true when the streaks cross as they emanate from multiple sources within the image.

Because of the differences noted between third- and fourth-generation machines, each generation is more prone to different types of sampling artifacts. Too few views will create view streak artifacts or view aliasing (see

Fig. 2-12). View aliasing is characterized by fine streaks emanating from high-frequency interfaces, with the streaks being more visible at greater distances from the point of origination. They are reduced by increasing the number of views (see Fig. 2-13) (this number is fixed at a satisfactorily high number on a fourth-generation machine) or using a convolution filter (see Chapter 7, p. 79), which creates a smoother image.

Too few samples create *sample aliasing* (also called just *aliasing*). Sample aliasing is usually characterized by fine streaks emanating from high spatial frequency interfaces, and these artifacts are clearly seen in the vicinity of the point of origination. Most third-generation machines increase the effective number of ray samples per view by using the quarter offset principle (see Chapter 7, p. 81). The Elscint system additionally uses the dynamic focal spot described above, thus producing extra ray samples for each tube position. Fourth-generation instruments increase the number of samples by increasing the number of times the detector is sampled (accepts data) as the tube moves.

The most frequently used names for the three choices of scan arc of about 220°, 360°, and 400° are the *half scan* (or partial scan), *full scan,* and *overscan,* respectively. The half scan (partial scan) is greater than the 180° of a half circle because the approximate fan angle of the field of view is added to the 180°. The full 360° scan obtains two samples 180° apart, which provide similar information. The rays taken at 180° contribute equally to the reconstruction process and improve statistical sampling characteristics as long as there are not significant inconsistencies in the data, which might be caused by patient motion or geometrical misalignment.

The overscan adds approximately the angular width of the field of view to a full scan (see Fig. 5-11). This is helpful because the registration between the first and last positions of the tube is never exactly the same, and the position of the patient and the patient's organs is most likely to be different. All materials have some flexibility, and the gantry actually deforms slightly as the tube and the detector array are rapidly whirled around the patient. Overscans permit some overlap of the data from the first and last tube positions, which are then averaged, reducing the artifact of misregistration.

As noted above, the fourth-generation machine uses some views acquired sequentially over time and some averaged between the beginning and the end of the scan. This increases the inconsistency of data within views and may account for our anecdotal impression that fourth-generation scanners are more sensitive to motion artifact than third-generation scanners using the same scan times. To compensate for this problem, fourth-generation manufacturers may recommend using overscans. When the scan angle is extended an additional arc about equal to the X-ray fan angle, even views from the beginning and the end of each scan can be created from continuous points in time (see Fig. 5-11). **Therefore, particularly in a fourth-generation scanner, increasing scan time may diminish motion artifacts if that extra**

time is used to perform an overscan. One advantage of a fourth-generation system that helps to compensate for this problem is that its fixed detectors reduce the mechanical engineering difficulties of a rapidly moving tube housing. Furthermore, the need for stability between detectors is decreased because each may be calibrated during the scan by receiving unattenuated X-rays.

The source of some artifacts from partial scans is the smaller number of angular samples or views obtained. In older units using smaller numbers of views or samples than theoretically optimized newer ones, there is a significant improvement in scan quality when the scan time and consequently the number of views or samples is increased. Changes in photon fluence at small numbers of views may be somewhat secondary in importance because the images are so severely degraded. By contrast, with newer units, more views or samples are obtained in 2 sec than were formerly taken in 10 sec. Therefore, increasing the scan time to 3 or 4 sec or more usually only improves image quality if the longer scan time is required to provide satisfactory mAs.

It is possible to separate promotional claims from fact about scan speed by asking users about scan times. Scanners may be advertised as "one-second" scanners even though such short scan times are actually impractical because of the tube output or sampling problems just discussed. The routine scanning times employed by users are more important than the fastest scan time of which the machine is capable. Thus some "one-second" scanners are really five-second scanners, whereas some "two-second" scanners may actually be two-second scanners.

To summarize, scan speed alone does not determine the severity of motion artifacts. Overscans may diminish motion artifacts on some full scans for the reasons mentioned. Also, the severity of motion artifacts on one model scanner at a specific scan speed may differ from that on another unit operating at the same speed. There is an interaction between scanner design, sampling frequency, and motion artifact, which is easier to observe than to predict from reviewing technical specifications.

Knowing the number of samples or views with which an image was obtained is valuable for assessing the reasons for poor image quality. It is probably impossible to obtain alias-free images with fewer than 400 views or samples per scan. Most newer scanners obtain routine scans with about 600 to 1,200 angular samples or views per scan. Fast scanning speeds may be combined with high sampling frequencies by keeping the X-ray tube on continuously during the scan, rather than pulsing the tube, because the tube continues to rotate during the interval in which the tube is off in a pulsed system, thus skipping small intervals. However, one disadvantage of a continuously operating tube is the inability to change kVp with alternating pulses. This technique is valuable for dual-energy scanning, which currently has limited clinical applications (4) (see Chapter 9, p. 113). An alternative to continuous tube operation is more rapid pulsing of the tube.

SELECTING mA AND kVp

Although every unit has some flexibility regarding mA selection, some units are more flexible than others. The mA may be freely chosen on a finely graduated scale, limited to a stepwise scale, or chosen only as one component of a technique factor "set." Also, a specific mAs setting may lead to images of differing quality and even different radiation exposure from scanner to scanner because of differences in tube geometry, focal spot size, detector efficiency, and the like.

Manufacturers usually have standard sets of recommended techniques. Being familiar with the routine or average technique will permit determining if suboptimal image quality is caused by poor mA selection (6). However, recommendations may not be optimal for specific clinical needs. For example, at one time in the past, two manufacturers recommended techniques for head scanning that varied by a factor of three to five. It is not surprising that radiologists might be less satisfied with the image quality from the scanner using the lower mAs and radiation dose technique.

Another important factor affecting image quality is kVp. Most early scanners employed a single kVp selection, usually between 120 and 130. However, newer scanners offer a choice of two or more settings between about 80 and 140 kVp. The greater penetrating power of the higher energy beams affords higher detected X-ray intensity, and thus better photon statistics and smoother images. It also decreases tube stress and heating for the same intensity. However, as with conventional radiography, contrast diminishes with higher energy beams.

The 80-kVp beam may be used in dual-energy scanning in which data is obtained with both an 80-kVp beam and a 120- or 140-kVp beam. Using this information, and knowing the absorption properties of various elements, one can produce tissue characterization information (see Chapter 9, p. 113). The reasons that the higher contrast, low-energy images cannot be used routinely are the poor penetration, the high mA requirements, greater tube heating, and greater patient radiation dose. Although added choice seems to be beneficial, each new combiantion of technique factors may require a new calibration sequence, which is inordinately time consuming in some units, although simple in others. The high (140 kVp) beam may be useful for dynamic studies where scans must be performed in rapid sequence with minimal tube heating. However, we virtually always scan at the single recommended kVp.

FOCAL SPOT AND TUBE GEOMETRY

The effects and importance of tube-object-detector geometry have already been discussed, but another factor affecting these choices is focal spot size.

As with the other factors mentioned, not all models offer choices. As focal spot size is decreased, spatial resolution is increased if all other factors remain unchanged (see Fig. 2-7). Also, the degree of improvement in spatial resolution depends on the radiographic magnification factor. As magnification increases, focal spot size becomes more important (see Fig. 2-7) (3). Third-generation scanners use a magnification factor of about 1.6 to 1.75, whereas the current conventional fourth-generation model uses a factor of about 2.3.

However, a small focal spot has a lower loading capacity and thus cannot produce a satisfactory photon fluence for routine scan times. The small focal spot is then usually reserved for special applications requiring high resolution in a small field of view, and when patient motion is less of a problem.

REFERENCES

1. Blumenfeld, S. M., and Glover, G. (1981): Spatial resolution in computed tomography. In: *Radiology of the Skull and Brain: Technical Aspects of Computed Tomography,* edited by T. H. Newton and D. G. Potts, pp. 3918–3940. C. V. Mosby, St. Louis.
2. Gamsu, G., Mark, A. S., and Webb, W. R. (1981): Computed tomography of the normal larynx during quiet breathing and phonation. *J. Comput. Assist. Tomogr.,* 5(3):353–360.
3. Gerlock, A. J. Jr., and Sloan, M. (1981): Angiography. In: *The Physical Basis of Medical Imaging,* edited by C. M. Coulam, J. J. Erickson, F. D. Rollo, and A. E. James, pp. 141–154. Appleton-Century-Crofts, New York.
4. Goldberg, H. I., Cann, C. E., Moss, A. A., Ohto, M., Brito, A., and Federle, M. (1982): Noninvasive quantitation of liver iron in dogs with hemochromatosis using dual-energy CT scanning. *Invest. Radiol.,* 17:375–380.
5. Goodenough, D. J. (1981): Psychophysical perception of computed tomography images. In: *Radiology of the Skull and Brain: Technical Aspects of Computed Tomography,* edited by T. H. Newton and D. G. Potts, pp. 3993–4021. C. V. Mosby, St. Louis.
6. Haaga, J. R., Miraldi, F., MacIntyre, W., LiPuma, J. P., Bryan, P. J., and Wiesen, E. (1981): The effect of mAs variation upon computed tomography image quality as evaluated by in vivo and in vitro studies. *Radiology,* 138:449–454.
7. Hanson, K. M. (1981): Noise and contrast discrimination in computed tomography. In: *Radiology of the Skull and Brain: Technical Aspects of Computed Tomography,* edited by T. H. Newton and D. G. Potts, pp. 3941–3955. C. V. Mosby, St. Louis.
8. Joseph, P. M. (1981): Artifacts in computed tomography. In: *Radiology of the Skull and Brain: Technical Aspects of Computed Tomography,* edited by T. H. Newton and D. G. Potts, pp. 3956–3992. C. V. Mosby, St. Louis.
9. Stark, D. D., Moss, A. A., Gooding, G. A. W., and Clark, O. H. (1983): Parathyroid scanning by computed tomography. *Radiology,* 148:297–299.
10. Zatz, L. M. (1981): Basic principles of computed tomography scanning. In: *Radiology of the Skull and Brain: Technical Aspects of Computed Tomography,* edited by T. H. Newton and D. G. Potts, pp. 3853–3876. C. V. Mosby, St. Louis.

6

Selectable Scan Factors: Dynamic Scanning

Most newer scanners permit scans to be obtained much more quickly in sequence than was previously possible. The term usually used for this rapid-sequence scanning is *dynamic scanning.* However, the term has been applied inconsistently. At one time, routine nondynamic scanning rates were about 1 to 3 scans per min. When dynamic scanning was first introduced, scanning rates of about 4 to 8 scans per min were possible. However, newer scanners may now acquire scans routinely at 4 to 8 per min, and the manufacturers reserve the term *dynamic* or its equivalent (e.g., Synerdyne™ for Picker, Autoscan™ for Siemens, DynaPak™ for General Electric) to special scanning programs that can achieve up to about 15 scans per min or even more. The inexact use of terms has caused confusion in the radiologic literature. For example, one author has claimed that one of his techniques avoids the need for dynamic scanning. However, he was actually using the same scanning rate as most previous investigators, although the manufacturer of his unit did not apply the term *dynamic* to that rate.

A faster than usual scanning rate is not the only feature of the dynamic scan; thus many units must still be programmed separately for a rapid scan sequence even if rapid scan rates are routinely available. The variables that define a dynamic scan are (a) scan time, (b) interscan delay, (c) total number of scans in a sequence, (d) table incrementation between scans, and (e) tube output. Not all dynamic scans should be done at the most rapid rate possible because of limitations of tube heat capacity, patients' breath-holding capacity and ability to lie motionless, image reconstruction times, and the distribution times of vascular contrast material.

SCAN TIME

Most scanners permit rapid scanning at variable scan times, but certain scan times, usually involving half scans and overscans, are often excluded from dynamic scans. Most scanners operate by rotating the tube assembly in one direction for one scan, and in the opposite direction for the succeeding scan. Thus, a 360° scan brings the tube back to the standard position of readiness for the succeeding scan, whereas extra interscan time is required to bring the tube back to the initial scan position for half scans and overscans (see Fig. 5-11). However, this is not a major technical problem, and the full range of scan times is available for dynamic scans on some scanners.

INTERSCAN DELAY

Most units permit selection of the interscan delay down to a lower limit. For these scanners, there is a minimum time that the computer needs to prepare for the next scan, and the tube or tube-detector assembly rotating around the patient needs time to decelerate and accelerate for the next scan. The time for these functions is commonly about 1.5 to 2.5 sec. Therefore, with a 2-sec scan and a 2-sec interscan delay, the maximum scanning rate is 60 sec divided by 4 sec per scan, or 15 scans per min. However, an additional interscan delay is required if the patient couch is moved (incremented) between scans. The additional delay may vary greatly from scanner to scanner. This may limit the maximum scan rate for 2-sec scans to about 10 to 12 scans per min or fewer.

The radically different designs of the Toshiba nutating scanner and the Imatron do not impose these limitations. The Toshiba system uses a tube that continues to travel in the same direction for successive scans, with no interscan delay. The Imatron, in which the X-ray source has no moving

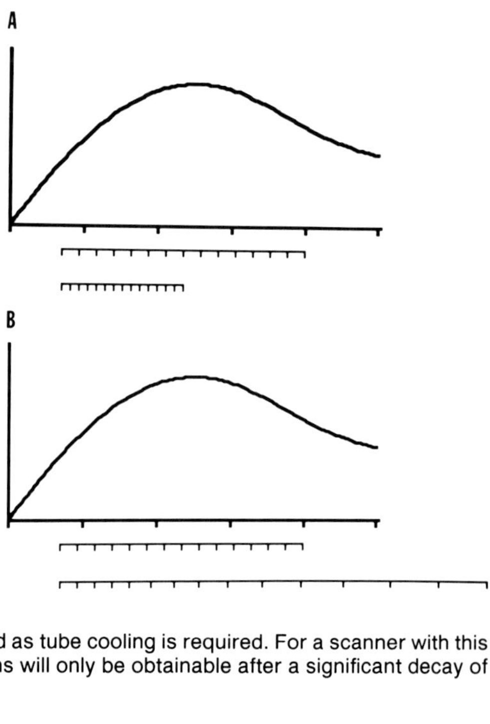

FIG. 6–1. Time-density curves illustrating the need for adjusting rates and timing of scanning for injection technique. **A**. The vertical axis represents the enhancement of liver parenchyma over precontrast levels. The horizontal axis represents time, with each hatch mark indicating 1 min. This approximates an enhancement curve for a 2-min injection of intravenous contrast. The line just below the graph represents the timing of 15 scans obtained at a rate of 4 scans per min. The bottom line indicates the entire scanning sequence for a scan rate of 8 per min. With the faster scanning sequence, the last scans are being obtained at the peak of contrast enhancement. It would be wiser to delay slightly the initiation of the first scan so that the majority of scans are obtained at or near the peak of enhancement. However, with the slower scanning rate, the enhancement curve is being used optimally. **B**. The identical curve as in **A**. However, the lower line indicates a 15-scan sequence in which the interscan delay is lengthened as tube cooling is required. For a scanner with this type of scanning mode, the last few scans will only be obtainable after a significant decay of enhancement has occurred.

parts, permits several simultaneous scans and successive scans at 50-msec intervals.

However, even if the system can mechanically accommodate very rapid rates, these rates may not be clinically desirable. Two seconds is insufficient time for most people to begin breathing and suspend respiration between scans. Therefore, one may prefer to extend the interscan delay to avoid motion artifacts as the patient attempts to return too rapidly to breath holding. Also, the time curve of contrast distribution from an intravenous injection must be considered. If the entire scan is obtained too rapidly, a signficant part of the scan may be inadvertently obtained before opacification is optimal, depending on the organ system being examined (Fig. 6-1). Extending the scanning sequence improves the likelihood that most of the scan will be obtained with satisfactory enhancement.

We have also found that injecting a specific volume of contrast material more rapidly shortens the time before which the peak of contrast enhancement is reached and increases the height of the peak. This type of information should be used in concert with the capabilities of the specific scanner when designing injection rates, volumes, and timing. Ideally, carefully planned timing rather than just faster scanning should lead to better results with dynamic scanning (2,4).

NUMBER OF SCANS IN DYNAMIC SEQUENCE

Dynamic scanning programs require planning for the total number of scans in a sequence. The levels are first selected from the scanogram or a preliminary series of nondynamic slices. Once the number and thickness of the slices are tentatively selected, some scanners' computers can calculate the heat loading capacity of the system and use the current heat status of the tube to indicate the maximum tube output possible for the number of scans required. Longer scans are possible at higher techniques when the tube is cold at the beginning of a sequence. Many newer scanners permit nondynamic scan rates of about 4 per min, equaling the performance of the older dynamic scan programs. However, the nondynamic routines differ from dynamic scans because as tube heat limits are approached with a nondynamic program, the scan rate declines as tube cooling is required (see Fig. 6-1). By contrast, dynamic programs produce a constant rate of scan acquisition throughout the scan sequence and are programmed to cut off when tube heat limits are reached or computer memory is consumed.

TABLE INCREMENTATION

The radiologist must decide whether table incrementation is to be used for a dynamic scan. The purposes of a dynamic scan at a single level (single-level dynamic scan) are different from a scan with table incrementation (incremented dynamic scan or survey dynamic scan). Single-level scans are usually done to follow the effect of a bolus contrast injection at a specific anatomic site or within a lesion (6,8). Incremented scans are usually done to survey an entire body region and take advantage of high levels of contrast enhancement after a bolus or rapid injection (1,3,6). The clinical purposes are more completely described in Part 2, but examples of single-level scans include examining liver lesions to observe typical patterns of enhancement of hepatic hemangiomata, or studying the thoracic aorta to detect and characterize flow patterns in the lumina of dissections. Incremented scans with the injection of a large volume of contrast material either by hand or with a power injector designed for CT are the routine technique in our facility to study the upper abdomen. The entire region is viewed near the maximum phase of vascular and parenchymal enhancement before significant diffusion and excretion have occurred.

Some dynamic scanning packages are capable of permitting scans of an entire body region with a single sequence. However, in most cases, the dynamic portion of the examination covers the most critical area (e.g., the liver or the mediastinum) and is followed quickly by a series of scans done at an ordinary rate to complete examining the region. Dynamic scans with intraarterial infusions are also commonly used in some institutions (7). This has been applied particularly to determine the exact location and number of liver primary or metastatic lesions in a patient being considered for partial hepatectomy.

TUBE OUTPUT

Perhaps the most significant technical problem with dynamic scanning is the limit on mAs levels imposed by tube heating. A sequence of scans over an average-sized organ or body region usually cannot be done with techniques as high as would be selected for nondynamic scans. Thus dynamic scan images are usually somewhat degraded by increased quantum noise. However, this noise is balanced by the improved spatial detail and increased subject contrast added by contrast media. The degree of degradation caused by fewer photons depends on the ability of the scanner to reduce the several other sources of noise (electronic noise, computer calculation approximations, filter functions, etc.). Therefore, some scanners can provide more satisfactory image quality at low X-ray doses than can others. Assessment of this machine capability is probably one of the most important, yet most difficult features to evaluate when comparing equipment.

When selecting dynamic scan techniques on a specific scanner, a rough rule of thumb we use is to perform a dynamic scan only if one can attain at least one-half to two-thirds of the mAs that would be routinely selected for a nondynamic scan (5). Also, a higher kVp can be used to improve tube capacity at a modest sacrifice of contrast resolution. However, this is not a solution we employ, because on some of our scanners time-consuming recalibration is required for each kVp change.

When selecting equipment, one may wish to apply the above mAs criterion for satisfactory dynamic scanning. Although a scanner may easily accomplish a rapid tube assembly rotation (fourth generation) or tube-detector array rotation (third generation) of 12 scans per min, the images will be of little clinical use if dynamic scans can only be done with 20% to 40% of the ordinary tube output.

Both the patient and the features of the particular scanner enter into the decision whether to do a scan dynamically or routinely. For example, larger patients require higher X-ray doses for penetration. To obtain satisfactory image quality, one may need to refrain from using a dynamic scan or perform a shorter sequence than would otherwise be done.

If a dynamic scan is necessary, but the scanner will not permit the desired number of slices at the desired tube output, there are several alternatives. First, one might try to schedule the patient at the beginning of the day or at other times when the tube is cool. Alternatively, simply waiting several minutes for the tube to cool may help, allowing more scans or higher techniques. Second, the dynamic sequence may be split into two or more sequences. However, the results of splitting injections are often unsatisfactory because this often leads to poor opacification with both sequences. We no longer employ this solution, but prefer only to minimize the number of slices done with the dynamic sequence and to increase the mAs to the maximum allowable for the scan sequence selected.

One must also appreciate that in some scanners the number of scans in a sequence may be limited by the computer memory for raw data. Because of the much larger requirements for storing information in the form of raw data, most machines attempt to delete those data as quickly as possible to create more space for the reconstructed image (display) data. When so constricted by memory, one may simply have to limit the number of scans in the dynamic portion of the examination and perform the remainder of the scans at a routine rate.

REFERENCES

1. Berland, L. L. (1984): Screening for diffuse and focal liver disease: The case for hepatic computed tomography. *J. Clin. Ultrasound,* 12:83–89.
2. Burgener, F. A., and Hamlin, D. J. (1983): Contrast enhancement of hepatic tumors in CT: Comparison between bolus and infusion techniques. *AJR,* 140:291–295.
3. Claussen, C. D., Banzer, D., Pfretzschner, C. Kalender, W. A., and Schorner, W. (1984): Bolus geometry and dynamics after intravenous contrast medium injection. *Radiology,* 153:365–368.

4. Foley, W. D., Berland, L. L., Lawson, T. L., Smith, D. F., and Thorsen, M. K. (1983): Contrast enhancement technique for dynamic hepatic computed tomographic scanning. *Radiology,* 147:797–803.
5. Haaga, J. R., Miraldi, F., MacIntyre, W., LiPuma, J. P., Bryan, P. J., and Wiesen, E. (1981): The effect of mAs variation upon computed tomography image quality as evaluated by in vivo and in vitro studies. *Radiology,* 138:449–454.
6. Hosoki, T., Chatani, M., and Mori, S. (1982): Dynamic computed tomography of hepatocellular carcinoma. *AJR,* 139:1099–1106.
7. Matsui, O., Kadoya, M., Suzuki, M., Inoue, K., Itoh, H., Ida, M., and Takashima, T. (1983): Work in progress: Dynamic sequential computed tomography during arterial portography in the detection of hepatic neoplasms. *Radiology,* 146:721–727.
8. Thorsen, M. K., San Dretto, M. A., Lawson, T. L., Foley, W. D., Smith, D. F., and Berland, L. L. (1983): Dissecting aortic aneurysms: Accuracy of computed tomographic diagnosis. *Radiology,* 148:773–777.

7

Image Creation and Refinement

Texts on CT physics often devote many pages to describing the image reconstruction process. However, the purpose of this book is to discuss factors that affect image quality. Knowing the intricacies of the reconstruction process adds little to this purpose, but most machines do provide a limited choice of image reconstruction techniques, and it is important to understand the nature, effects, and importance of those choices.

RAW DATA, RAYS, AND VIEWS

As described in Chapter 5, p. 59, the raw numerical data used to create an image consist of the detected X-ray transmission values from all the rays of each view. For a third-generation scanner, each ray of the X-ray fan beam strikes a single detector in the array, and each set of rays with the tube in one position constitutes a view (see Fig. 5-12) (11). For a fourth-generation scanner or its variants, a view is the set of rays striking a single detector. The value for each ray is a number that is directly proportional to the X-ray energy fluence absorbed in the detector. This energy fluence depends on the percentage of X-rays absorbed by the detector (the fraction of X-ray energy striking the detector array that is absorbed in the detectors) and also on the X-ray absorption by the patient (which varies for each ray of each view).

The following simplified examples show how the number of pieces of raw data may be calculated for a third- or fourth-generation scanner. For example, if there are 700 detectors in a third-generation scanner, and 1,000 views are taken at different positions in the 360° rotation, then there are 700 rays $\times$ 1000 views, or 700,000 samples of information composing the raw data for each slice. For a fourth-generation scanner with 1,200 detectors, if 1,000 samples are obtained, then each view provides 1,200,000 pieces of data for an image.

RECONSTRUCTION

The basic method of reconstructing an image (part of the reconstruction algorithm) from the raw numerical data in the computer is limited to one or several choices for each scanner. All modern scanners use their own type

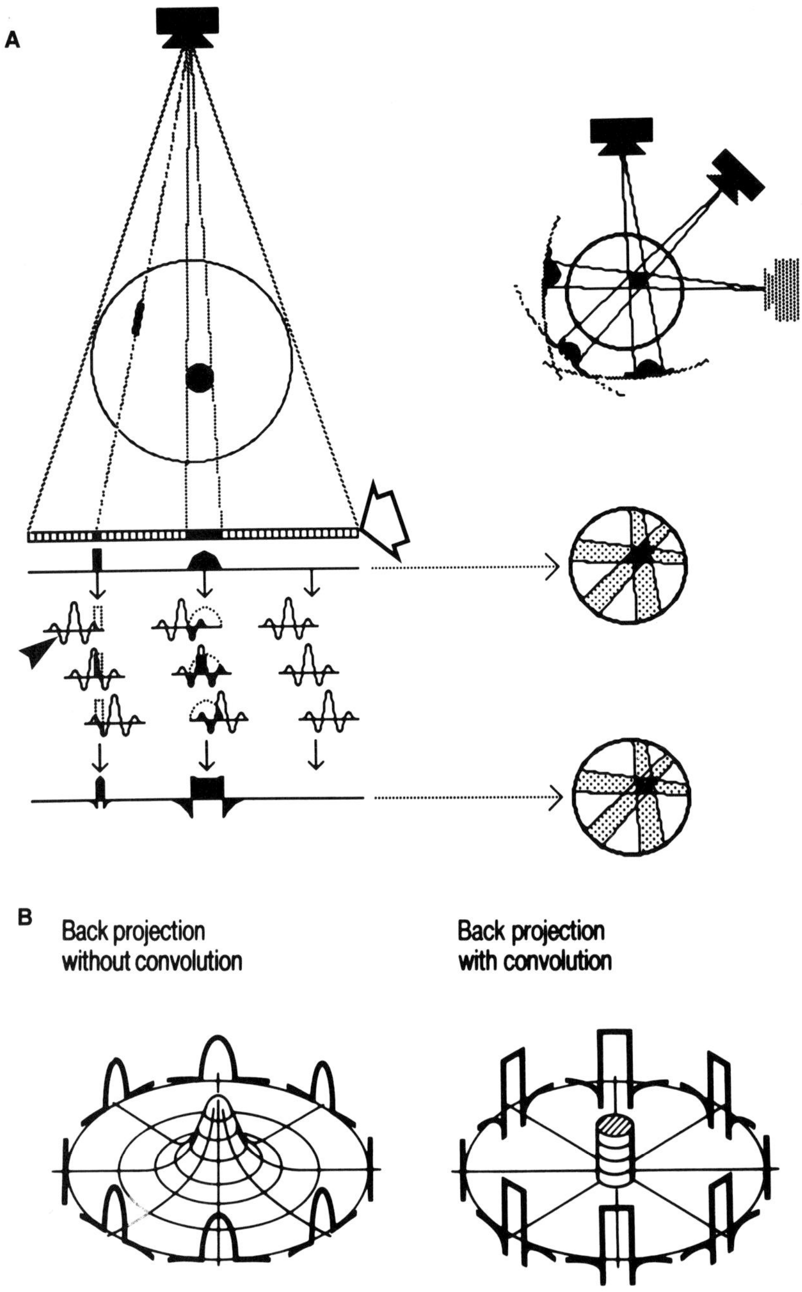

FIG. 7–1. The back projection and filtration process. **A**. The upper left-hand illustration indicates two hypothetical objects within a scanning field, projected on a detector array (open arrow). On the line immediately below the detector array is indicated the direct detector response. The image at upper right illustrates the projections of an object in three selected views. If the raw detector response (raw data) is then back-projected into the field of view, it will create an image similar to that indicated by the dotted arrow. Even though the hypothetical object is round, the resulting image is star shaped. Because the data are projected back across the entire image, in line with the rays, streaks radiate from the object.

of "filtered back projection," or "convolution back projection" (8,9). A simplified description of back projection and filtration is illustrated in Fig. 7-1. One way of conceptualizing the method by which these numbers are translated into an image is to think of projecting the number for each ray back across the entire line of the ray from the tube to the detector. The resulting two-dimensional array of numbers is then superimposed and averaged, and then each resulting number is converted into a shade of gray. However, if one were to do this back projection alone, the structures in the image would have blurred edges and inaccurate attenuation numbers (6). A number of corrections must be made to make the image more closely approach a real display of anatomy. The first and most important of these corrections is the spatial filtration of each view. This edge-enhancing step is applied to the raw data before the image is reconstructed with the back projection method just described.

RECONSTRUCTION FILTERS

A reconstruction filter (also called a kernel) is applied to the raw data to optimize a balance between spatial resolution and contrast resolution to best represent clinically relevant detail. The process of applying filtration to the data is termed *convolution* and is similar to the process of convolving the scanogram image with an edge-enhancing kernel as discussed in Chapter 3, p. 33. One difference is that, with the CT scan, the data are convolved with a one-dimensional or linear series of measurements from adjacent detectors. With the scanogram, the filter is applied to the two-dimensional array of pixels representing the scanogram.

Convolution with a filter is performed by sliding a mathematical curve (function) over the actual detector response curve, multiplying the areas of the overlapping curves together, and using the resulting value to define a point on a new curve (1). The mathematical curve is called the filter function or kernel, and the process is called convolution. When one is applying the filter to the data curve, one is convolving or spatially filtering the data.

As shown, filtration of the data from a view weights the value from a ray according to the value of nearby rays. If one enhances the differences

←

To suppress these false data, filtration is performed on the raw detector data before back projection. This is illustrated immediately beneath the line indicating the raw detector response. A predesigned filter function curve (arrowhead) is passed sequentially across the raw data. The area in which these curves intersect is multiplied and used to create a filtered data response curve as noted on the bottom line. The shape of the filtered function has a negative component on either side to suppress the star artifact. Also, where the filter is passed over a zero raw data response, this is translated as no filtered response.

When the final filtered data are back-projected, a more faithful representation of the object is obtained, as in the lower right image.

B. Effect of convolution with a filter function on the back projection. (**B** courtesy of Siemens Medical Systems, Inc.)

between adjacent ray samples, the edges are enhanced and noise is increased in the final image. This is done to differing degrees for various applications. Filters are often complex and nonlinear. For example, one may select how many of the nearby samples will be used to apply to the other values by adjusting the width of the filter. One may subtract a weighted value of the immediately adjacent ray sample but simultaneously add a weighted value of the sample two or three rays away on either side (10).

When software engineers design convolution filters to create sharp differences from pixel to pixel, they are seeking to enhance higher spatial frequencies and to sacrifice the display of lower spatial frequencies, producing better defined edges and noisier images (5). This may be termed a "sharp" kernel, or "high-pass spatial filtering." Using sharp kernels theoretically hinders the detection of low-contrast lesions by increasing noise, but improving edge sharpness also often improves low-contrast detectability (2,4). Therefore, the clinical or perceptual result of changing a filter is not always clear. In general, sharp kernels are preferable for looking at intrinsically high contrast areas such as the temporal bones, or other bones where noise does not significantly interfere with interpretation. Soft kernels are preferable for examining low-contrast areas such as brain and abdominal structures.

Whereas some systems apply the same kernel to most images, others vary the filter function depending on the application. For example, one kernel may be chosen for head scanning, another for body scanning, and another for high-resolution spine scanning. However, the manufacturers' recommendations may not reflect local preferences. Also, unless one diligently seeks information from the proper person in the company, it may be difficult to obtain a coherent explanation of the difference between, for example, "algorithm number 4" and "algorithm number 11." The term *algorithm* refers to the entire process of reconstructing, spatial filtering, and applying corrections, and the algorithm choices may primarily reflect changes in the filter function. The number of choices available from different manufacturers varies widely, and different kernels may be automatically selected as a component of a computerized protocol.

It may be best to experiment with several slices at different kernels when such choices are available. The most convenient way to do this is by saving on magnetic tape the raw data from a relatively good quality scan and performing several "second" or "retrospective" reconstructions with various filters. This may be tedious and should be done when idle computer time is available. We sometimes use alternatives to the manufacturers' recommended filters based on information obtained by such experimentation.

OTHER PROCESSING CORRECTIONS

The reconstruction process has several other components, some of which are mysterious because they are proprietary and are peculiar to each unit. A series of programs called pre- and postprocessing corrections are designed to suppress artifacts such as rings, which are an inherent problem in third-generation systems. These corrections also include offset and gain corrections as discussed in Chapter 2, p. 24. Other components of the corrections affect CT number inaccuracies caused by beam hardening (3,7,10), including the cupping artifact, which is discussed in Chapter 8, p. 93, and Chapter 11, p. 153.

SPECIALIZED RECONSTRUCTION ALGORITHMS

Special back projection algorithms (such as bone detail) may be available to enhance one feature of the image appearance (such as spatial resolution). The bone detail back projection method used with third-generation scanners is permitted by a special technique of interleaving ray data samples from views taken at 180° from one another. This is possible because of an ingenious method of slightly offsetting the detector array so that views taken on opposite sides of the patient are not exactly in line with one another (Fig. 7-2). This offset is one-quarter of a detector width on both the tube and the detector sides, leading to the term *quarter-quarter offset* (7). This technique effectively increases the number of ray samples per view, providing an image with a higher spatial resolution, but coarser in texture. Although this algorithm is termed "bone detail," studying bone (Fig. 7-3) is not necessarily its only application. It may be used for any area containing a high inherent subject contrast such as bone or lung. However, it is most commonly used to examine areas with fine bony detail such as the petrous bones. The quarter offset method is not applicable to fourth-generation geometry, but ray sampling can be increased on these machines by taking more samples as the tube rotates.

IMAGE MAGNIFICATION VERSUS "TARGETING"

Specialized reconstructions are nonstandard reconstructions of the raw data used for higher resolution. Various companies' names for these include ReView™, target, and zoom. These reconstructions may be done on the original raw data before or in lieu of the standard reconstruction or may be done as additional images. The raw data must be saved on the magnetic disk or on magnetic tape because it is the entire reconstruction process that must be performed. Raw data are not routinely saved for secondary reconstructions because doing so consumes about four times as much computer memory as the reconstructed display data. The data are normally discarded almost immediately after the image is reconstructed, or saved in a limited memory buffer until displaced or saved on magnetic disk or tape.

The purpose of specialized reconstructions is to obtain better detail over

A

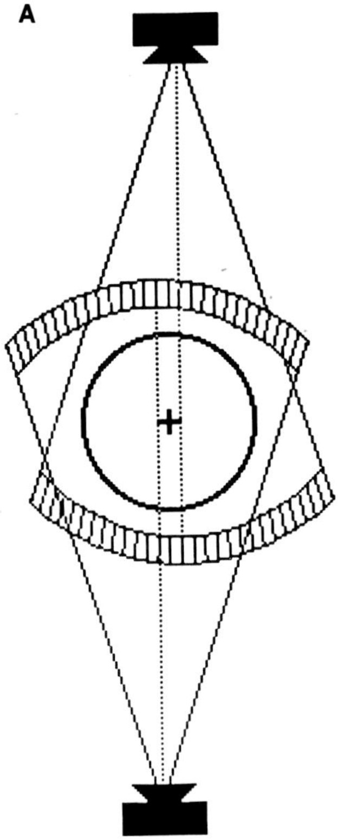

FIG. 7–2. The quarter offset principle. **A**. A third-generation system shows exaggerated offset of the axis of the tube-detector assembly from the center of rotation. **B**. Close-up of the detector arrays in 180° orientation illustrates the effect of offsetting the assembly by one-quarter of a detector width. A central ray with the detector array in the lower position strikes primarily the lightly shaded detector. When in the upper position, the central ray strikes primarily the heavily shaded detector. Because each is offset one-quarter of a detector width, this sums to a one-half detector width shift between these opposite rays. This slight difference in position provides more samples to satisfy the Nyquist frequency illustrated in Fig. 5–15. This information can also be used to reconstruct images with higher spatial detail as illustrated in Fig. 7–3.

B

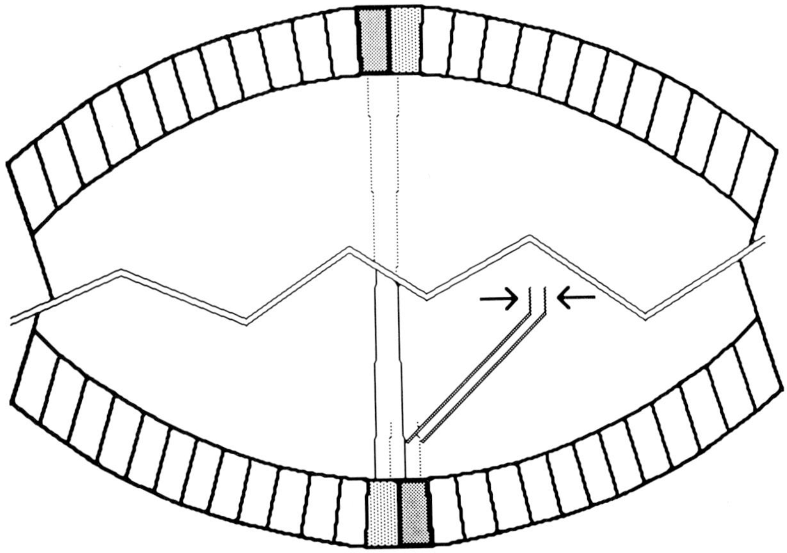

A B

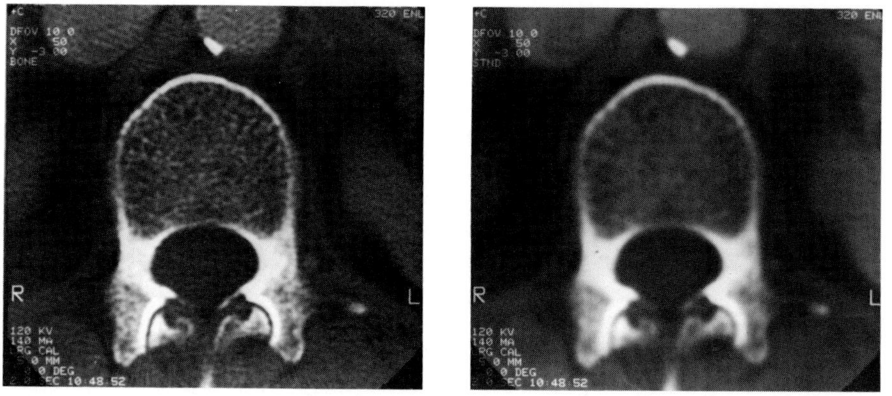

FIG. 7–3. Two images reconstructed with different algorithms and filter functions from the same raw data. **A**. This image was reconstructed with an algorithm using the quarter-offset principle, which enhances edges and improves spatial detail. The 180° rays are considered separate because of the offset. **B**. This image was reconstructed with the standard filter and algorithm, which suppresses noise and streak artifact but produces less spatial detail. The 180° rays are reconstructed on the assumption that they are essentially the same ray.

a smaller field of view. As mentioned before, there is often more information available in the raw data than can be accommodated on the limited matrix display. However, when the field of view is limited, the information in the field can be displayed over a larger number of pixels than on the standard display, thus improving depiction of detail by decreasing the amount of tissue represented in each pixel. These may be termed "soft tissue detail" reconstructions and are similar to primary reconstructions done with a small displayed field of view, although slightly differing spatial filters may be used (see Chapter 5, p. 47). This is the basis of most special reconstruction techniques, although pixel size reduction may be combined with kernel changes. Some systems arrange for selecting the field of view by entering a numerical value for field size and coordinates for the center of that field. Options on some machines include the display of a box, which may be changed in size or position, from which the "zoomed" image is created.

When specialized reconstructions are used after the initial reconstruction they are termed *secondary* or *retrospective.* They are done when it is important to see both the full field of view and a limited field of view for enhanced spatial resolution. When it is hard to localize the particular small area of interest until the whole scan is viewed, or when the standard reconstruction leaves doubts that might be answered by higher resolution, then both primary and secondary reconstructions may be done (2). Prospective special reconstructions are done when the purpose of the examination is well directed to an easily localized area of anatomy such as the lumbar spine.

Most scanners permit the targeted field of view to be selected in the center of the routine field, or off-center as is required of temporal bone studies.

Targeted reconstructions are usually unnecessary for head scans because the image is already displayed over a relatively small field of view. However, targeting is very popular for spine scanning because of the limited area of interest combined with the need for high resolution. We have also begun to use a limited field of view for body scans when our attention is directed to a specific area such as the pancreatic head. In these cases, we usually define the area of interest with a series of scans done before intravenous contrast injection. This is followed with a scan during contrast injection using a small field of view and thin slices to help define details in the area of complex anatomy around the pancreas (Fig. 7-4; see Chapter 14, p. 210).

The specialized reconstruction differs from simple image magnification. The latter process involves simply enlarging the information from one pixel and displaying it over several pixels, then smoothing or interpolating the data so that the image does not appear too "boxy" (see Fig. 5-5). Unlike in the target-type reconstructions, no new information is in the magnified image. The process does not require the raw data but simply the standard display data. Therefore magnification may be done at the physician's console on any available image and does not require as much computer time as do reconstructions. Thus reconstructions actually improve resolution

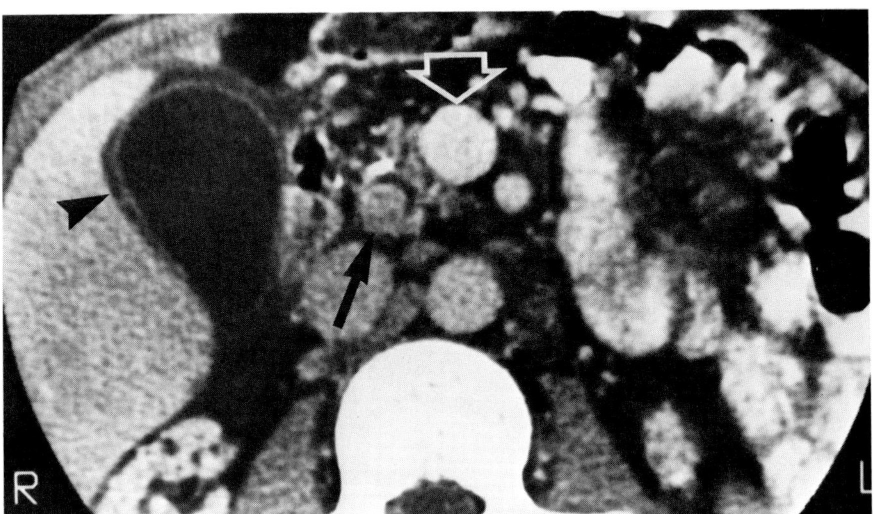

FIG. 7-4. Secondary reconstruction using a small field of view. In this 3-mm slice through a common bile duct stone (arrow), the thin crescent of bile (curved arrow) remaining would be difficult to appreciate with the standard field-of-view image but is better seen with secondary reconstruction. The gallbladder wall (arrowhead) is also thickened, and the superior mesenteric vein (open arrow) is unusually large.

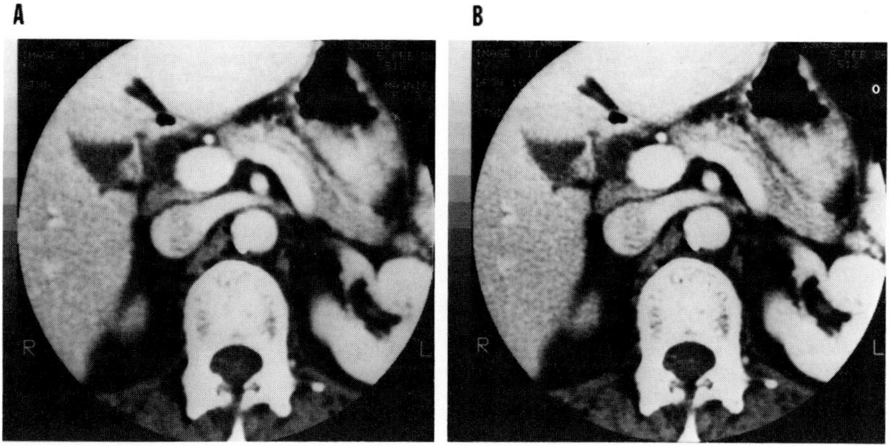

FIG. 7–5. Images demonstrating the difference between image magnification and direct reconstruction to a small field of view. **A**. Image directly reconstructed to a large field of view and magnified by a factor of 3.2. **B**. Image using the same data directly reconstructed to a 15-cm field of view. There is a modest but definite improvement in the image directly reconstructed to the small field of view. When a smaller magnification factor is used to simulate a small field of view, the differences are less noticeable. Differences between magnification and direct reconstruction are more noticeable with older scanners and smaller matrices.

whereas magnification changes it very little. However, both offer improved perceptibility of clinically relevant detail because of enlargement of the area of interest.

The greater the magnification factor used, the poorer the quality of the image compared to a computer reconstruction performed for the same field of view. For example, enlargement of a portion of an image by a factor of two may appear similar to a direct reconstruction to the same field of view. However, magnification by a factor of four may be considered unsatisfactory for clinical use compared to a direct reconstruction to the smaller field of view (Fig. 7-5). The advantages of magnification compared to secondary reconstruction are the better perception offered by a larger image, ready availability, and ease of use. One confusing fact is that the term *zoom* is applied by some manufacturers to the simple image magnification-interpolation process rather than the special reconstruction.

RECONSTRUCTION SPEED

The speed with which a scanner converts raw data into an image is one of the most important features of a CT scanner. Some scanners provide choices of reconstruction speed from the same raw data. However, the faster reconstruction options on any specific machine are essentially always done at the cost of image quality. Factors affecting reconstruction speed include the computer and gantry system configuration, the rate of analog-to-digital conversion of the detected X-ray signal, the amount of data accumulated (which is related to the cost of the data acquisition system), the speed of the various computer components, the reconstruction algorithm, and the corrections chosen. The pressure felt by most manufacturers to match the very fast reconstruction speed available from some scanners testifies to the importance of this feature.

Reconstruction speed strongly depends on the number of data samples used to reconstruct the image, and on technological innovations. The quantity of data may vary severalfold. For example, one older model scanner used a total of over 294,000 data points for a 10-sec scan, leading to a reconstructed image in about 40 sec. The 2-sec scan on the newer model from the same company takes about 1,008,000 data samples, yet can reconstruct an image in under 10 sec. Clearly, major strides have been made in the intervening years.

If rapid reconstruction is not a standard feature of a specific machine and speed options are available, one may wish to compromise image quality at times to improve reconstruction speed. A faster than ordinary reconstruction with diminished detail or increased noise may be acceptable if the scans are used solely to localize organ limits before diagnostic scanning or to localize needles for percutaneous biopsy. We also use a fast reconstruction feature on one of our scanners, which ordinarily would provide a standard reconstruction time of 50 sec. Because this was too long for efficient patient care in our institution, we selected a 35-sec reconstruction, which economizes by averaging some adjacent detector readings before reconstruction. This increases aliasing and other artifacts.

REFERENCES

1. Blumenfeld, S. M., and Glover, G. (1981): Spatial resolution in computed tomography. In: *Radiology of the Skull and Brain: Technical Aspects of Computed Tomography,* edited by T. H. Newton and D. G. Potts, pp. 3918–3940. C. V. Mosby, St. Louis.
2. Coulam, C. M., and Erickson, J. J. (1981): Image considerations in computed tomography. In: *The Physical Basis of Medical Imaging,* edited by C. M. Coulam, J. J. Erickson, F. D. Rollo, and A. E. James, pp. 189–211. Appleton-Century-Crofts, New York.
3. Coulam, C. M., and Erickson, J. J. (1981): Equipment considerations in computed tomography. In: *The Physical Basis of Medical Imaging,* edited by C. M. Coulam, J. J. Erickson, F. D. Rollo, and A. E. James, pp. 213–229. Appleton-Century-Crofts, New York.
4. Fu, T. Y., and Hayworth, M. (1986): The digital image: Its structure, storage, and transmission. In: *The Computer in Radiology,* edited by T. B. Hunter, pp. 94–120. Aspen Systems, Rockville, MD.
5. Glenn, W. V., Harlow, C. A., Dwyer, S. J. III, Rhodes, M. L., and Parker, D. L. (1981): Image manipulation and pattern recognition. In: *Radiology of the Skull and Brain: Technical Aspects of Computed Tomography,* edited by T. H. Newton and D. G. Potts, pp. 4326–4354. C. V. Mosby, St. Louis.
6. Herman, G. T. (1981): Principles of reconstruction algorithms: Section II. Advanced prin-

ciples of reconstruction algorithms. In: *Radiology of the Skull and Brain: Technical Aspects of Computed Tomography,* edited by T. H. Newton and D. G. Potts, pp. 3888–3903. C. V. Mosby, St. Louis.

7. Joseph, P. M. (1981): Artifacts in computed tomography. In: *Radiology of the Skull and Brain: Technical Aspects of Computed Tomography,* edited by T. H. Newton and D. G. Potts, pp. 3956–3992. C. V. Mosby, St. Louis.
8. Macovski, A. (1981): Principles of reconstruction algorithms: Section I. Basic concepts of reconstruction algorithms. In: *Radiology of the Skull and Brain: Technical Aspects of Computed Tomography,* edited by T. H. Newton and D. G. Potts, pp. 3877–3887. C. V. Mosby, St. Louis.
9. Swindell, W. (1986): Computed tomography hardware and software. In: *The Computer in Radiology,* edited by T. B. Hunter, pp. 124–142. Aspen Systems, Rockville, MD.
10. Zatz, L. M. (1981): Basic principles of computed tomography scanning. In: *Radiology of the Skull and Brain: Technical Aspects of Computed Tomography,* edited by T. H. Newton and D. G. Potts, pp. 3853–3876. C. V. Mosby, St. Louis.
11. Zatz, L. M. (1981): General overview of computed tomography instrumentation. In: *Radiology of the Skull and Brain: Technical Aspects of Computed Tomography,* edited by T. H. Newton and D. G. Potts, pp. 4025–4057. C. V. Mosby, St. Louis.

8

Image Quality

When clinicians are trying to learn about the value of an imaging examination they often are interested in understanding how small a lesion can be seen, the spatial resolution of the machine, and how large a lesion can be missed. Whereas the answers to the first and third questions lead to a better, albeit incomplete understanding of the ability of a machine to depict clinically relevant detail, the second question is asking about a quite different aspect of image quality (2).

SPATIAL AND CONTRAST RESOLUTION AND NOISE

The spatial resolution of an instrument is actually represented by a set of values determined from measuring the ability to visually separate small, high-contrast structures in test objects from one another (Fig. 8-1). This set of values can be displayed on a modulation transfer function (MTF) curve just as is done with conventional radiography. This curve plots the MTF on the vertical axis against the spatial frequency on the horizontal axis (Fig. 8-2). Most radiology residents I have known have feared the term "modulation transfer function" more than any other because of a belief that it is fundamentally incomprehensible. I believe that the difficulty is largely due to a failure to understand the concept of spatial frequency. Spatial frequency (see Chapter 3, p. 33) is a way of representing the size of an object, the sharpness of its edge, or its degree of homogeneity. That is, small objects show abrupt, frequent changes in density as one passes over them. This is represented as a high-frequency wave (one with frequent changes that are not necessarily of high amplitude). Large objects change their density less often, that is, with a lower frequency (Fig. 8-3) (3). The MTF is a measure of how faithfully the inherent spatial frequencies of the object can be represented as a change in spatial frequency on an image (5).

Another technical term that may be used to define this concept of spatial frequency is modulation. Small objects produce a greater modulation or change of the transmitted beam per unit distance, indicating a higher spatial frequency. Thus, in a specific CT scanner, certain spatial frequencies will be better represented than others. When the object's actual spatial frequency and imaged spatial frequency are identical, the MTF is given a value of 1. Any frequency less well seen is given a lower value, and a curve is thereby

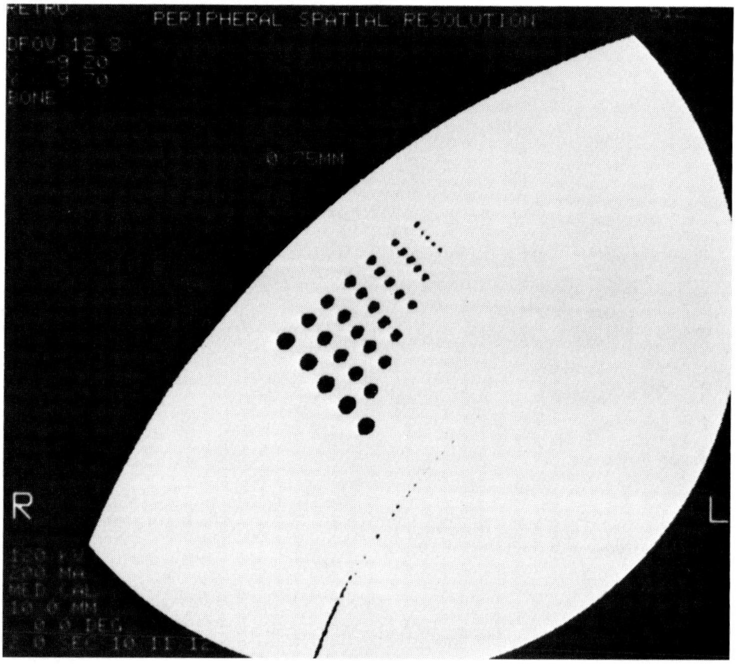

FIG. 8–1. CT scan of a spatial resolution test object. This is an off-center small field-of-view reconstruction of a set of holes in a dense object. The holes are placed at the periphery of the scanned field of view. Spatial resolution differs between the center and the periphery of the field for reasons cited in the text. This is one important difference between scanners. However, information about the degree of degradation at the periphery of the field is not readily available.

defined. The relative "modulation" is "transferred" from the real object to the image. The curve so defined is the modulation transfer "function" (22).

Measuring contrast resolution involves determining how easy it is to see large, low-contrast objects whose CT density is similar to that of their surroundings (1,22). Contrast resolution, like spatial resolution, is related to but cannot be equated with the ability to perceive clinically relevant detail. Contrast resolution is measured by determining the best spatial resolution that can be obtained when cylinders of varying sizes are placed in an environment of water density. These cylinders are of a known density slightly different from that of water (Fig. 8-4). Contrast resolution may be better understood by thinking of a graph that plots object (actual inherent) contrast on one axis versus detectable object diameter on the other (Fig. 8-5). Spatial resolution measurements use inherently high contrast objects to determine the smallest objects detectable, whereas contrast resolution measurements use large, low object contrast structures to determine how well faint structures can be perceived.

Contrast resolution is usually limited by noise. Noise is generally characterized by graininess, or a salt-and-pepper, random statistical pattern superimposed on the image (11). Noise can obscure borders, thus affecting edge discrimination, and can obscure underlying differences in shading, thus affecting contrast resolution.

Noise intrudes from a variety of sources. Quantum noise is a result of the limited number of photons (quanta) contributing to an image. Electronic noise occurs because of random electrical interference within the myriad electronic components in the system. Computational noise may occur as a result of approximations used in the measurement and averaging process and in the lack of exact geometrical coordination between the oblique, diverging rays and the positions of the pixels. Noise is also seriously influenced by reception of scattered X-rays as alluded to in Chapter 1. Several of these types of noise should be monitored as a quality assurance procedure. Structural noise refers to the confusion contributed by overlying structures superimposed on the tissue of interest. This component of noise is largely eliminated by sectional imaging techniques.

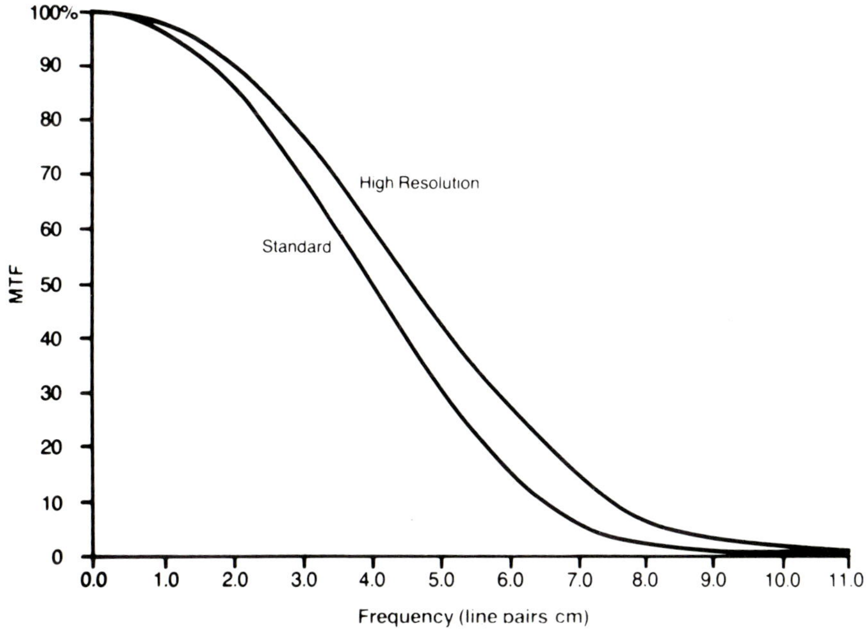

FIG. 8–2. Typical CT modulation transfer function (MTF) curves. The vertical axis represents the MTF factor, with a maximum of 100% or 1.0. The horizontal axis represents spatial frequency. Note that the high-resolution curve has higher values throughout most of the curve, indicating a more faithful representation on the image of actual spatial frequencies. However, the cutoff frequency of 11 line pairs per cm (0.45 mm resolution) is about the same. Therefore, one must not overemphasize the importance of the cutoff frequency when comparing units. (Graph courtesy of Philips Medical Systems. Note that these curves do not represent current specifications of any Philips Systems, but are used for illustration only.)

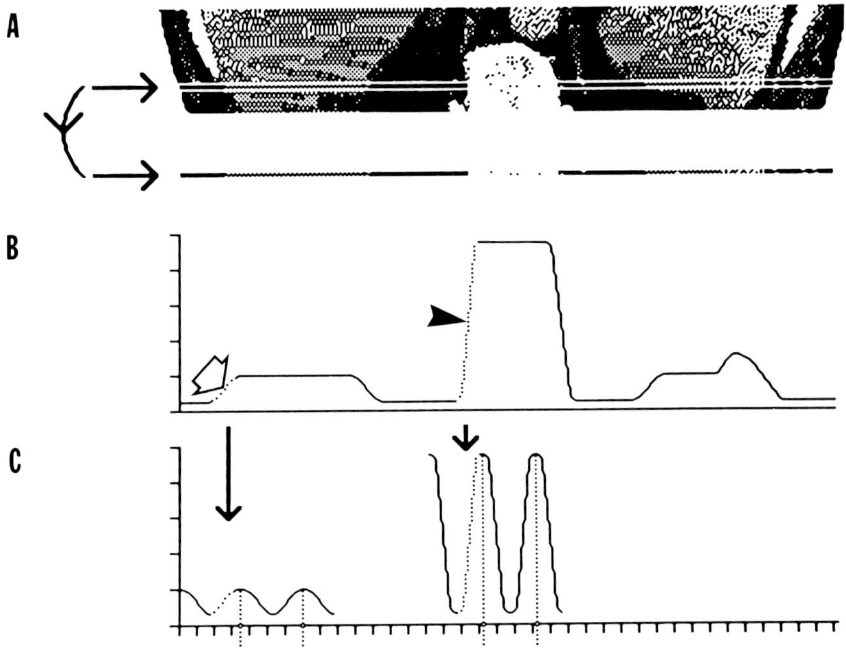

FIG. 8–3. **A** represents a segment of a CT slice. A horizontal line has been selected (arrows) and is displayed separately beneath the CT scan. The set of curves beneath the image (**B** and **C**) represent how the images may be translated into spatial frequencies. The vertical axis represents image density. Each point on the horizontal axis corresponds to the points on the CT scan line directly above it.

Near the midline is an abrupt change in density from paraspinal muscle to the bone of the vertebral body. This abrupt change is represented as the nearly vertical dotted line (arrowhead) on the curve. If one isolates just this abrupt transition from low to high density, one can convert this change to a periodic wave form as noted in **C**. This wave has a high amplitude and a short wavelength (high frequency). Thus, abrupt changes are considered to have high spatial frequency. By contrast, along the left-hand portion of the image there is a less abrupt change, represented by a sloping dotted line in **B** (open arrow). In **C** this may be translated to a low-amplitude, low-frequency wave and thus is an area within the image of low spatial frequency.

The visual perception of noise is affected by modifying the display. As the window width is narrowed, the contrast of the noise increases. The interplay between spatial and contrast resolution, noise, and visual perception is complex, and some aspects are poorly understood. This topic and radiographic image perception in general have been elegantly discussed and illustrated in a monograph by C. Carl Jaffe (13) and in a chapter on visual perception of CT images by David J. Goodenough (10).

The answer to the curious clinician about how well we can see lesions is that "it depends." It depends on the spatial resolution, contrast resolution, noise, visual perception, and other factors, and on the ability to resolve clinically relevant detail, which changes from patient to patient and from application to application. The clinically relevant answers must come from empirical observations made when the examination technique has been optimized by understanding and employing the capabilities of the unit. It is not sufficient to respond to the clinician by quoting the technical spatial and contrast resolution figures printed in the manufacturers' specifications.

ATTENUATION NUMBERS

One of the uses for CT envisioned by its developers and early users was the specific characterization of tissues by attenuation numbers. The currently accepted unit for CT attenuation is the Hounsfield unit (HU) (15,18), named after Geoffrey Newbold Hounsfield, Nobel laureate and the acknowledged pioneer in CT development. The numbers are set on a scale so that

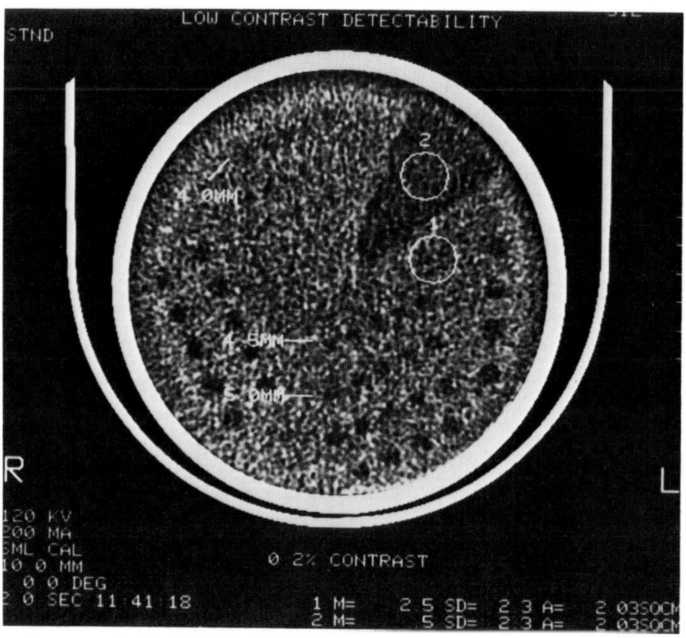

FIG. 8–4. Scan of a contrast phantom used to measure contrast resolution. This is done with large objects that differ slightly in attenuation from one another. The wedge at upper right is 2 HU(0.2% contrast) lower in attenuation than its surroundings. Holes 4.5 and 5.0 mm in diameter are also visible at this same level of contrast. This image was filmed at a very narrow window width of 30 HU. (Scan courtesy of General Electric Company, Medical Systems.)

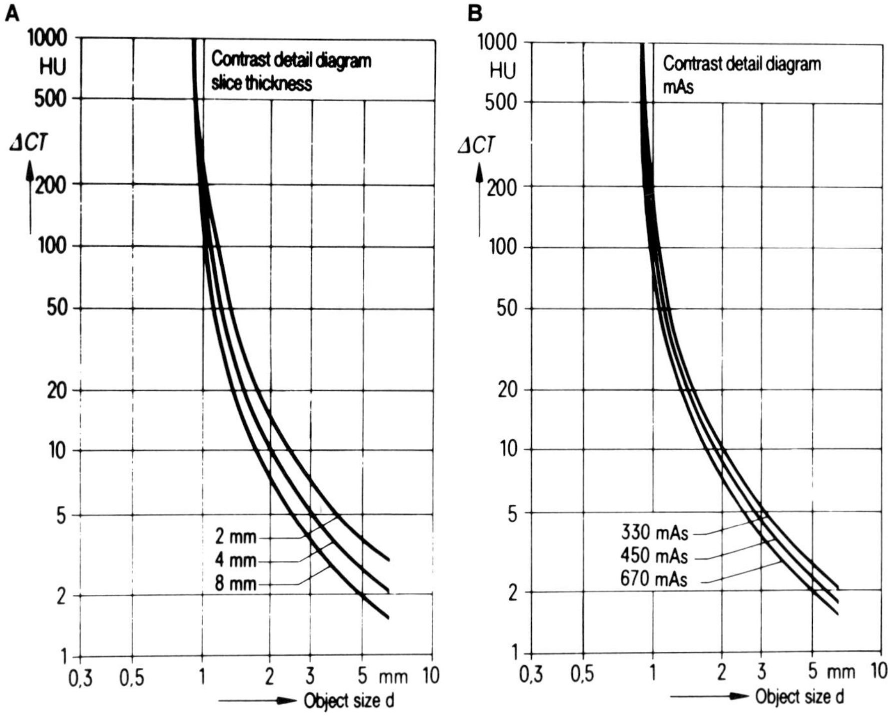

FIG. 8–5. Typical CT contrast-detail curves, which plot image contrast on the vertical axis against detectable object diameter on the horizontal. Both scales are logarithmic. These curves demonstrate the ability to perceive an object of varying diameters at varying levels of contrast. As expected, as contrast (difference in value in Hounsfield units) on any of the three curves is increased, smaller objects are resolvable (**A**). Also, as mAs is increased (**B**), the curve shifts to the left, also indicating the ability to resolve smaller objects. Such curves may be plotted for variations in factors such as object size and slice thickness. (Graphs courtesy of Siemens Medical Systems, Inc.)

the density of air is represented by −1,000 and that of pure water by zero. With these standards, bone density is usually found within a range between about 800 for normal cortical bone up to 3,000 for dense petrous bone. An older system of units was the EMI unit, which used values one-half those in the Hounsfield system (22). This system was used very briefly on the earliest systems and has been completely abandoned. The current scale of CT attenuation numbers from about −1,000 to 3,000 can be displayed with 12 bits of computer data. That is, with a binary system such as is used in computers, 12 bits provides 2^{12} combinations, or 4,096. Thus, numbers from −1,024 to 3,071 are used, with each number assigned to a specific combination of bits in the "on" or "off" position.

Unlike plain film radiography, in which more X-ray intensity makes the film darker, and less makes it lighter, more X-ray intensity on CT makes the image less noisy but should not change the average attenuation number of a region of tissue (11) (see Chapter 5, p. 68). Thus one might expect that the shade of gray represented on each pixel would correspond to the actual linear X-ray attenuation coefficient of that element of tissue independent of the X-ray dose. However, this goal cannot be reached with current CT technology, and the hope of finding specific CT attenuation numbers for a wide variety of normal and abnormal tissues with single kVp techniques has not been realized (19,21). Inaccuracies and inconsistencies caused by artifacts as great as 70 HU have been measured (16). The uses of CT numbers for making diagnoses are very limited, and in most situations CT numbers should be one of the last diagnostic criteria used to evaluate lesions.

The evaluation of relative tissue density by CT is indeed quite valuable, but much damage has been done by overdependence on absolute numbers when the weight of diagnostic evidence points elsewhere. I have seen several disturbing examples of how faith in CT numbers took precedence over good judgment, leading to unfortunate clinical results. However, in certain cases, numbers can be clinically helpful. For example, fat attenuation within a renal lesion may make the diagnosis of a benign angiomyolipoma nearly certain, and numbers consistent with fluid will help accurately diagnose benign renal cysts. CT numbers have also been used effectively to diagnose osteoporosis from measurements of spinal density. However, one can arrive at most clinical conclusions without resorting to direct computer readings of attenuation if one visually compares the shades of gray in the structure in question to nearby structures of known density such as subcutaneous fat (about −70 to −100 HU), muscle, bone, or bile (about 0 to 20 HU or higher). Thus, numbers are more reliable when used only relative to other tissue numbers in the same or comparable slices. If the visual impression is inconclusive, comparison measurements may be used, but the absolute numbers should be interpreted *extremely* cautiously.

There are many artifacts that may lead to inaccurate CT numbers (11,12,22). These include beam hardening, noise, volume averaging, kVp variations, scatter, motion artifact, aliasing, and geometric inconsistencies. The position of an object within the scan field, the composition and shape of beam filters (19), and careless measurement techniques can also affect the CT number values.

The most significant single source of inaccuracy is the use of the single kVp for each scan and a polychromatic X-ray source. Because the beam is polychromatic (composed of photons with numerous different X-ray energies), it is subject to shifting of the average energy as it penetrates the patient. This average energy shift is termed *beam hardening* (see Chapter 11, p. 153) and depends on the composition and thickness of various body parts. The beam is "hardened" because lower energy photons are preferentially absorbed in tissue, leaving the residual transmitted beam with photons of higher average energy even though much of the intensity of the beam is attenuated (many of the photons are absorbed) in the patient (see Fig. 2-5). Beam hardening is a problem with CT imaging because the degree of beam hardening depends on the thickness of the body part and its relative composition of fat, muscle, bone, and other tissues, which cannot be computed by a fixed correction factor. Thus the intensity reaching the detector depends not only on the actual attenuation coefficient of a voxel of tissue being examined, but also on the thickness and beam filtering nature of the surrounding tissue. The beam hardening corrections are based on idealized models of patients composed of an average combination of fat, muscle, fluid, and bone. Naturally, few real people fit that description, and inaccuracies result. Second-order corrections are described below and reduce some of the inaccuracy.

Some of the error in CT numbers partly caused by beam hardening is a systematic variation in CT numbers from the center to the periphery of the field. This is often termed a *cupping artifact* (3,12,14), because the concentric variations with a dip in the center of the reconstructed field is analogous to the dip in the center of a cup. The source of the cupped shape of the artifact relates to the geometry of the beam. The peripheral parts of the fan beam travel through the least quantity of tissue and are therefore least affected by hardening. The central part of the beam is most severely affected (Fig. 8-6).

The severity of this artifact depends largely on patient size and composition. The beam is hardened less by fat and more by bone. Components of higher atomic number such as calcium increase beam hardening.

As mentioned, the initial correction for beam hardening depends on the assumption of an idealized patient of a certain composition, which is usually a poor approximation. Therefore, a second correction process, termed a *second-order correction* is often done (23). This involves using the first-order reconstruction to estimate the effect of body composition on beam hardening and correcting for it.

As discussed above, various other processing corrections are included in the reconstruction process: for example, making the image appear smoother or suppressing rings. Each type of correction may lead to errors because certain assumptions are made. CT numbers may also be severely affected by the presence of tissue outside the reconstructed field of view (the out-of-field artifact; see Fig. 5-1). Electronic drift of the components of the system also occurs. Sophisticated and accurate beam hardening and scatter corrections are essential to producting high-quality images. This can be practically assessed by radiologists only by carefully studying images.

Serious errors may result from poor measurement techniques by those unfamiliar with the limitations of CT number accuracy. One error is that of measuring a structure too small relative to the thickness of the slice; another is measurement of a structure at its most cephalad or caudad extreme. This inaccuracy is a volume averaging artifact or partial volume artifact caused by the inclusion of some tissue above or below the structure, but still within

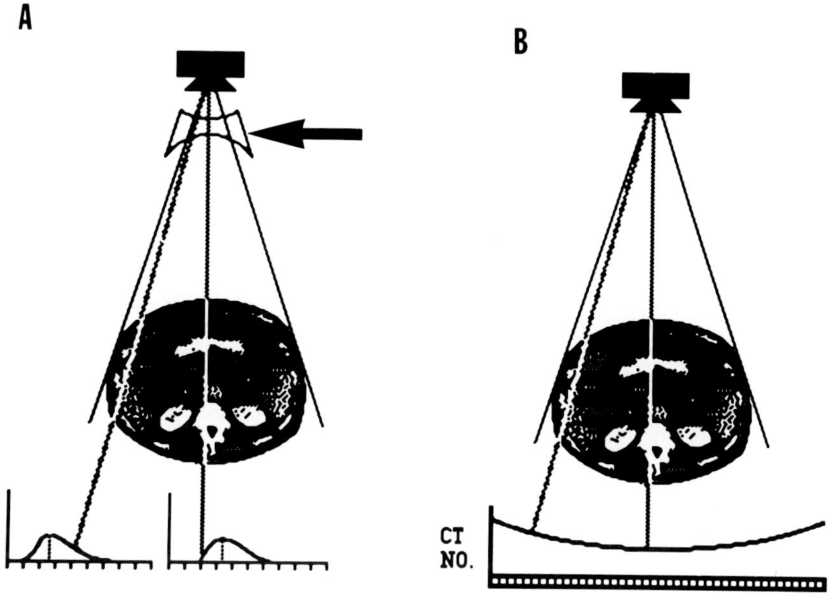

FIG. 8–6. Effects of and compensation for beam hardening. **A**. A prepatient beam-shaping filter (arrow) partly compensates for the beam hardening effect illustrated in Fig. 2–5. Because the filter is thicker in the periphery of the beam, it is already partly filtered before arriving at the patient. In the periphery of the patient there is less filtering, and thus the combination of prepatient filtering and reduced patient filtering somewhat balances the effect of the beam passing through the central portion of the patient. However, this effect cannot be completely eliminated. **B**. Without a prepatient shaping filter, CT attenuation numbers are artifactually decreased through the central portion of the image, because as the beam is hardened and the average energy of the beam increases, the reconstruction algorithm leads to the false interpretation that the higher energy beam actually has a higher intensity (number of photons). This is interpreted as lower attenuation through the center of the patient and leads to the cupping artifact. (*Figure continues* on page 98.)

the slice, into the measurement (Fig. 8-7). A way to avoid such errors is to measure structures only when the thickness of the slice is about one-half the size of the lesion or less. Thus, an 8-mm lesion should be studied with consecutive slices of 4 mm or less.

However, if the measured value would be expected to be lowered by the adjacent tissue, and a clinical threshold is exceeded nevertheless, then the measurement still provides diagnostic clinical information. For example, if a pulmonary nodule only 8 mm in size is seen in a 10-mm slice and is found to have a density of 200 HU, that number may be falsely low because of averaging of adjacent lung. However, the inaccurate reading of 200 HU would still suffice to indicate that the lesion was calcified, even though the actual attenuation of the lesion is much higher.

Volume averaging artifacts are still possible with larger lesions if the edges of roughly spherical lesions are included in the measurement. The edges

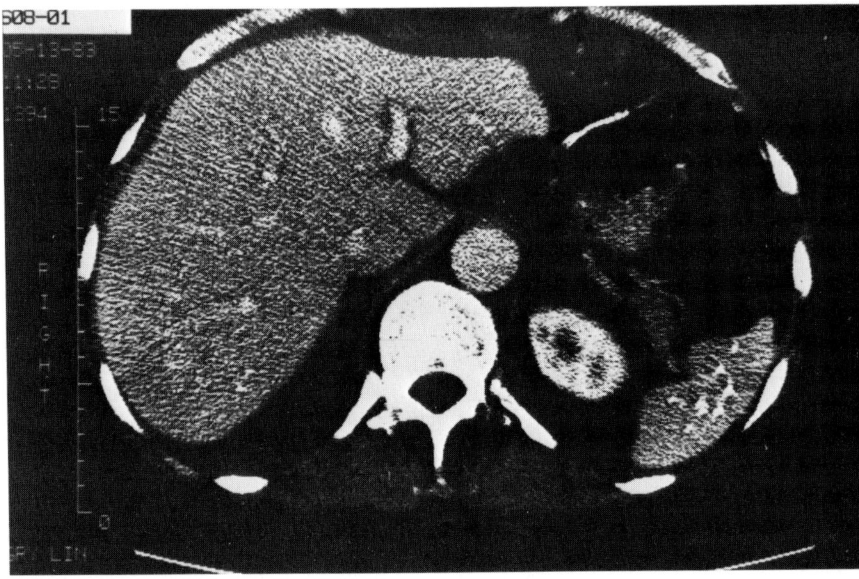

FIG. 8–6. (*cont.*) C. Abdominal scan illustrating the artifact. This image is viewed at a very narrow window width, which accentuates the cupping effect and image noise. The periphery of the liver is apparently increased in attenuation compared to the central portions.

may be subject to volume averaging, whereas the center is not. Therefore, regions of interest should be confined to areas several pixels away from lesion borders.

The type of volume averaging discussed above may be termed a *linear partial volume effect.* That is, a correction factor could theoretically be applied based on the amount of tissue included within the slice. However, nonlinear partial volume effects also occur when irregular shapes project into the scan slice, causing streak artifacts (14).

It has been found that the surroundings of a mass may slightly affect the measured density of the mass itself. This is termed the *environmental density artifact* (19,21). For example, the density measurement of a small renal cyst may differ before and after the administration of intravenous contrast material, despite the lack of vascularization of the cyst or volume-averaging effect, suggesting that the cyst enhanced as if solid. The convolution filter and beam hardening corrections, among others, create this potentially clinically confusing situation.

Characterization of tissue is also limited by the inherent composition of the tissue, which may be a blend of various tissues. For example, CT attenuation measurements of livers with fatty infiltration may show densities that would be expected for pure water. The liver is not fluid in these cases, but is a mixture of fatty (negative) densities and solid (positive) densities, which average to near zero.

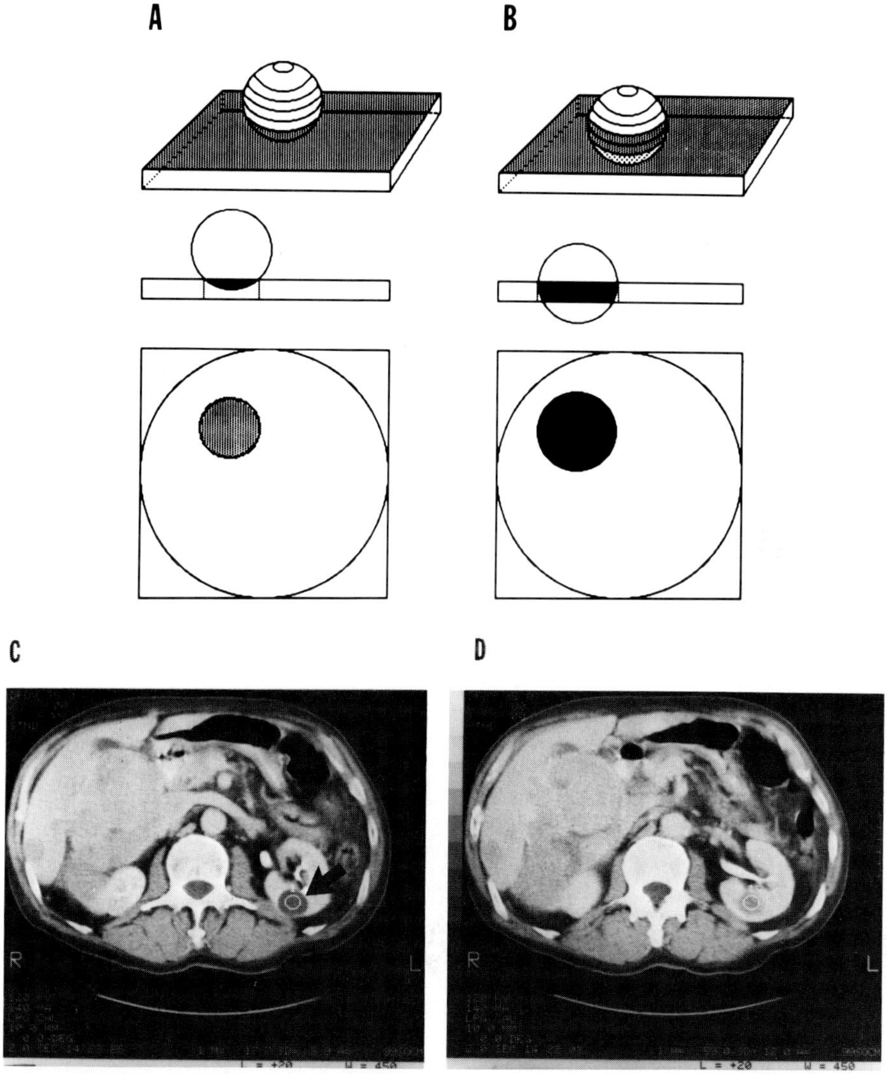

FIG. 8–7. Volume averaging or linear partial volume effect. **A**. The image in perspective illustrates a sphere that only partly projects into the slice. In the next diagram below, this arrangement is viewed in profile. The bottom diagram indicates the CT scan appearance, in which the sphere is represented as smaller than its true diameter, with an attenuation that is averaged with the other tissue within the slice, and with a vague margin caused by the sloping of the sphere within the slice. **B**. When the sphere is located in the middle of the slice, the CT image indicates its true diameter and attenuation. **C**. A CT slice of a patient with a renal cyst (arrow). A circular cursor is located through the midportion of the renal cyst, which measures about 18 HU. **D**. The same cyst measured at the next most cephalad level has an attenuation number of 59 HU because there is partial volume averaging with the adjacent enhanced renal parenchyma. Also, the cyst boundaries are less well defined, and the lesion is apparently smaller. An extremely large right-sided adrenal mass and liver metastases are also seen in this patient.

A

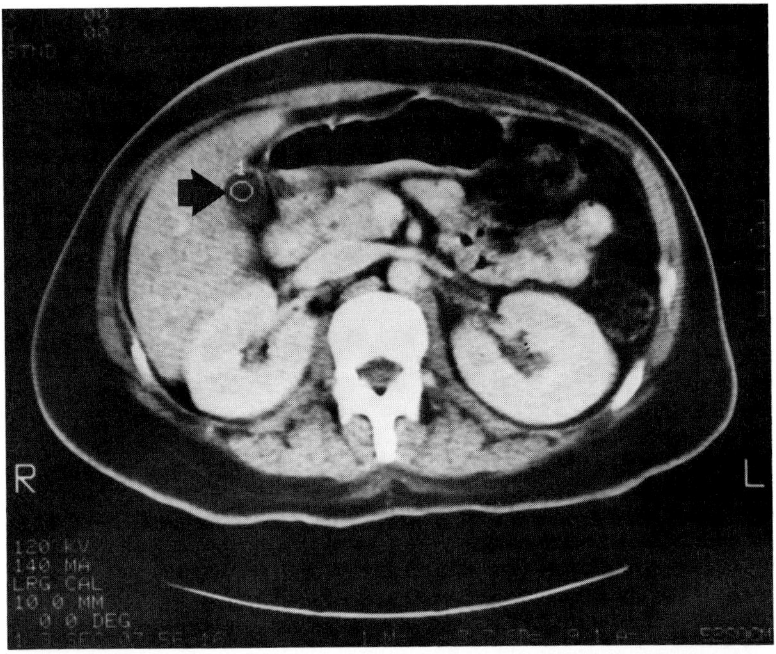

B

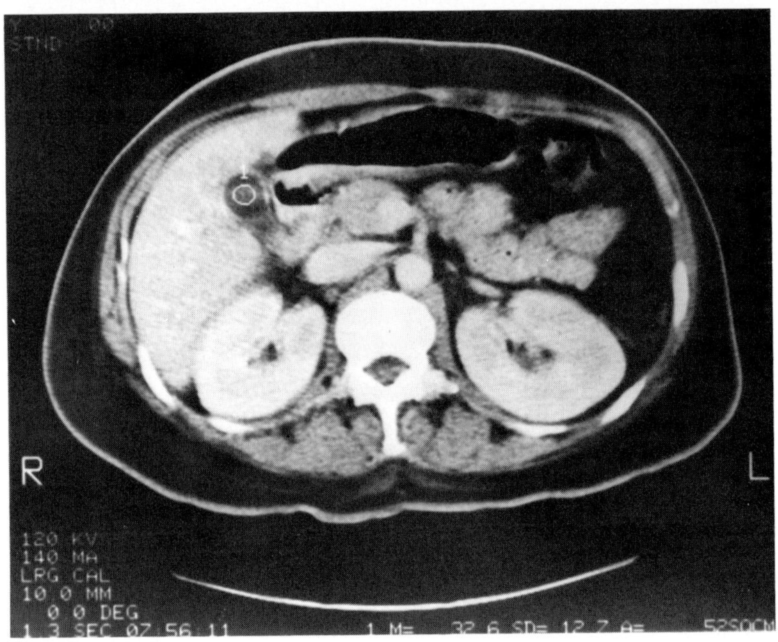

FIG. 8–8. Variability of CT attenuation numbers due to subtle artifacts. **A**. The ROI circle (arrow) within the gallbladder indicates an attenuation of about 9 HU. **B**. The ROI circle in an adjacent slice with a subtle artifact radiating from the duodenum indicates an attenuation of 33 HU. One must be extremely cautious when using CT attenuation numbers for diagnosis.

Another common error of measurement is the inclusion of areas of streak artifacts wtihin the region of interest (ROI) cursor. Such streaks may markedly change the value of some pixels from their true value, skewing the average measurement for the whole lesion (Fig. 8-8).

Test objects are available to check the accuracy of numbers. Some may be placed on the patient couch during scanning, thus providing an internal reference for known numbers (Fig. 8-9). However, these phantoms may themselves be affected by artifactual streaks, and they do not help correct for errors in measurement occurring because of variations in the position of the ROI within the field.

Specialized, rigorously controlled methods of measuring the CT numbers of pulmonary nodules have been advocated (24). One system involves the use of thin sections, with careful machine calibration, and direct pixel-by-pixel displays of CT numbers with averages. Threshold CT attenuation numbers are determined for each machine. Patterns of distribution of calcifications are also considered in the final clinical conclusion of whether a lesion is benign or indeterminate.

A second system uses a phantom constructed from a commercially available kit of component parts of various sizes and densities including those of subcutaneous fat, chest wall, lung, and nodules (9,17). A combination of components is assembled to resemble the slice in which the real pulmonary nodule was seen in the patient. The purpose of this exercise is to overcome the limitations of beam hardening by placing an object representing the nodule with a known attenuation at the threshold density of calcification in virtually identical conditions as the unknown nodule. If the real nodule is found to be higher in attenuation than the phantom nodule, then the real nodule is diagnosed as benign.

A third system uses CT scans taken at two X-ray energies through the pulmonary nodule (4). If the information from the two scans is properly calculated, then an actual elemental nodule composition can be calculated. There are significant difficulties with each of these systems. Slight changes in registration from scan to scan may lead to misregistration of small nodules within thin slices. All techniques require great attention to details of scanning and calculation and at least a modest amount of faith that uncontrollable artifacts will have a negligible effect on the results. Perhaps the greatest problem is that each of the three techniques requires additional time, expense and expertise.

Many practitioners of CT, including this author and others performing CT at our institution, believe that the infrequency with which additional information is offered by such demanding techniques does not warrant their widespread application. We perform maneuvers no more complex than simple ROI measurements of pulmonary nodules using thin sections. Furthermore, recent studies with an experimental dual-energy digital radiographic unit have demonstrated a high accuracy and reproducibility for demonstrating calcification within pulmonary nodules (6). If this technology becomes

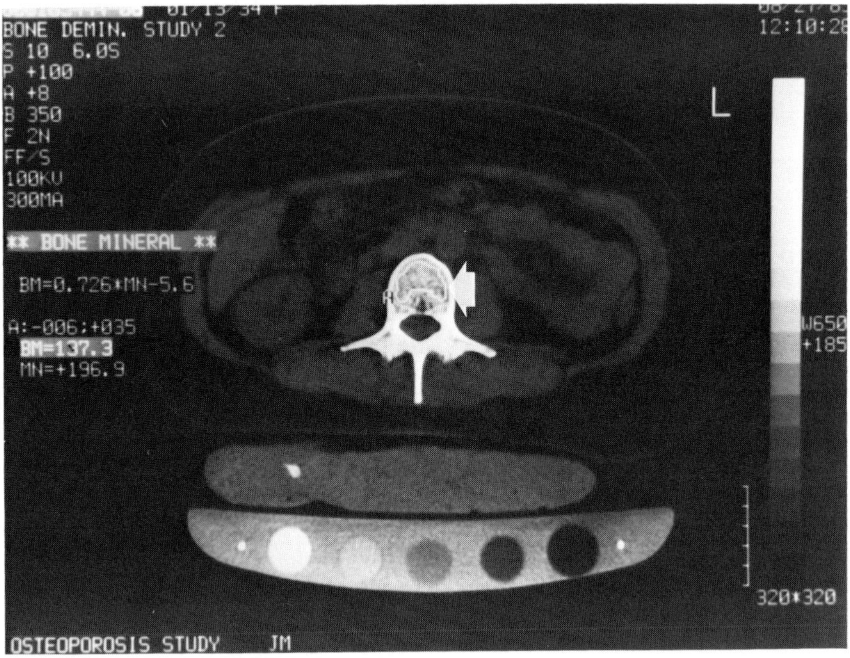

FIG. 8–9. Use of a CT attenuation number reference object. The object replaces a portion of the patient cushions and contains cylinders with substances of known attenuation. This information can be used to calibrate for accurate CT attenuation numbers. However, the object itself may be somewhat affected by streaks radiating from the patient couch. Also, CT attenuation numbers vary with position within the scanning field, because of cupping artifact. Therefore, such test objects can correct attenuation numbers only to a limited degree. Nevertheless, this reference object permits the satisfactorily accurate analysis of bone mineral content as used in this case. Note the freehand ROI cursor (arrow) in the vertebral medullary space and the associated measurements and calculations. (Image courtesy of Philips Medical Systems.)

more widely available, it may be the best and simplest solution to the clinical problem of diagnosing the nature of pulmonary nodules.

Techniques to measure bone density have been developed and clinically applied to evaluating osteoporosis (7,8,20). These techniques are discussed in Chapter 9, p. 113.

REFERENCES

1. Bergstrom, M. (1981): Performance evaluation of scanners. In: *Radiology of the Skull and Brain: Technical Aspects of Computed Tomography,* edited by T. H. Newton and D. G. Potts, pp. 4212–4227. C. V. Mosby, St. Louis.
2. Blumenfeld, S. M., and Glover, G. (1981): Spatial resolution in computed tomography. In: *Radiology of the Skull and Brain: Technical Aspects of Computed Tomogaphy,* edited by T. H. Newton and D. G. Potts, pp. 3918–3940. C. V. Mosby, St. Louis.

3. Boyd, D. P. (1981): Transmission computed tomography in: *Radiology of the Skull and Brain: Technical Aspects of Computed Tomography,* edited by T. H. Newton and D. G. Potts, pp. 4357–4371. C. V. Mosby, St. Louis.
4. Cann, C. E., Gamsu, G., Birnbert, F. A., and Webb, W. R. (1982): Quantification of calcium in solitary pulmonary nodules using single- and dual-energy CT. *Radiology,* 145:493–496.
5. Coulam, C. M., and Erickson, J. J. (1981): Image considerations in computed tomography. In: *The Physical Basis of Medical Imaging,* edited by C. M. Coulam, J. J. Erickson, F. D. Rollo, and A. E. James, pp. 189–211. Appleton-Century-Crofts, New York.
6. Fraser, R. G., Hickey, N., Niklason, L. T., Sabbagh, E. A., Luna, R. F., Alexander, C. B., Robinson, C. A., Katzenstein, A. A., and Barnes, G. T. (1986): Calcification in pulmonary nodules: detection with dual-energy digital radiography. *Radiology,* 160:595–601.
7. Genant, H. K. (1985): Assessing osteoporosis: CT's quantitative advantage. *Diagnostic Imaging,* (August) 52–57.
8. Genant, H. K., Cann, C. E., Ettinger, B., Gordan, G. S., Kolb, F. O., Reiser, U., and Arnaud, C. D. (1985): Quantitative computed tomography for spinal mineral assessment: Current status. *J. Comput. Assist. Tomogr.,* 9(3):602–604.
9. Godwin, J. D., Fram, E. K., Cann, C. E., and Gamsu, G. G. (1982): CT densitometry of pulmonary nodules: A phantom study. *J. Comput. Assist. Tomogr.,* 6(2):254–258.
10. Goodenough, D. J. (1981): Psychophysical perception of computed tomography images. In: *Radiology of the Skull and Brain: Technical Aspects of Computed Tomography,* edited by T. H. Newton and D. G. Potts, pp. 3993–4021. C. B. Mosby, St. Louis.
11. Hanson, K. M. (1981): Noise and contrast discrimination in computed tomography. In: *Radiology of the Skull and Brain: Technical Aspects of Computed Tomography,* edited by T. H. Newton and D. G. Potts, pp. 3941–3955. C. V. Mosby, St. Louis.
12. Hemmingsson, A., Jung, B., and Ytterbergh, C. (1983): Ellipsoidal body phantom for evaluation of CT scanners. *J. Comput. Assist. Tomogr,* 7(3):503–508.
13. Jaffe, C. C. (1984): Medical imaging, vision, and visual psychophysics. *Med. Radiogr. Photogr.,* 60:1–48.
14. Joseph, P. M. (1981): Artifacts in computed tomography. In: *Radiology of the Skull and Brain: Technical Aspects of Computed Tomography,* edited by T. H. Newton and D. G. Potts, pp. 3956–3992. C. V. Mosby, St. Louis.
15. McCullough, E. C. (1977). Factors affecting the use of quantitative information from a CT scanner. *Radiology,* 124:99–107.
16. McCullough, E. C., and Morin, R. L. (1983): CT-number variability in thoracic geometry. *AJR,* 141:135–140.
17. Proto, A. V., and Thomas, S. R. (1985): Pulmonary nodules studied by computed tomography. *Radiology,* 156:149–153.
18. Pullan, B. R., Ritchings, R. T., and Isherwood, I. (1981): Accuracy and meaning of computed tomography attenuation values. In: *Radiology of the Skull and Brain: Technical Aspects of Computed Tomography,* edited by T. H. Newton and D. G. Potts, pp. 3904–3917. C. V. Mosby, St. Louis.
19. Rao, P. S., and Alfidi, R. J. (1981): The environmental density artifact: A beam-hardening effect in computed tomography. *Radiology,* 141:223–227.
20. Rosenthal, D. I., Ganott, M. A., Wyshak, G., Slovik, D. M., Doppelt, S. H., and Neer, R. M. (1985): Quantitative computed tomography for spinal density measurement: Factors affecting precision. *Invest. Radiol.,* 20:306–310.
21. Young, S. W., Muller, H. H., and Marshall, W. H. (1983): Computed tomography: Beam hardening and environmental density artifact. *Radiology,* 148:279–283.
22. Zatz, L. M. (1981): Basic principles of computed tomography scanning. In: *Radiology of the Skull and Brain: Technical Aspects of Computed Tomography,* edited by T. H. Newton and D. G. Potts, pp. 3853–3876. C. V. Mosby, St. Louis.
23. Zatz, L. M. (1981): General overview of computed tomography instrumentation. In: *Radiology of the Skull and Brain: Technical Aspects of Computed Tomography,* edited by T. H. Newton and D. G. Potts, pp. 4025–4057. C. V. Mosby, St. Louis.
24. Zerhouni, E. A., Spivey, J. F., Morgan, R. H., Leo, F. P., Stitik, F. P., and Siegelman, S. S. (1982): Factors influencing quantitative CT measurements of solitary pulmonary nodules. *J. Comput. Assist. Tomogr,* 6(6):1075–1987.

9

Programs and Features

The basic functions needed for CT software may seem obvious to radiologists. However, those who direct the writing of CT system software may have little or no direct contact with users. Therefore, CT software is often not "user friendly" and comes with time-consuming, apparently meaningless "bells and whistles" while lacking important basic features. Most operators have strong feelings about the user friendliness or hostility of their machines and will freely share their opinions.

BASIC PROGRAM FEATURES

The computers used in current CT systems are capable of doing much more than they have been programmed to do. However, many companies have limited budgets and have trouble finding high-quality software engineers, and even when enough manpower is available, management may misdirect resources to developing apparently unimportant features. Therefore, one cannot assume that, because one scanner has a simple feature that seems of obvious value, another manufacturer will adapt that feature to its unit, even though the hardware may be capable of it. For example, a common feature permits the console operator to retrieve a succeeding slice without waiting for the last slice to be completely painted on the screen. That is, the image paint process may be aborted to save display time. Most operators like this time-saving feature. However, at least one manufacturer has failed to implement this simple program. Another manufacturer programs the console to completely rewrite the list of slices for the examination each time a new image is called for, adding several unnecessary seconds to the display of each image. A third company has strongly supported hardware development but has delayed in developing an easily learned operating system. Thus, rather than being provided with simple function keys or clearly written menus, operators have had to learn computer codes to perform routine display functions.

Some manufacturers boast about the flexibility of their system configuration for adding upgraded software. However, the flexibility of the system is no guarantee that the upgraded software the users most desire will ever be written, or that when upgrades are produced they will be compatible with current hardware.

Therefore, if one is considering equipment purchase, it is useful to ask users about the quirks of the system being considered. These idiosyncrasies related to software may materially affect the usability and desirability of the system. The following are several of the features that are most important for efficient scanner use.

Priority Reconstruction or Priority Processing

For units capable of very rapid reconstruction, the order in which images are reconstructed (processed) is unimportant because they are all available for review quickly. However, if such fast reconstruction is not implemented, it is important to be able to select (prioritize) the order in which slices are reconstructed separately from the order in which they are acquired. For example, it may be useful to reconstruct the last slice obtained in a series before all of the others are reconstructed. This capacity will permit a decision to be made whether to terminate the scan because the area of interest has been completely covered. One cannot assume that such a program will be available, and I strongly recommend that one inquire about its inclusion when considering purchase of a scanner with a reconstruction time of about 15 sec or longer per slice.

Speed of Image Display and Recall

It is important to be able to display an image rapidly. Some scanners require unnecessarily complex procedures to first find and then display an image. Then, the image paint time may be excessive—up to 10 sec on some units. It is also important to be able to easily select the next image one wishes to display. It is often desirable to view images out of sequence, and some scanners require several frustratingly time-consuming steps to perform this operation. When testing the efficiency of image recall in a system, one should be able to display an image quickly whether or not it is first in the series of scans. It should then be a simple matter to view slices sequentially backward or forward, to skip several slices backward or forward, or to select slices within the series at random.

Window and Level Controls

The ease of using window width and window level controls can greatly affect how images are viewed, and therefore how well subtle findings are diagnosed. Simple controls encourage the routine use of special features, whereas complex controls inhibit them. I believe that the easiest controls to use are those of the dial or trackball type, because one can quickly shift to the desired target window or level and then make minor adjustments. Button or paddle controls, in which the desired window or level is slowly continuously approached as the key is depressed, are more cumbersome. With these systems it may take several seconds rather than a split-second to reach the vicinity of the desired level, and then one is likely to overshoot the desired number. Such frustrating devices discourage viewing at more than one setting and thus may lead to missing lesions that might be seen better at other settings.

Some systems also employ a feature that permits instant switching between different window width and window level settings. This feature facilitates examining and filming slices of, for example, the chest at both lung and soft-tissue settings or of limbs at both soft-tissue and bone settings. The user may view each image quickly at the two settings rather than have to paint the image set twice.

Linear and Attenuation Measurements

Size and attenuation number readings are frequently valuable adjuncts to scan interpretation. Although all scanners provide them, some are easier to use than others. The measurements may be controlled by a light pen touched to the screen, a trackball, or a joystick. Linear measurements are generally marked with a simple cursor, but average density measurements of areas (regions of interest, ROI) may be done with a circle, square, oval, or freehand contour. One system uses a crosshair that can be quickly and freely moved around the screen with a joystick, giving instantaneous attenuation readings of the average of the pixels composing the crosshair itself. This feature is useful, but its use is limited to objects larger than the crosshair.

One advantageous feature is the ability to display multiple linear or attenuation measurements on a single image. This saves time and film but can be somewhat confusing to those not familiar with the data display format. Such confusion could result in misdiagnoses. For example, on one of our systems, the data displayed include the average attenuation number, the standard deviation, and the number of pixels used for the average (Fig. 9-1). These are labeled with obscure abbreviations, and on an older version of software two spaces were left between the minus sign and the number for attenuation. A serious interpretive error was made in one case because the minus sign was not perceived, and a second error in another case because the number of pixels was taken to be the attenuation average.

Image Annotation

The essential information to be annotated on each image consists of the patient's name and identification number, date, slice number, computer

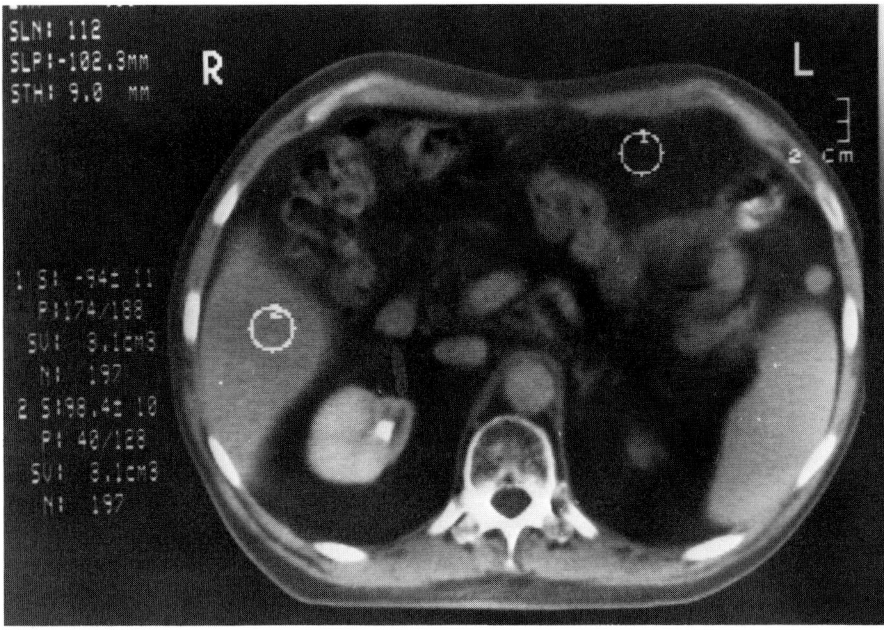

FIG. 9–1. Abdominal scan illustrating the potential complexity of ROI measurements. Two ROI circles placed simultaneously on the image produce many numbers annotated along the left-hand side of the image. The abbreviations may be obscure and confusing. For example, both circles contain an "N" of 197. This number may be mistaken for the average attenuation of the ROI although it simply represents the number of pixels used to create the average.

examination or run number, right and/or left indicators, and position index relative to some external landmark. Other information should be available for optional display, including the time of scan acquisition in hours, minutes, and seconds; the technique factors including slice thickness, scan time, kVp, mA, and mAs; and whether or not intravenous contrast was used.

We often use this timing and slice location information to determine the cause of suboptimal images. For example, we check the adequacy of timing for a dynamic scan, clarify whether the proper slices have been scanned, or determine whether images have been inadvertently omitted from the film. When image noise is high, mAs values are inspected to determine whether proper tube output technique factors were used.

Furthermore, a grid or linear measurement marker should be available, and the displayed field of view should be noted or available. A measuring reference of satisfactory length is an important feature because small errors from short markers can be compounded. For example, if one attempted to use a caliper with a 2-cm marker scale to measure a 30-cm body diameter, then a 1-mm error in measuring the 2-cm marker would be magnified to a 15-mm error in measuring the body. A 1-mm error with a 30-cm marker would result in only a 1-mm error overall. One system provides only a 2-cm marker (see Fig. 9-1), which not only introduces inaccuracies but is awkward. It is impractical to do all measuring with the console software; thus a convenient system for measuring with calipers from films is necessary. One should also be able to superimpose words and arrows on an image for display and teaching purposes.

Reformatting or Multiplanar Reformation

Reformatting or reformation is a feature of CT software that is now standard on most scanners. The computer performs this function by figuratively stacking consecutive scans upon each other within the computer memory. The appropriate pixels from each slice are then retrieved to project an image in a plane other than the axial, from which the data was originally obtained (Fig. 9-2). Thus, coronal, sagittal, parasagittal, and other oblique planes may be viewed to appreciate a different anatomic perspective. These views are usually termed reformatted images rather than reconstructed images because the term *reconstruction* is reserved for the process of reconstructing the original image from the raw data. The reformation process uses only the already reconstructed display data. The quality of these images is almost always poorer than the original scan data, because the thickness of the slice fixes the maximum spatial resolution perpendicular to the slice, and the thinnest slice thickness is still greater than the worst spatial resolution. For example, if one were performing a coronal reconstruction of axial slices 5 mm in thickness, then the cephalocaudad spatial resolution could be no better than 5 mm, compared to under 1 mm on the original slices. Also, if there is any misregistration between slices caused by patient breathing or motion, the image is further degraded. Because of the large slice thickness relative to normal axial detail, the reformatted images are interpolated to smooth the discontinuities.

For these reasons, reformatting has found little use in body imaging, in which most scans are 8 to 10 mm thick. However, reformatting is more popular for head and spine scanning because these areas may be more easily held motionless, thus avoiding misregistration, and thinner slices of 1 to 5 mm are more commonly used. The orientation of clinically relevant anatomy in these areas requires either using the reformatted image or scanning directly in the unusual plane. Reformatting may have some applications in the body to facilitate appreciation of the relationships of organs to lesions, particularly for nonradiological clinicans, and to display complex anatomy with thin sections, such as may be used for the larynx or feet.

Reformatting images is often a time-consuming task. If one is considering equipment purchase with the expectation of performing reformatting frequently, it would be worthwhile to ask users as well as salepersons about the practical aspects of this technique. Although the process is considerably more streamlined than with earlier scanners, there are still marked differ-

A

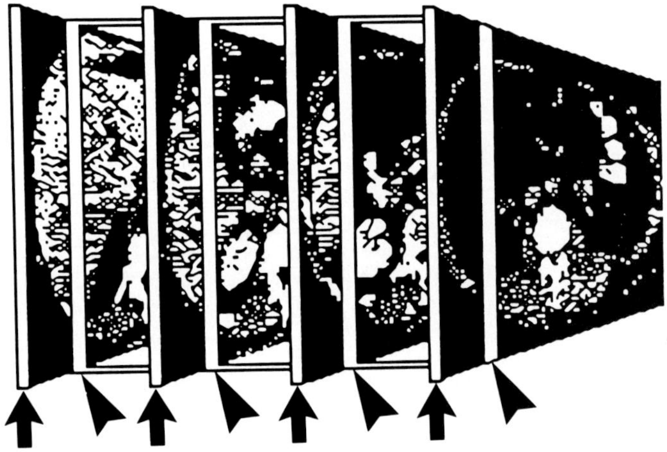

B

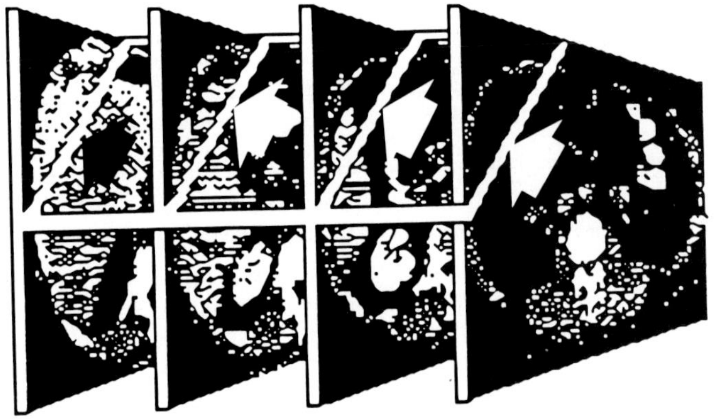

FIG. 9–2. Illustrations of the principle of reformatting. **A**. Successive CT slices (arrows) are figuratively stacked adjacent to one another. A plane (arrowheads) may be cut in any orientation within this figurative stack and the information from within this plane used to create a new image. **B**. An oblique plane (arrows) has been defined through the same set of slices. **C**. A slightly obliqued set of coronal views through the spinal canal is defined on the upper left image. Five sections through this area are then displayed simultaneously. (Image courtesy of Picker International, Inc.)

ences in usability between scanners, and even in different units marketed by the same manufacturer.

Magnification

Magnification is discussed in Chapter 7, p. 81. This feature permits variable enlargement of portions of the image, but it uses only the data previ-

C

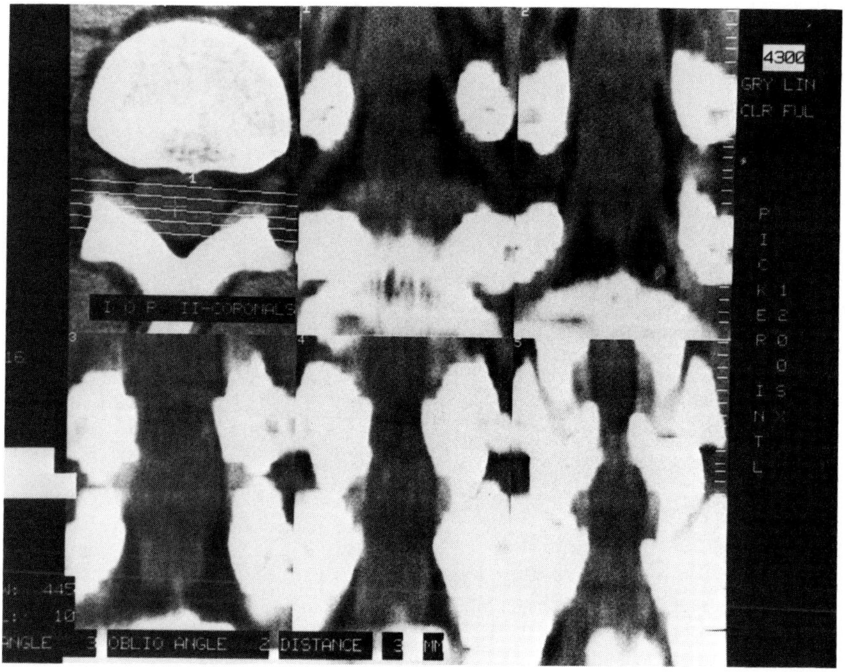

FIG. 9–2. (*cont.*)

ously reconstructed, and an interpolation is also usually done. Targeted images require a separate reconstruction from the raw data.

Multiple Image Viewing

Virtually all systems offer methods for viewing more than one slice on a screen at one time. These vary greatly in style. Some may offer a fixed format choice of four ("4-on-1") or six ("6-on-1") images per screen. Other systems may be more flexible. Some permit viewing of multiple images, but the image is minified, and so spatial resolution is reduced. Choosing the portion of each image to be displayed may not be possible. Some systems permit viewing images at different window width and window level settings on the same screen. This feature is primarily a convenience, time saver, and film saver for those doing examinations with many slices or creating many reformatted images.

ADDITIONAL COMMON PROGRAM FEATURES

I believe that the value of some of the less utilized program features depends more on their ease of use than on their sophistication. A feature that is difficult to learn or is time consuming to perform (which in a computer context may be only a few seconds) will be used infrequently. This section provides a brief review of the nature and use of some of these features.

Clip Artifact Suppression

If surgical clips obscure a critical anatomic area, a second reconstruction of the raw data is available from some manufacturers to suppress the resulting star artifact (10). The location of the clip is manually marked, and the detector readings from the rays through this clip are recalculated during the second reconstruction as though the clip were not present.

Density Contour

The density contour feature allows one to select a point and automatically highlight the set of contiguous pixels within a definable range of that point. The computer may then calculate the number of and the area of the pixels so highlighted, and the average attenuation of the irregular region. This feature may be used to calculate organ or lesion areas or volumes on a slice-by-slice basis.

Image Flip

The image flip feature reorients the screen image right to left and/or top to bottom. This facilitates viewing of examinations done with unusual patient positioning, such as hyperextension for coronal head scans.

Inset Images

In some systems, the scanogram or another reference image may be displayed in a small box in a corner of the screen. This facilitates localization of slices by radiographic or other landmarks.

Pixel Highlighting

The pixel highlighting feature permits all pixels within a programmable range of CT number values (using window width and level selections) to be highlighted by causing them to blink or appear brighter. This is a quick technique to find the average attenuation value of an area of interest by adjusting the level until the maximum number of pixels are highlighted.

Pixel Histogram

The pixel histogram plots a graph of pixel values against the number of pixels with that value for a selected ROI or for an entire image. An example of its use is in pulmonary nodule evaluation.

Screen Annotation

Screen annotation is the capability of superimposing letters or arrows directly over the image. This is generally used for demonstration or teaching.

Screen Save

If specially tailored images have been created (such as magnifications, multiple images, reformations, or screen annotations), the screen save feature permits these images to be saved for archiving onto the system disk or tape.

Time-Density Plotting

With the time-density plotting feature one can graph CT numbers against time. This is done for a specified ROI over several slices during a dynamic scan with contrast injection. The dynamic sequences can be either single-level or incremented scans.

SPECIALIZED FEATURES

This section outlines some of the features that apply to specialized examinations. Some of these require expensive additional hardware components besides the software. The sophistication of these programs and knowledge of their diagnostic utility continue to evolve rapidly.

Three-Dimensional Reformatting

New, sophisticated programs are available or in development that take conventional reformatting one major step further, displaying scan data in a three-dimensional format so that bone and organ contours are viewed (Fig. 9-3) (4). This feature has been most extensively applied to the reconstruction of facial deformities, but it is also applicable to other body areas such as the pelvis for open repair of fractures, the temporal bone, the vertebral column, the wrist, the knee, and the ankle.

The features and ease of use of three-dimensional systems vary consid-

A

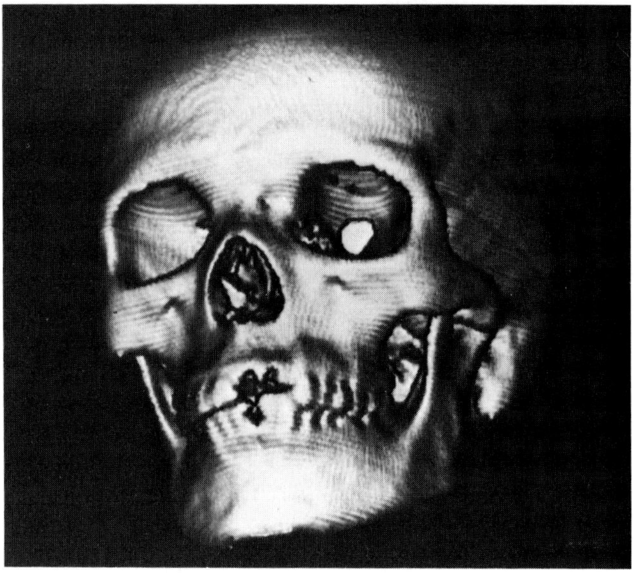

B

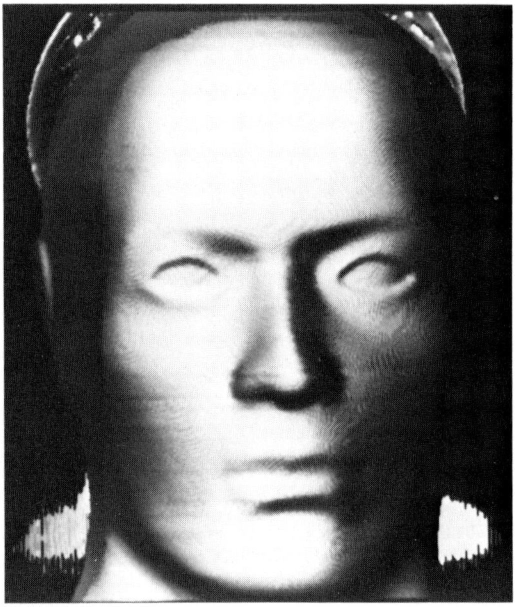

FIG. 9–3. Three-dimensional image reformatting. **A**. The data from successive slices have been stacked, as with standard reformating. However, contours of similar density are selected and displayed as though one were physically viewing the object scanned from the left anterior aspect. The shading provided gives the visual impression of three dimensions. **B**. The same head phantom with the soft tissues rather than bone selected for display. (Images courtesy of Elscint, Inc.)

erably. Features to evaluate include the speed of reformatting, the ability to display soft-tissue and bony contours, the use of color, the method of shading, the availability of transparent representation of bones and soft tissues, and the ability to change the perspective of viewing under real-time control and to view through cutaway areas.

Three-dimensional reformatting is available from some companies as a paid service. These companies accept scan data on magnetic tape acquired by a detailed protocol. They then reformat the data and may even supply a physical model to aid in surgical reconstruction. Entire computer consoles and auxiliary units are also being marketed to work in conjunction with various CT scanners.

Dual-Energy CT

As discussed in the preceding section, the most important reason for inaccurate CT attenuation numbers is the polychromatic nature of the X-ray beam and the use of a single kVp. An ideal CT source would produce a monochromatic X-ray beam, that is, one in which all of the photons had a single energy. Such beams can be produced. However, one source of these, the synchrotron, is an enormous and prohibitively expensive unit, which cannot produce an easily steered beam as is required with CT. The most commonly used source of monochromatic X-radiation is radionuclides. These are not practical to use with CT because a sufficiently strong source in the desired energy range cannot be compressed into a size small enough to produce satisfactory resolution. Therefore polychromatic beams are the only practical solution.

However, beam hardening problems can be virtually eliminated by using two separate polychromatic beams of different kVp (7,8). If nearly simultaneous images can be obtained with two different energy beams, one may derive information about the specific characteristics of X-ray absorption in tissues of differing composition, because X-ray absorption in tissues involves both Compton (incoherent) scattering and photoelectric absorption. Photoelectric absorption in elements of high atomic number depends strongly on X-ray energy, whereas in tissues composed of primarily low atomic number compounds it does not. Thus relating the densities on a pixel-by-pixel basis (subtracting them and using correction factors) can indicate whether a structure with a high attenuation is a structure of high atomic number (such as calcium) or a dense structure of low atomic number (such as carbon). A problem with dual-energy techniques is that the noise level in the resultant images is increased over that of a single-kVp scan. This is caused by the complex processing of information.

Also, obtaining a usable image depends on obtaining images with both energies without motion of the area of interest. With body parts that can be immobilized, such as the spine and the limbs, this is usually not a problem. However, with other areas the only reliable technique is to obtain images nearly simultaneously. This can be done if the X-ray generator is capable of switching the kVp back and forth extremely rapidly for successive pulses or views. This can be done only with pulsed X-ray systems. Units in which X-rays are produced continuously rather than in pulses are not capable of this rapid switching, and one must settle for making successive images with differing energies.

At present, the only clinical application for which dual-energy CT scanning has been studied extensively is bone densitometry (1,6). For dual-energy bone densitometry examinations, the attenuation of cancellous bone in the spinal medullary space is measured. With single-energy scanning, the contribution of medullary fat to overall attenuation is difficult to gauge. Dual-energy scanning permits the nonbony components of the image to be subtracted, leaving only the bone to be measured. This application can be performed by both continuous and pulsed systems. Nevertheless, some researchers in this area currently believe that this technique has no clinical advantage over single-energy quantitative CT.

Other possible applications for dual-energy techniques include the calculation of iodine content in the thyroid or in other organs after the administration of intravascular iodinated contrast agents. Dual-energy scanning can also minimize several types of artifacts caused by beam hardening, but only at the cost of increased noise levels.

Cardiac Gating

Experimental cardiac gating programs have been developed for some CT systems. There are several techniques used, but the basic principle involves collecting CT data over several cardiac cycles coordinated with the EKG so as to reconstruct several images from these data, with each image from one phase of the cycle. The series of slices can then be displayed in a movie format, dramatically depicting cardiac contraction as though from fluoroscopic CT. This technique permits assessment of coronary artery bypass graft patency, quantitative cardiac contractility, focal areas of myocardial thinning or hypokinesis, and, theoretically, myocardial perfusion.

However, the technique has several disadvantages (11). It is expensive and very cumbersome compared to other currently available methods to study the heart such as radionuclides and sonography. Although the movie display simulates real-time imaging, it does not represent actual real-time information. Thus, because data are acquired over several cycles, the technique is subject to error from minor arrhythmias. A moderately high radiation dose is administered, some motion artifacts are present, and intravenous contrast must be given. However, especially in the newest CT units, the image quality can be excellent (Fig. 9-4). Despite the demonstrated capa-

A

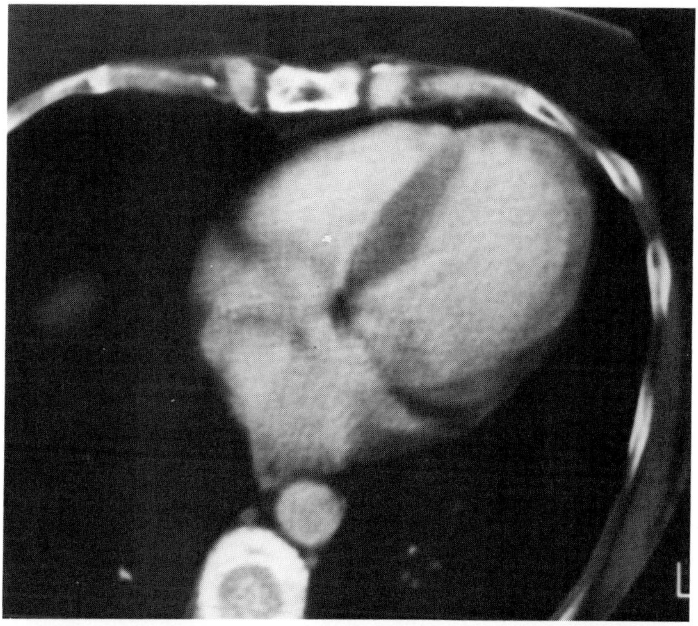

B

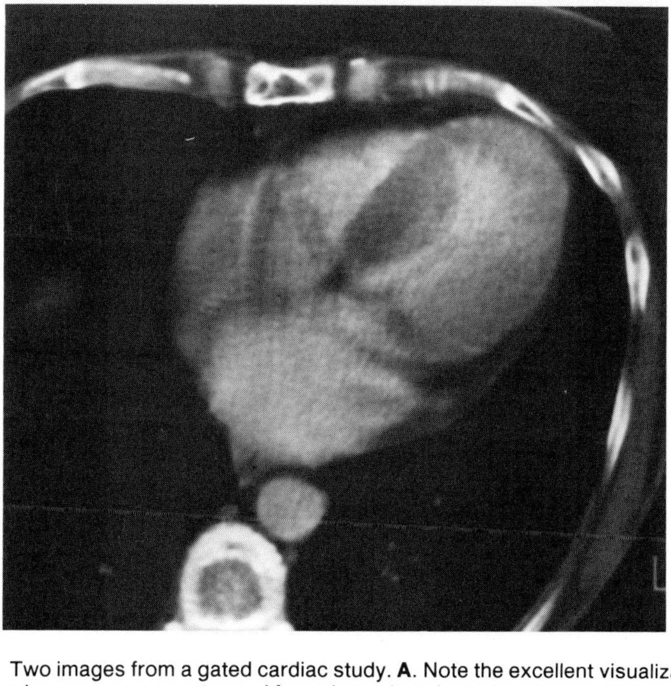

FIG. 9–4. Two images from a gated cardiac study. **A**. Note the excellent visualization of the myocardium. Images are reconstructed from data taken through several cardiac cycles. Each image is a reconstruction from separate points in a cycle; this image was reconstructed from the diastolic portion of the cycle. **B**. This image was reconstructed from data obtained during systole.

bility to display cardiac anatomy, this technology appears to be a solution in search of a problem, because very few applications have been found for it that cannot be done as well by more established means, or better by magnetic resonance imaging.

An alternative to gating is offered by the high-speed Imatron scanner, which can acquire eight simultaneous images in 50 msec. This scanner was initially limited in practice to examining the heart, but improvements in the standard of image quality have permitted its use for more general purpose examinations. The clinical utility for such high-speed scanning in the heart and elsewhere is still under investigation.

Correlative Imaging from Scan to Scanogram

Programs have been developed by at least two manufacturers that allow one to indicate the location of a lesion on a series of CT slices and have that information automatically translated into an outline on the scanogram (see Fig. 3-4). The General Electric trade name for this program is CORRELATE ™; the program is also available from Siemens in a different form. This program can be very useful for CT radiation treatment planning because radiation ports can be outlined on the scanogram and this information transferred to the radiation therapy simulator (12). It can also help in surgical planning because lesions can be displayed in reference to known bony and soft-tissue landmarks.

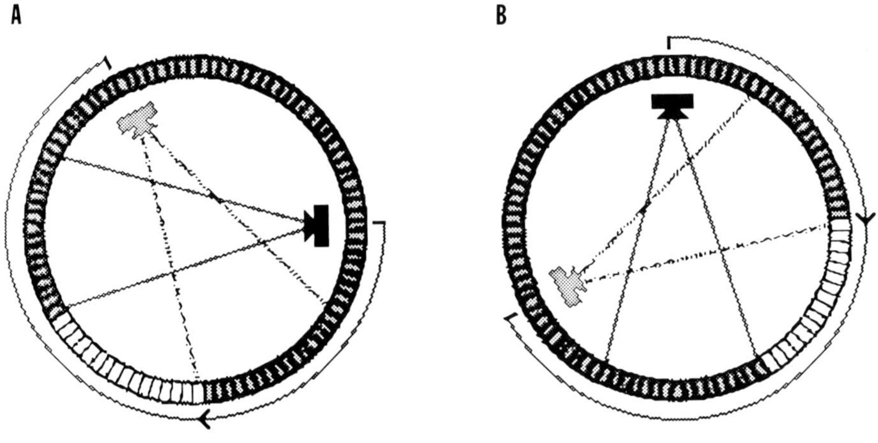

FIG. 9–5. Diagrams of two half-scans done with the tube position at different beginning and end points. By selecting such segments of data from various parts of full scans, half scan images can be reconstructed to provide more precise curves of changes in contrast enhancement over time.

Dynamic Scan Segmentation

Some scanners permit full 360° scans to be broken down into images created from various segments of the scan. As mentioned before, an image can be created from a half or a partial scan. Segmentation uses the data from the equivalent of a half scan worth of data to construct an image. Any partial contiguous views can be selected, and so the scans can be broken into many images (Fig. 9-5). One may then view temporal changes, usually in the passage of a bolus of contrast, in shorter time intervals than can be achieved with successive full scans. For example, if a dynamic scan were done with 2-sec scans and 2-sec interscan delays, then 15 scans could done per minute. If each of these 360° scans were broken into three scans encompassing the beginning 220°, the middle 220°, and the final 220°, then 45 separate images could be produced showing the passage of a bolus of contrast. However, each successive partial scan would overlap by 150°. This software can theoretically produce precise data regarding blood flow and organ perfusion over time. However, it has not found widely accepted clinical applications.

Xenon Blood Flow Imaging

Because xenon has a high atomic number relative to soft tissue and can be safely inhaled in controlled concentrations, it can act as a radiographic contrast agent. Xenon also has a high fat solubility and crosses the blood-brain barrier, and therefore is useful to study regional cerebral blood flow and function (Fig. 9-6) (5). Xenon contrast inhalation studies have demonstrated a wide variety of cerebral disorders, but the technique is particularly useful in evaluating regional perfusion in cerebrovascular disease and in studying brain metabolism. It may find a significant clinical role in dementia, degenerative and sleep disorders, migraines, and epilepsy. This technique has the highest resolution of the several methods to measure cerebral blood flow such as positron emission tomographic (PET) scanning and two-dimensional radionuclide evaluation.

Xenon scanning may also be useful to examine regional pulmonary function with CT, and to evaluate perfusion in parenchymal organs such as the liver. To perform xenon CT scanning one needs an inhalation device and specialized software. These additions and the xenon itself may be costly.

Radiation Therapy Treatment Planning

Techniques of radiation therapy planning with CT may be quite complex and vary from center to center (9). One may use CT to help determine the extent of a lesion to undergo therapy, to confirm the proper placement of ports, or to plan isodose curves. Examinations related to planning for radia-

A

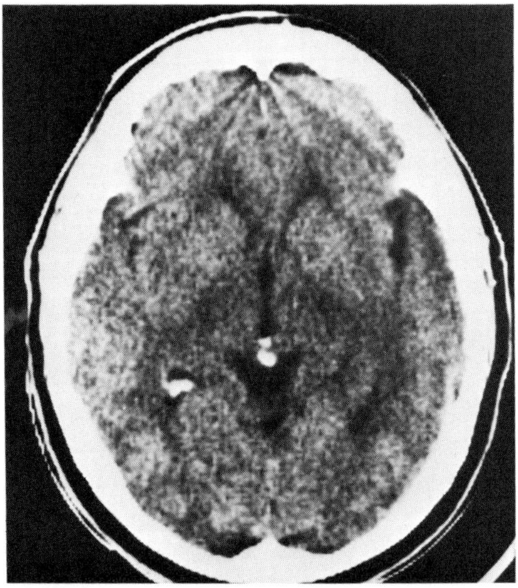

B

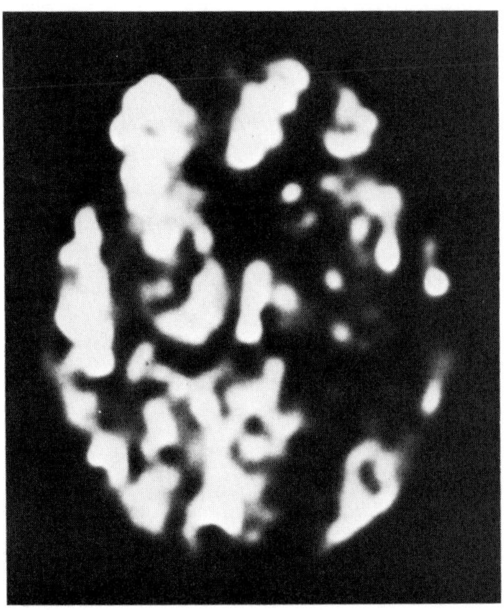

FIG. 9–6. Xenon perfusion study. **A**. Normal CT scan of a patient with a clinical left hemispheric stroke. **B**. Xenon perfusion study done at the same time shows marked asymmetry, with decreased perfusion of the left hemisphere. (Images courtesy of General Electric Company, Medical Systems.)

tion therapy may be extensive, for diagnosis, or brief, simply for localization. Specialized hardware and software may be offered, or data may be transferred to dedicated radiation therapy computers. This topic is touched upon briefly in Part 2, but local needs and approaches are so variable and potentially complex that imaging professionals must confer and work with therapists to design the best approach locally.

Stereotactic Biopsy

Stereotactic biopsy is most commonly applied to the head and requires the purchase of specialized hardware, which may be available from the manufacturer of the CT scanner or through other companies. The device and software permit simple calculations of the appropriate angle and depth of entry of a biopsy needle and a physically adjustable guide for the actual placement of the needle.

Off-Line Processing

Many scanner manufacturers offer add-on console and computer systems that can work in conjunction with the main system. These systems can be linked with the main computer so that data can be transferred freely between computers without the need for manual handling of recording media such as floppy disks or magnetic tapes. The value of such systems is that they permit ongoing analysis and recording of data and scans without the interference of waiting (time-sharing) or other, higher priority functions such as scanning or image archiving to proceed. As the use of many of the newer specialized techniques described in this section grows, the need for additional time for analysis also grows. Also, in many busy scanning facilities, the added capacity offered by independent computer console systems significantly enhances efficiency for the routine functions of reviewing and filming cases.

Bone Mineral Analysis

Bone mineral analysis with quantitative CT has been gaining in popularity because of recent interest in osteoporosis, particularly in postmenopausal women (1–3). Quantitative CT bone analysis is competitive with other radionuclide examinations such as dual photon absorptiometry. The CT method involves performing low radiation dose scans through the vertebral column followed by calculation of the average attenuation of medullary bone. A reference object containing materials of known attenuation is placed within the field of view with the patient on the table. The purpose of the reference object is to control the accuracy of measurements. This technique has been demonstrated to be accurate and clinically valuable and is likely to become more widespread.

Mobile CT

Numerous independent companies have been formed nationwide to provide mobile CT services. The technology of CT permits all of the necessary components of a CT scanner to be placed on a truck trailer. This type of service is popular in rural areas served by small hospitals, which cannot justify permanent installation of a scanner.

As indicated, many of the forthcoming innovations for CT will be in the realm of new ways of transferring, storing, and displaying data. Software developments will also certainly be among those changes that will most significantly affect the value of CT in future years.

REFERENCES

1. Fourth International Workshop on Bone and Soft Tissue Densitometry Using Computed Tomography. (1985): Proceedings. *J. Comput. Assist. Tomogr.,* 9(3):602–641.
2. Genant, H. K. (1985): Assessing osteoporosis: CT's quantitative advantage. *Diagnostic Imaging,* (August) 52–57.
3. Genant, H. K., Cann, C. E., Ettinger, B., Gordan, G. S., Kolb, F. O., Reiser, U., and Arnaud, C. D. (1985): Quantitative computed tomography for spinal mineral assessment: Current status. *J. Comput. Assist. Tomogr.,* 9(3):602–604.
4. Glenn, W. V., Harlow, C. A., Dwyer, S. J. III, Rhodes, M. L., and Parker, D. L. (1981): Image manipulation and pattern recognition. In: *Radiology of the Skull and Brain: Technical Aspects of Computed Tomography,* edited by T. H. Newton and D. G. Potts, pp. 4326–4354. C. V. Mosby, St. Louis.
5. Gur, D., Good, W. F., Herbert, D. L., Yonas, H., Wozney, P., Van Thiel, D. H.,, and Wolfson, S. K. Jr. (1985): Blood flow mapping in the human liver by the xenon/CT method. *J. Comput. Assist. Tomogr.,* 9(3):447–450.
6. Laval-Jeantet, A. M., Cann, C. E., Roger, B., and Dallant, P. (1984): A postprocessing dual energy technique for vertebral CT densitometry. *J. Comput. Assist. Tomogr.,* 8(6):1164–1167.
7. Marshall, W. H. Jr., Alvarez, R. E., and Macovski, A. (1981): Initial results with prereconstruction dual-energy computed tomography (PREDECT). *Radiology,* 140:421–430.
8. Marshall, W., Hall, E., Doost-Hoseini, A., Alvarez, R., Macovski, A., and Cassel, D. (1984): An implementation of dual energy CT scanning. *J. Comput. Assist. Tomogr.,* 8(4):745–749.
9. McCullough, E. C. (1981): Computed tomography in radiation therapy treatment planning. In: *Radiology of the Skull and Brain: Technical Aspects of Computed Tomography,* edited by T. H. Newton and D. G. Potts, pp. 431–4311. C. V. Mosby, St. Louis.
10. Morin, R. L., and Raeside, D. E. (1981): A pattern recognition method for the removal of streaking artifact in computed tomography. *Radiology,* 141:229–233.
11. Peck, W. W., Lipton, M. J., and Higgins, C. B. (1985): Cardiac computed tomography: Its potential use in evaluation of ischemic heart disease. In: *New Concepts in Cardiac Imaging 1985,* edited by G. M. Pohost, J. L. Ritchie, C. B. Higgins, H. R. Schelbert, and J. Morganroth, pp. 229–252. G. K. Hall Medical Publishers, Boston.
12. Shuman, W. P., Griffin, Br. R., Yoshy, C. S., Listerud, J. A., Mack, L. A., Rowberg, A. H., and Moss, A. A. (1985): The impact of CT correlate scoutview images on radiation therapy planning. *AJR,* 145:633–638.

10

Image Display, Recording, and Storage

Image display, recording, and storage is probably the area of technology that has lagged the furthest behind during the rapid development of CT. Forms of display and recording similar to those designed for some of the earliest scanners are still being used. Because of this lag, it is likely that some of the most significant advances in CT over the next several years will occur in image display and recording. Such developments may have great relevance to diagnostic quality and should not be dismissed as of ancillary importance. In this chapter I will describe (a) TV monitors, (b) the window-level concept, (c) film, (d) copy film, (e) film base, (f) format cameras, (g) setting monitor and camera controls, (h) magnetic tape and disk storage, and (i) some of the important developments on the horizon and how to evaluate their utility.

CATHODE RAY TUBE MONITORS

The CT image is displayed on a cathode ray tube (CRT) monitor. Currently available scanners have monitors that have been modified to accommodate the higher number of raster lines (about 600 to 1,200 rather than the standard TV's 525) and higher resolution necessary for satisfactory imaging. They also have incorporated flicker-free images by doubling the frame rate from 30 to 60 frames per sec (60 Hz) (7). The problem of the objectionable display and filming of raster lines has also been successfully addressed by recent innovations in monitor and camera technology (4).

CRT monitor viewing provides the most faithful reproduction of the display data and the most flexible means of image manipulation, but is limited by the inability to display more than one or two full-sized images simultaneously. Because of restrictive computer configurations and limited memory in viewing systems, some units are also slow at painting new images on the screen, making review of entire scans cumbersome. Also, there usually are severe clinical demands for use of the viewing console, making routine case review at the monitor impractical in most clinical facilities.

WINDOWS AND LEVELS

The viewing monitor is the only place to adjust the appearance of the image before filming. Because changing the mAs affects only the overall noise in the image and not the shades of gray, the monitor settings are virtually independent of the X-ray technique factors. However, with inherently noisy images, one is more likely to use wide window settings, which suppress the display of contrast of the noise. Because of this relative independence of technique and viewing, the filming process may be standardized to a large degree.

However, there is commonly confusion about the importance of the brightness and contrast controls on the monitor. These controls affect the image on the screen but do not directly affect the brightness and contrast on the film. Changing them adds nothing to the diagnostic content of the film. Brightness and contrast adjustments for the viewing monitor and camera are further discussed below.

The window and level controls are based on the CT attenuation number system described in the previous chapter. They are the means for translating the numbers assigned to each pixel into levels of gray displayed on the screen. The meaning of the terms *window* and *level* is illustrated in Fig. 10-1. The approximate range of attenuation of tissues is from −1,000 HU for

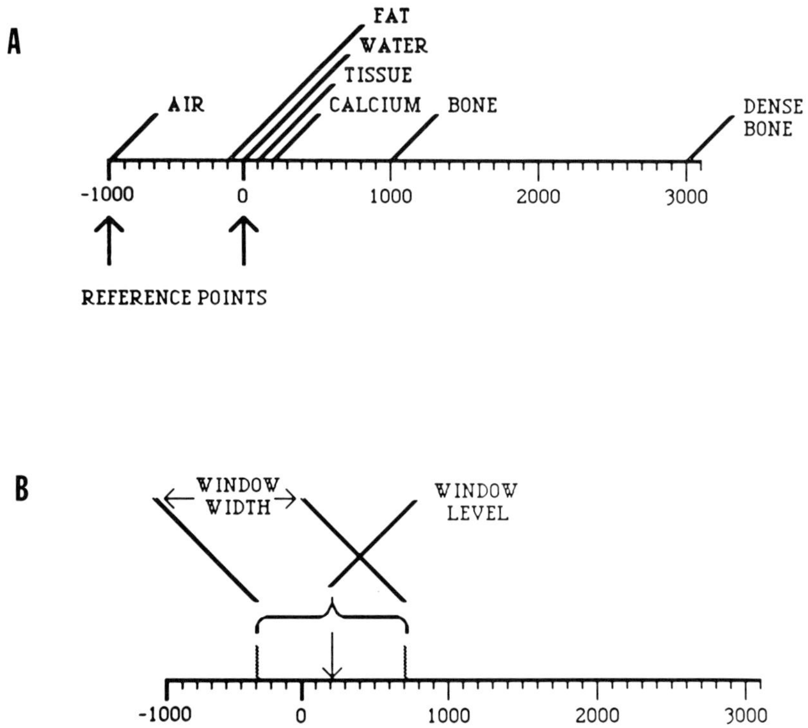

FIG. 10–1. The Hounsfield unit system and the concepts of window width and window level. **A.** The scale of Hounsfield units ranges between about −1,000 and about +3,000. Standardized reference points are −1,000 HU for air and 0 HU for water. The approximate scale locations of other tissues are indicated. **B.** A window that might be appropriate for visualization of bone is indicated. Window width and window level are noted.

air to about 3,000 HU for dense bone. However, the full range of these values is rarely displayed simultaneously. Instead, one can focus on the tissues of primary interest. This is done by controlling the window width (sometimes shortened to "window") and the window level (sometimes shortened to "level"). The window (7) is the range of values chosen for display (Fig. 10-2). If display of a broad range of values is required, such as one might find in the chest, then a window of about 2,000 HU within the available range of 4,000 is chosen. If we are interested in tissues with a narrow range of attenuation values, such as the brain, we may choose a window of only about 100 HU.

The center position within the specified range of values is the window level. Specifying the two parameters of window width and window level sets the top and bottom of the window for gray level assignment. For example, if the window width is set to 1,000 HU and the window level to zero, then any pixel assigned a number above 500 would be represented as pure white on the screen whether it was 5 HU or 500 HU above the range. Similarly, any pixel with a number below −500 HU would be black. Only pixels with values between −500 and 500 HU would be displayed in shades of gray (see Fig. 10-2). The methods for selecting window width and window level for various applications are discussed below.

Narrowing the window increases the contrast. As an example, if the window width were narrowed from 1,600 to 160, and 16 gray level steps were being used, then each level of gray would represent 10 rather than 100 individual attenuation numbers. Thus, two pixels differing by 20 HU difference

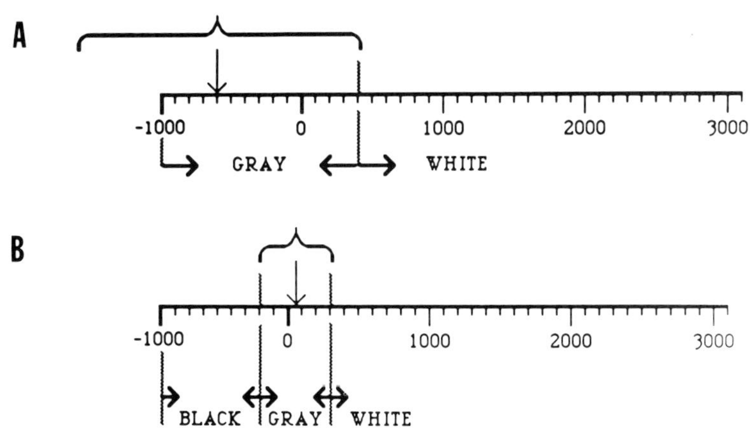

FIG. 10–2. Two different windows in common clinical use. **A**. A lung window with a level of −600 and a window width of 2,000. Because the scale does not extend below −1,000, there is no true black on the film, and the actual window width is less than the 2,000 that has been set. Not even all the shades of gray are utilized because a large block of the window is below the −1,000 reference point for air. **B**. A typical soft-tissue window. This window is relatively narrow, and a large portion of the scale is displayed either in all black or all white, thus providing no useful clinical information in this range. However, contrast between soft tissues within the window is enhanced.

would be displayed as separate shades with the narrower window, whereas they would be the same shade if the wider window were chosen. Superfically, it would seem ideal to maximize contrast, and therefore detectability, and always use narrow windows. However, the narrow window sacrifices the meaningful display and contrast of pixels with attenuation values above and below the window (Fig. 10-3). Also, narrowing the window enhances the contrast of the noise. This can acually hinder interpretation by inserting

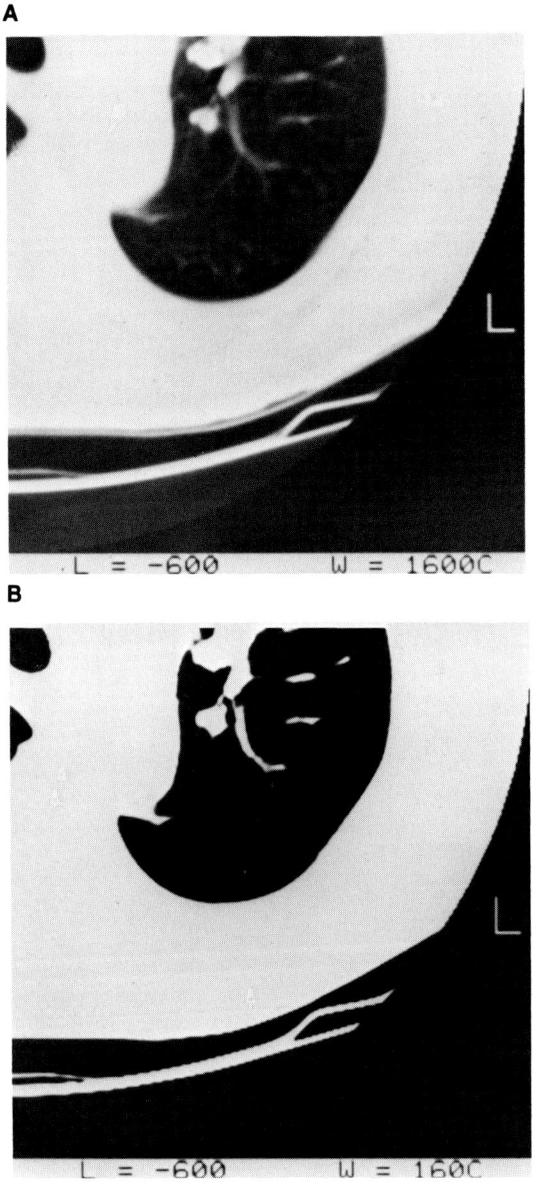

FIG. 10–3. Effect on image quality of changing window width and window level. These images demonstrate the critical nature of level selection when the window is narrowed. **A**. At the most appropriate setting of a window level of −600 and a window width of 1,600, lung structures are well seen. **B**. When the level is held constant at −600, but the window is narrowed to 160, the image becomes so contrasty that little useful information about lung tissue is displayed. **C**. By adjusting the window level to a lower setting (−800) more closely centered on the average attenuation of lung and vessels, more clinical information can be preserved.

C

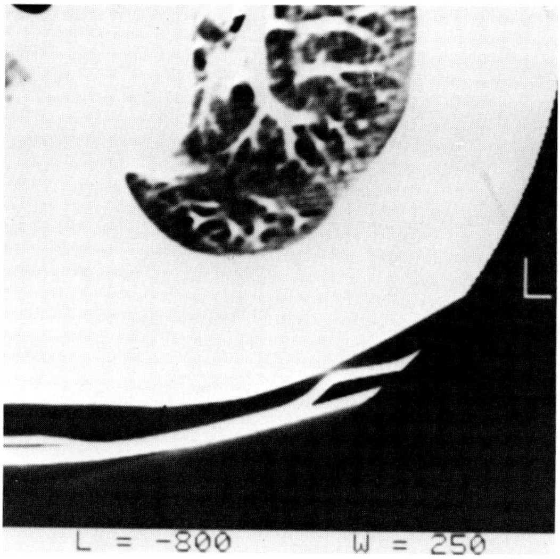

FIG. 10–3. (*cont.*)

confusing edges and shading, which can lead to overinterpretation of lesions (Fig. 10-4). The use of narrow windows might also require viewing or filming at multiple window levels centered on various tissues of interest.

Using the above information, the principles behind using windows and levels properly are as follows: (a) Wide windows (400 to 2,000 HU) should be used when trying to encompass tissues of greatly differing attenuation within the image. For example, body scans are usually filmed at 350 to 600 HU to encompass the attenuation numbers of fat, fluid, and muscle. Lung and bone are filmed at 1,000 to 2,000 to include air spaces and vessels for lung, and cortex and marrow for bone. (b) Narrow windows (50 to 350 HU) should be used to display soft tissues within structures containing different tissues of similar densities. For example, brain may be displayed at 80 to 150 HU to show differences between gray and white matter. Liver may be viewed at 100 to 250 HU to highlight liver metastases. (c) Levels should be centered near the average attenuation of the tissues of interest. For example, body scans may be viewed at about a level of 0 to 60 HU because fat has attenuation numbers from about −60 to −100 HU whereas those of muscle and organs may range from about 60 to 150 HU with intravenous contrast. Lung is viewed at a level of about −600 to −750. Specific guidelines for filming are offered in Chapter 14, p. 212.

However, windows and levels do not solely determine the appearance of the image. Various manufacturers' systems appear to display images quite differently. For example, body images appear best on one unit at a window of 500 and on another at 350. This may not vary only with the manufacturer. Different machines built by the same manufacturer may display images best at different windows. The wider windows in the older units help

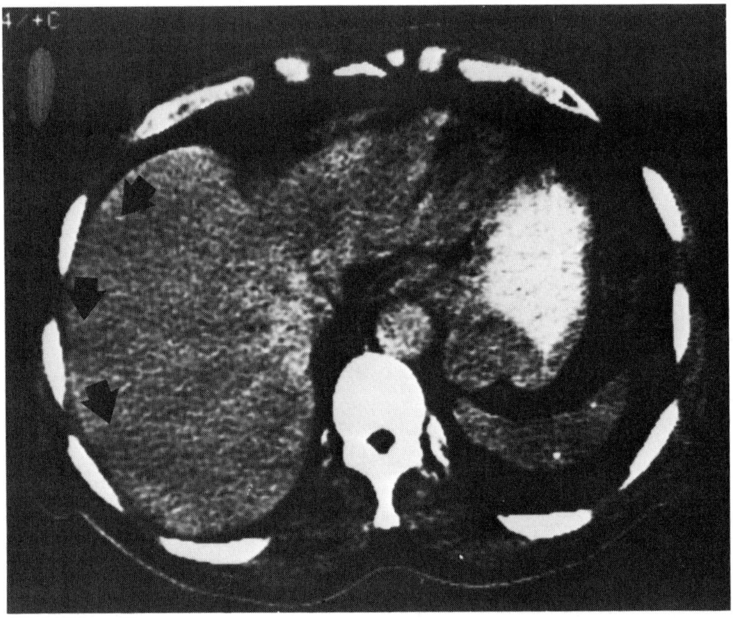

FIG. 10–4. Abdominal scan filmed at a narrow window width. The appropriate level for this narrow width has been selected. However, the prominence of beam hardening artifacts (arrows) adjacent to ribs has been enhanced, leading to the possible misinterpretation of intrahepatic lesions.

suppress some of the noise inherent in these older systems. The lower noise levels in newer units permit using the narrower window to improve image contrast wtihout giving the noise excessive contrast.

Image appearance also depends on the monitor's brightness and contrast settings. Therefore, although the above rules are good guidelines, the eye must be the final judge, and one should not fear changing the settings from long-used standards. Without conscientious quality control efforts monitors may drift, or they may be readjusted by others in your absence. Even with satsfactory maintenance, monitors deteriorate over time, and this degradation may be partly compensated for by changing monitor settings.

Although standardized settings may be changed for a particular case to improve the image appearance, one should avoid the temptation to change the settings from image to image on one case. Unless one is specifically highlighting an area of suspicion with a narrow window, for example, the settings should be left alone while filming a single body region. This makes viewing films easier because visually referring to structures of known densities such as fat or muscle should be done frequently. If the settings change from image to image, these visual standards are lost.

Manufacturers differ about whether to provide continuous variability in window width (in increments of single attenuation numbers), or only fixed-step controls (in 50- to 250-HU increments). Some provide both choices as programmable options. This is a matter of personal preference and ease of use.

Some units provide a dual window capability, which allows one to display, for example, lung at its best setting and mediastinum at its best on the same image by establishing two nonintersecting windows using the full gray scale. That is, a window width setting of 1,000 may be centered at a window level of −700 (window of −1,000 to −200) to view the lung, and another window of 400 may be centered at 50 (window of −150 to 250) to view the mediastinum (Fig. 10-5). (Note that there is no Hounsfield value of −1,200; thus a window width setting of 1,000 can lead to an actual window of 800). However, when dual windows are used, there is a distracting and visually confusing band at the junction between the areas where the two windows are displayed, such as the periphery of the lung between the lung and the chest wall. We do not use this type of dual window display for this reason.

The term *dual window* has also been applied to the technique of displaying two images on the monitor simultaneously with independent selection of the window and the level for each. Some facilities use this method as a convenience and to save film. We prefer to film images that require separate settings on separate frames.

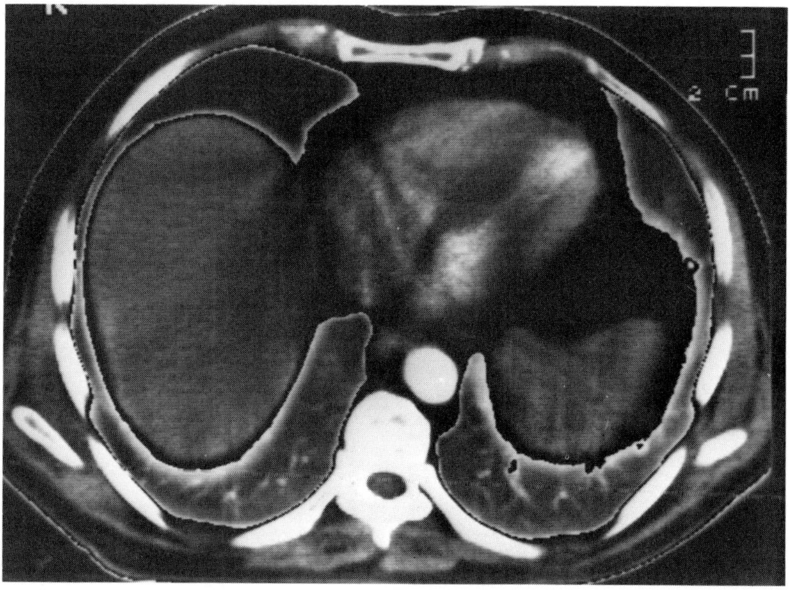

FIG. 10–5. Image filmed with a dual window. Both lungs and soft tissue may be displayed with this dual window technique. However, because the windows must not intersect on the scale, choices of width and level are restricted. Furthermore, prominent black-and-white borders, which are visually distracting and confusing, are inserted between tissues. Although this technique may be useful for some applications, we prefer not to use it for body imaging.

The most common method of assigning levels of gray within the window is to distribute the levels of gray evenly so that the same number of Hounsfield units is given each step on the gray scale. For example, as noted above, if there are 16 levels of gray and the window is 1,600, then each level represents a range of 100 HU. However, some manufacturers have begun to explore using nonlinear assignment of Hounsfield units (5). The most promising method is termed histogram equalization. This method assigns gray levels by the number of pixels found to have attenuation numbers within a certain range rather than by assigning them to any number of pixels having a certain attenuation (Fig. 10-6) (8). That is, in a conventional system, if numerous pixels occupy a small range of attenuation numbers, then all of these pixels will be assigned the same level of gray. In a histogram equalization image, this large number of pixels will be separated into several shades of gray, and other pixels occupying a wider range of attenuation numbers may be assigned only one gray level if there is a smaller number of pixels in this separate range. This has the effect of enhancing visual contrast in areas where there is little inherent contrast, and of suppressing contrast in areas with high attenuation differences. Thus, for example, a histogram equalization image may simultaneously display lung, mediastinum, and bone near optimum levels of contrast, which cannot be done with conventional systems. The advantages of such a system are that the great flexibility of display on a single image may allow compression of information in the computer for more efficient storage and transfer, and may make

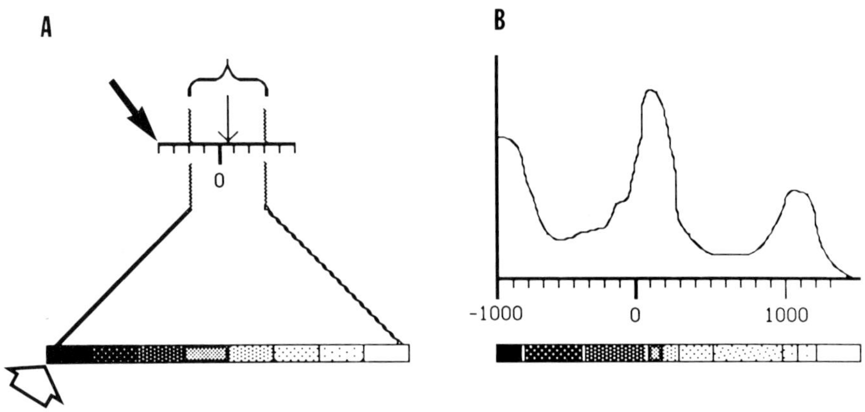

FIG. 10–6. Methods of gray level assignment. **A**. A small portion of the Hounsfield scale (arrow) is illustrated, and the depiction of gray level assignment is based on a linear scale (open arrow) relative to these units. **B**. Histogram equalization. A hypothetical curve of pixel assignments is constructed, with the horizontal axis showing the Hounsfield scale and the vertical axis representing the number of pixels with the attenuation values indicated. The bar at the bottom indicates that gray levels are assigned to pixels based on the number of pixels at each value, with more gray levels assigned to areas where there are a large number of pixels.

unnecessary the displaying of images at more than one setting, thus saving film and time. One disadvantage is the difficulty in obtaining attenuation measurements on images processed in this way.

FILM

What would a radiologist do without film? We may someday find out, but this form of recording is durable and portable, and is usually the medium from which most aspects of diagnosis emanate. Therefore, it holds a position of importance that must be fully appreciated. CT film appears physically similar to plain X-ray film. However, it is a single-emulsion film designed to record visible light from a CRT monitor. Therefore, the CT film emulsion is more like conventional photographic film whereas the film base is more like the conventional X-ray film base (3).

Photographic film needs only one emulsion because the brightness of the monitor or the exposure time can be easily adjusted to produce satisfactory film exposure. Two emulsions are used with X-rays to decrease the amount of X-ray exposure needed to achieve the desired film darkening.

Using single-emulsion films has important implications for image quality and the quality of copied film. When loading the film cassette, the duller emulsion side must be loaded facing out toward the camera monitor face. Thus, when the cassette is loaded, the dull side should be facing up. If this is not done, the light passes through the film base before striking the emulsion, and the film will be underexposed. This problem will be easily detected by looking at the background on each image on a film and at the notch along the edge of the film. If the film has been loaded improperly, the notch will be on the wrong side compared to properly exposed films. The emulsion side is facing up when the notch is in the upper right-hand corner as the film is being loaded. However, it depends on the style of camera whether the emulsion side is facing toward or away from you as you view the film after it has been developed so that the lettering and orientation are correct. The reason is that some monitors or lens systems present a mirror image to the film.

Another recording medium is the conventional Polaroid photograph of the monitor, but these are quite cumbersome to handle routinely. However, paper film is now commercially available that is routinely viewed with reflected light, although transmitted light is also satisfactory. The quality of the reproduction is good, and the film may be processed with conventional X-ray automatic processors. Paper film has the advantage of a markedly lower price, currently about 40% below that of conventional film. The disadvantages are that it is less durable, produces glare when viewed with reflective lighting, cannot be copied with ordinary X-ray film copiers, and cannot be projected with conventional overhead film projectors.

COPY FILM

Failure to appreciate the properties of single-emulsion film is also the source of many poorly copied films. To produce a good copy, the single emulsion of the original film must be placed in direct contact with the single-emulsion side of the copy film. The emulsion side is recognized in a safety light as the dull side. The two films in contact must than be placed so that the duplicator light shines through the original film to strike the copy film. The emulsions must be in contact to minimize blurring caused by gaps between one emulsion and the other (Fig. 10-7). The light must be transmitted through the original to the copy to produce an image. Also, if the films are not in emulsion-to-emulsion contact, the copy film will be underexposed. This will lead to a film that is too dark (Fig. 10-8) rather than too light, for reasons to be discussed below.

For most copying units, the light is projected from below upward. Thus, when preparing to copy a film, the original film should be placed on the table with the emulsion side facing up. The copy film should then be placed on top of the original with the emulsion facing down before the two films are placed in the copier.

Copy film works by the principle of solarization. Copy film has already been exposed to light (solarized) during the manufacturing process, making

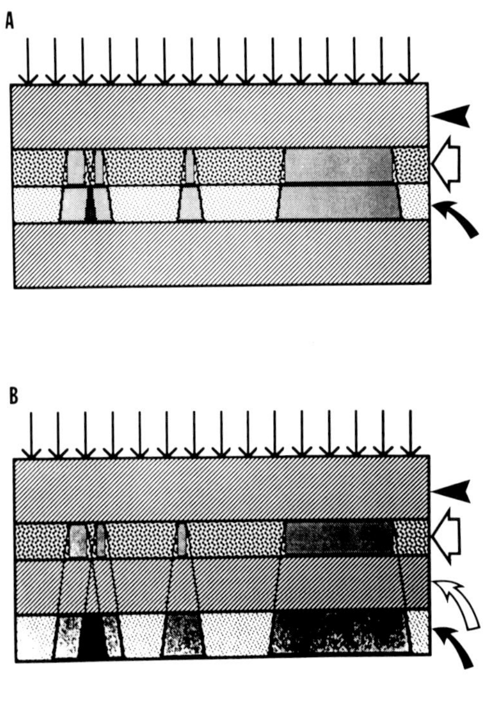

FIG. 10–7. Importance of proper techniques for copying film. **A**. Proper placement of original and copied film for reproduction. The entrance of light is indicated by the multiple arrows. This light first passes through the cross-hatched film base (arrowhead) of the original film. It then reaches the emulsion level of the original film (open arrow), where various images of different sizes are already imprinted and developed. Because of the slight divergence of the light beams, there is only minimal distortion of the images on the copy film emulsion (curved arrow). **B**. Light is again depicted entering through the film base (arrowhead) of the original film. However, the copy film has now been placed with its film base (curved open arrow) rather than the emulsion (curved black arrow) in contact with the original film emulsion (open arrow). This leads to greater blurring of the original image and decreased transmission of light because the light must pass through an additional layer of film base before the copy film emulsion is exposed.

it black if developed. However, before the film is processed, it is exposed to more light during the copy exposure. The brighter or longer the copy exposure (after solarization), the lighter the processed film will be, rather than darker as occurs on ordinary photographic film. Therefore, if the copy film appears dark, the exposure time should be lengthened, and vice versa. Because of the reversal of the usual pattern of exposure and results on development, the resulting film is a direct positive rather than a negative.

A

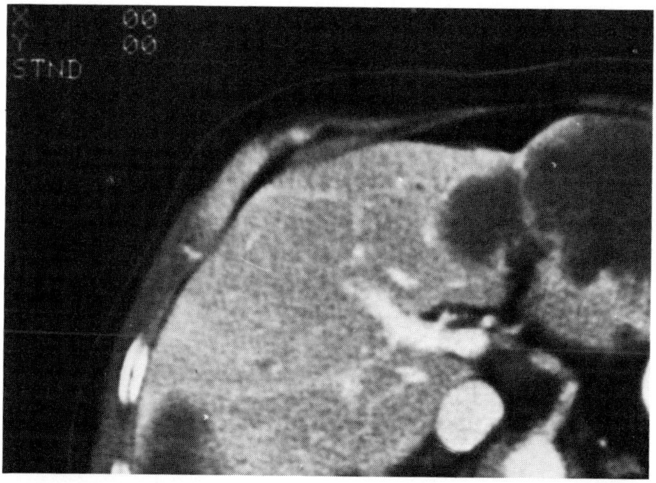

B

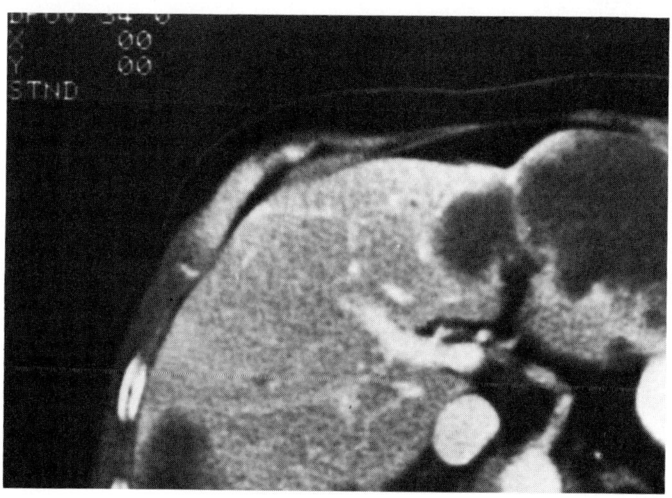

FIG. 10–8. Three images representing an original (**A**) and two copies. **B**. The first copy is done properly and faithfully represents the original image. **C**. The second copy was done with the film bases of the original and copied films in contact rather than the emulsion sides. This produces a much darker and more blurred image.

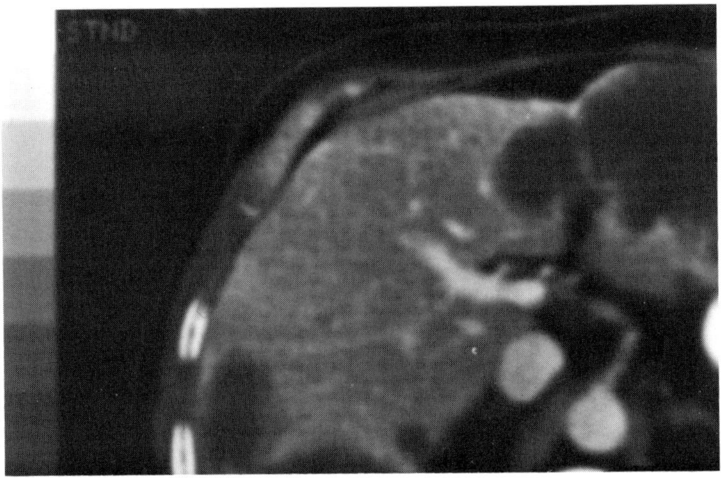

FIG. 10–8. *(cont.)*

FILM BASE

One must decide whether to use clear base or blue base film for original and copy film. I prefer clear base film for both original and copied films. The reason for this relates to the nature of the blue base. Adding a base color to an original film elevates the density of all of the gray levels of the image. However, the human eye is more sensitive to lower density levels. This effect is somwhat counterbalanced by the reduction in background transmitted veiling glare through the clear part of the film. The selection of clear versus blue base for original films appears to be largely an issue of personal preference.

However, using a blue base original for copying has a real, although slight effect on image contrast. The effect is analogous to slightly fogging a film before development (6). Nevertheless, properly exposed copies can be satisfactory with any choice of base color.

CAMERAS

The term commonly and often incorrectly applied to some cameras employed for CT is *multiformat cameras.* Many cameras do provide several formats on which images can be filmed. Other allow only one format and are thus better called *format cameras.* Although 8 × 10, 11 × 14, and 14 × 17 inch films are used, the last two are in more common use for CT. The most commonly used formats for the 11 × 14 inch film are the 6-on-1 and 9-on-1 displays, which display six or nine images per film, respectively. The

14 × 17 inch film usually is printed with a 12-on-1 or 15-on-1 display. I find that scans printed with more than 12 images on the 14 × 17 film or more than 6 images on the 11 × 14 film may be difficult to interpret because the images are too small. However, the format will depend on the shape of the display peculiar to the unit. Many systems use a rectangular display box with patient and scan data written on the right- and left-hand sides of the box. This precludes using the 12-on-1 format, which is possible for square boxes.

The crucial components of the format camera include a "slave monitor," which displays whatever is seen on the console viewing monitor, a lens and shutter system for projecting the image onto the film with the proper exposure, and a mechanism for moving either the film or the monitor-lens system into place for each separate exposure. Current-model cameras use a flat face monitor to provide the best quality reproduction of the image with the least distortion. Older, curved monitor images project distortions onto the film, which are most pronounced at the edges of the images and which limit the accuracy of measurements from films.

The most recent development in cameras is the laser format camera. In such systems, the image is exposed on an ordinary CT film directly with a laser. This permits a very precise and accurate representation of the image on film. In standard cameras, before light reaches the film it passes through lenses, which slightly blur the image. Such lens systems may go out of focus, cause ghost reflections, and lead to "blooming" in areas of high density. These standard cameras are also subject to the accumulation of dirt on the monitor faces and to drift in monitor density.

These defects of standard cameras are eliminated in laser cameras, which also blacken the background interspaces between images, decreasing glare. Also, the cameras are supplied with a computer memory in which to store sets of slices or entire examinations. This may make generation of multiple original films simpler than copying.

Although laser-generated image quality is superb, modern conventional cameras also produce excellent images. Laser cameras are currently more expensive and have longer exposure times than standard cameras and are not yet adaptable to all scanners. They also have features that limit the flexibility of filming because images need not be viewed on the monitor individually. Laser camera manufacturers have also not satisfactorily determined the optimal pixel matrix for medical imaging. However, it seems likely that these cameras will improve and decrease in relative price and be compatible for use on two scanners simultaneously. For all these reasons, laser cameras are likely to become the preferred cameras for CT.

Setting up the standard format camera for optimal image quality will be discussed below, but much of image reproduction is beyond the control of the radiologist and is the responsibility of the service engineer. One should be cautious in purchasing a camera not recommended by the scanner manufacturer. There may be a fundamental video incompatibility, which will preclude use other than on the intended systems.

Once the proper camera brightness and contrast are established on a conventional format camera, there are many points at which problems can arise. For example, the monitor itself or any component of it can fail, just as with any TV. The lens system may be out of alignment. The camera shutter or mechanics may be functioning improperly. The brightness and contrast controls may drift out of adjustment. Improperly shielded cables may create interference artifacts. The problem may be as simple as a dirty monitor face or mirror, or it may be outside the camera altogether—in the film processor, for example. It is primarily the responsibility of the quality control personnel in a department to check periodically for such problems, but the radiologist or technologist often first identifies the problem and must describe and document it well enough for the service engineer to approach it effectively.

Defects that can be recognized on films include improper image density, contrast, or brightness; white specks on images; image blurring; varying density from image to image on a single film; distortion or bands through the image; and film fogging. Density, brightness, or contrast problems may be caused by loading the film backward as discussed above, or by improper settings as are discussed in the following section. Image specks are usually caused by dust on the monitor face. This problem occurs frequently when the monitor face is mounted horizontally and facing up, where it easily collects dust and other stray particles. Other orientations minimize dust catching.

Scattered small, sharply defined white specks represent dirt particles lying directly on the monitor face or the film (Fig. 10-9). The extremely crisp

A

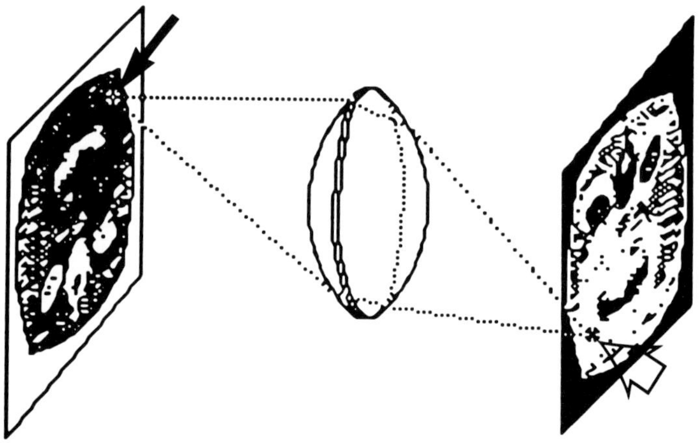

FIG. 10–9. Camera monitor artifact. **A**. In a simple photographic lens system, the only two points at which a structure is in focus are at the monitor face (black arrow) and on the film (open arrow).

B

FIG. 10–9. (*cont.*) **B**. Therefore, if small, crisp artifacts (open arrows) are seen at exactly the same point and are identical in shape on multiple images, they are most likely caused by a particle of dirt on the face of the camera monitor.

appearance of these specks indicates that these are the only two locations in which the problem can be occurring, because these are the only points at which the image is in focus. Dirt on a focusing lens between the monitor and the film would be out of focus on the final image. If the specks are found in the same position on each image, the dirt is on the monitor face and it should be cleaned. If the specks are randomly distributed on the film irrespective of the location of images, then the dirt is on the film, and conditions in the darkroom or the camera should be checked. One common problem is having darkroom personnel who smoke and drop ashes on the film. Lightinsulating felt or metal shavings from grinding mechanical components in the camera may also cause dirty films. One manufacturer uses a mirror in addition to lenses within its format camera. This mirror is mounted at an angle. Because of this it is prone to catching dirt particles, and this causes blurred spots on images.

If the image itself is blurred or gradually changes density over time, the monitor face may be exceptionally dusty. I have also encountered a problem in which an internal camera lubricant repeatedly became sprayed in a fine mist on the lenses, leading to a diffusely blurred and gray image.

Varying background densities, blurring of the image and graphics, or changes in the gray scale between images on a single film are caused by mechanical or electronic problems with the shutter or monitor, which must be corrected by a service engineer.

If the unexposed part of the film at the points between and around images is unusually dark, this indicates a malfunctioning film processor or diffuse light fogging prior to exposure or processing. Dark streaks on the film may indicate a light leak causing film fogging. This can occur anywhere that the unprocessed film is present before or after exposure, including the film bin, the cassette (perhaps because of a broken dark slide), the camera which may be leaking light through light seals, or the darkroom before processing.

The origin of a light leak can usually be deduced by examining the pattern of the streaks on the film. For example, if it occurs on the same spot on the film, but only on occasional films, it is probably a faulty cassette. If it occurs in the same location and usually at an edge, it is probably a faulty seal in the cameras. If the fog outlines but does not cover the area where the side slots hold the film in place in the cassette, then the fogging is taking place while the film is in the cassette. If the rectangular outline of the images is distorted along with several of the images themselves, the film has been improperly loaded in the cassette film guides and has sagged away from the cassette surface while being exposed (Fig. 10-10).

SETTING MONITOR AND CAMERA CONTROLS

Most CT cameras permit clinical users limited access for adjusting density. Controls are usually more accessible on the 8 × 10 inch film style cameras commonly used for ultrasound. However, when the controls are accessible, it is worthwhile to understand how to set the camera. The principles are simple, although the practice may be somewhat more confusing. The following is a suggested approach to adjusting a black-and-white monitor and camera.

The objective of adjusting the monitor and the camera is to create an image on film that corresponds closely to what is seen on the properly set viewing screen. As stated earlier, there is no direct relationship between the

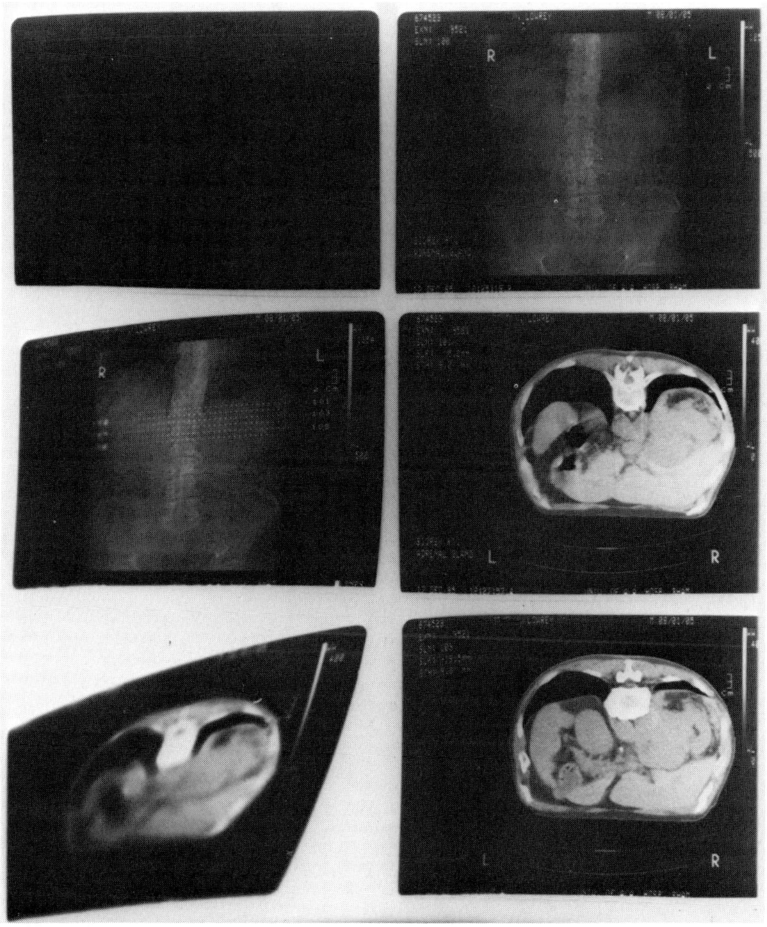

FIG. 10–10. When one or several frames on a film are grossly distorted in an unusual pattern, as in this case, the film has sagged out of the slots that hold it in place in the cassette when the dark slide is removed. The film has been improperly loaded, and darkroom technique should be checked.

brightness and contrast settings on the viewing monitor and the camera monitor. However, one may erroneously attempt to readjust the camera monitor to compensate for an improperly set viewing monitor.

Therefore, first adjust the viewing monitor (the CRT monitor on the operator's or filming computer console). As will be seen after a little practice, this procedure requires literally no more than 5 sec on a properly functioning monitor. The two controls available on virtually all black-and-white monitors are brightness and contrast. Remember the following principle: **The brightness control is used to set the black areas on the image, and the contrast control to set the white areas. Increasing brightness lightens the black. Increasing the contrast lightens the white.** If the brightness and the contrast are set to zero, the screen will be black. (Inadvertently brushing against the brightness or contrast controls and setting them to zero is sometimes the cause of an apparent system malfunction.)

If displaying the gray scale (gray bar) is under software control, the option to display should be selected. It will be useful for adjusting the monitor and the camera. Then the brightness on the monitor should be slowly turned up until the black background begins to lighten slightly. One memory aid is to recall that B is for black, and B (brightness) should be adjusted before C (contrast). If the brightness is set too low, with too black a background, then the low-level white areas will be suppressed. Then the contrast should be turned up slowly until the white areas are satisfactorily bright. This can be determined by looking at the gray scale. On a step-type gray scale, one should be barely able to discern the final steps at both the black and white ends of the scale. The midpoint of the scale should display the midlevel of gray. Then only minor adjustments need to be made to make the image most aesthetically pleasing.

Adjusting a camera is more confusing than adjusting a monitor because the camera monitor is of opposite polarity (that is, black and white are inverted) so that the developed film negative appears the same as the viewing monitor. The film must be processed to determine whether the adjustments are correct, and so it is considerably more time consuming to adjust the camera than the viewing monitor. However, the same principle applies to the camera monitor that applies to the viewing monitor, that brightness controls the black and contrast the white, but because the film is a negative, on the film the brightness now controls the white and the contrast controls the black.

The same approach of adjusting brightness first and then contrast should be taken for setting the camera monitor (Fig. 10-11). The process may be speeded up if it is possible to view the camera monitor while the rough adjustments are being made. However, this is not always possible and not as helpful as with the viewing monitor because of the reversed polarity and the contribution of exposure time to image density. The exposure time setting has an effect similar to the brightness setting, with longer exposures corresponding to higher brightness settings. Higher brightness on a camera monitor dims the whites on the films. Exposure time, brightness, and contrast should be adjusted while carefully recording the camera settings for each exposure.

Exposure time should be set so that it is not too long or too short, but the exact value is not that critical. One-quarter second is a common value, but manufacturers' recommendations should be followed. If the exposure time is shorter than the time it takes to refresh the image on the screen, streaks will appear on the film. If the exposure is too long, it becomes more time consuming to film. Once exposure time is set, again set the brightness and contrast to zero. Then slowly increase the brightness until the black on the camera monitor begins to lighten slightly. This will be represented as a slight dimming of the white on the film at the upper end of the gray scale. Then adjust the white on the monitor by turning up the contrast until the last steps on the gray scale are barely discernible from one another. The brightest white should be as clear as the film base. The last steps at the black end of the scale should also become barely discernible from one another. Fine adjustments may then be made by carefully trying to compare the filmed image with the monitor image and determining whether the full range of gray, white, and black is displayed identically on the film and on the monitor. Quality control personnel should save a film and record film densitometry readings and camera setting values once you are happy with the images. This will be the basis for resetting the camera whenever necessary.

If the camera needs only minor adjustments, the following is a technique to remember how to make them. First decide what is wrong with the image. For example, if the white is too bright on the film, then think, "The white needs to be darker, which means that on the monitor the black needs to be lighter. Therefore, because brightness controls the black, the brightness should be turned up." If the background black is too light, the approach would be, "The black on the film needs to be blacker, which means that on the camera monitor the white needs to be whiter. Therefore, because contrast controls the white, the contrast should be turned up." A summary follows:

1. If the black is too dark, turn the contrast down.
2. If the black is too light, turn the contrast up.
3. If the white is too dark, turn the brightness down.
4. If the white is too light, turn the brightness up.

Many cameras have separately programmable settings for positive- and negative-polarity images. Thus, if images do not appear to respond to changing brightness, contrast, and exposure settings, check whether the correct controls are being adjusted. Complications arise in some cameras that interlock the brightness and contrast controls to some degree or use phototimers to help set density. These systems are trickier to set up because the results of changing one control are not as predictable. However, the same basic principles still apply.

MAGNETIC STORAGE MEDIA

Forms of information storage other than film are central to operating the scanner, but are handled mostly by technologists. These forms of computer storage of information are usually magnetic media, including the hard disk, the floppy disk, and the magnetic tape (8). The disk is the usual form of on-line storage of images and data for immediate computer recall. The data are

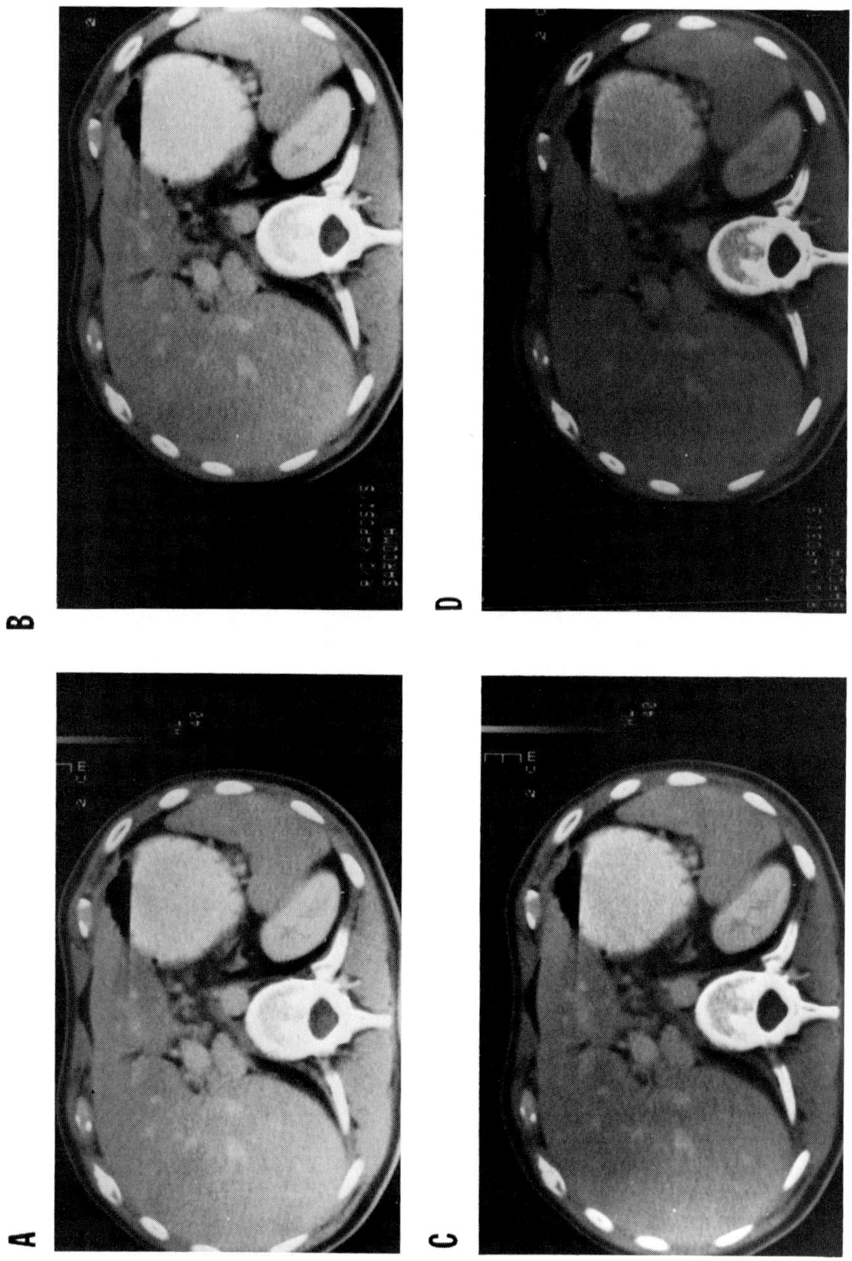

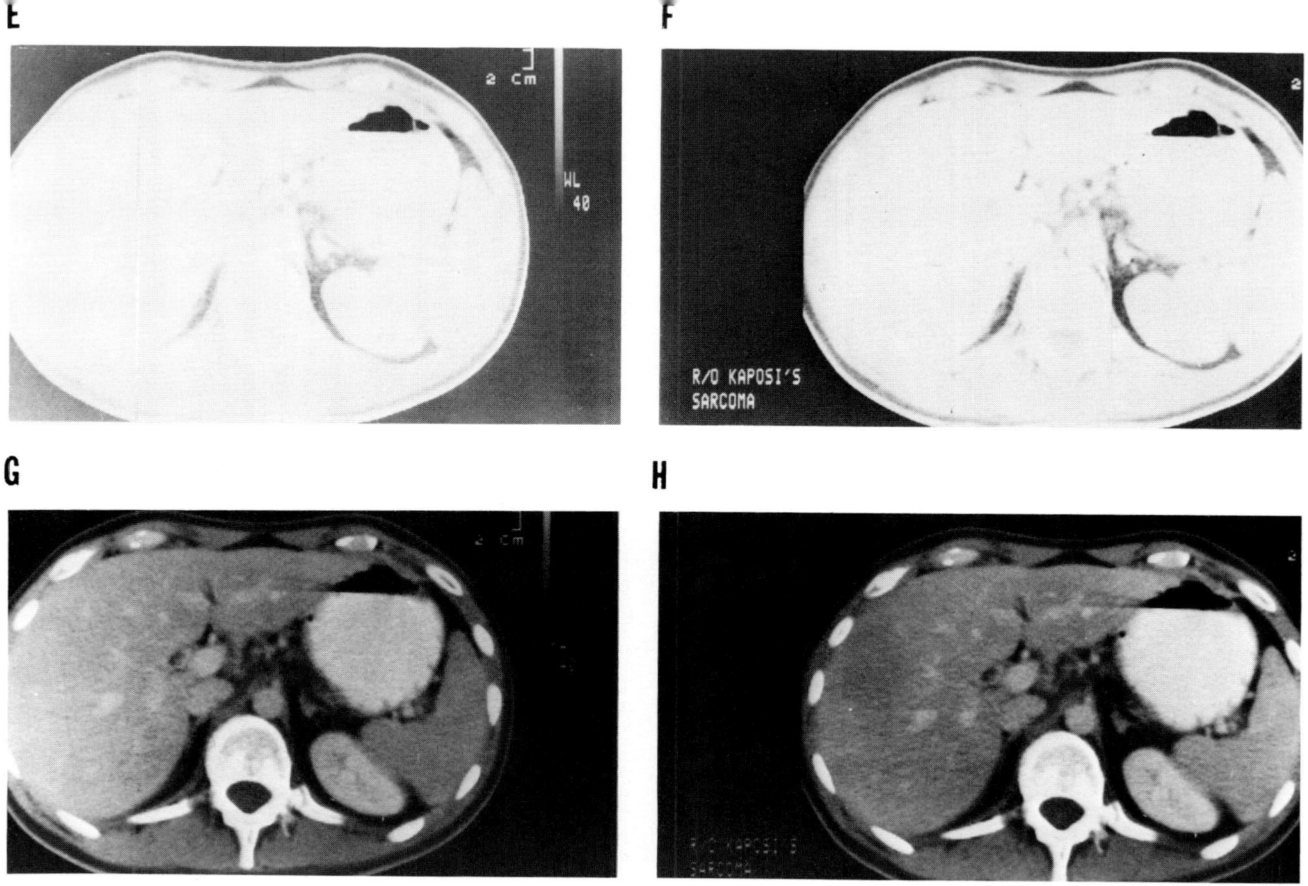

FIG. 10–11. Effect of contrast and brightness adjustments on image quality. **A–D.** In these four images the brightness has been successively increased while contrast was held constant. Because brightness controls the black on the camera monitor, it controls the white on the film. Thus, as brightness is increased, the white components of the image become darker whereas the black background is changed very little. **E–H.** In this series of four images the contrast was increased while brightness was held constant. Because the contrast controls the white on the monitor, it controls the black on the film. Therefore, as contrast is increased, the black background becomes darker whereas the white components of the image change very little.

rapidly accessible, and most systems are designed to hold a minimum of several hundred images, or from several cases to several days' worth of cases. This disk is directly connected to the computer and consists of rigid platters, which spin at high speed and are read by magnetic heads, which never come in direct contact with the disk. Data and reconstructed images are usually directly and immediately transferred to this disk and are the source of the images displayed on the physician's console.

The floppy disk is a small, flexible disk in a plastic housing; it can usually store several images or enough for a single examination. This medium is often not provided, depending on the scanner. Because these disks are so easy to use and are portable, they are convenient for transferring cases from one component of the computer to an independent console for filming, for example. They are also used for saving individual images or cases for short-term review or for teaching purposes. However, they are somewhat time consuming to use, are vulnerable to injury and thus loss of data, and carry a relatively small amount of data.

The most widely used method for long-term storage of data is magnetic tape. These large reels of tape are mounted on the computer tape drive, and data are dumped from the hard disk onto the tape. One can later load the data back onto the system disk for review at the console. These tapes can hold data from several patients' examinations. Most departments recycle these tapes after several months to a year or two. Two years is about the longest reasonable storage time, because if tapes sit unattended, information may be lost, although tape life can be extended by careful storage and periodic rewinding (2). Tapes consume much storage space and are often time consuming to use, because if a case is recorded at the end of the tape it may take several minutes for the computer to find the case before loading it onto the system disk.

What all of these forms of storage have in common is a flexibility that allows later manipulation of the data and image, which cannot be done from film. The magnetically stored data allow one to change windows and levels, measure the size of lesions directly with computer software rather than calipers, measure the CT attenuation numbers, and even perform reformatting of slices in sagittal or coronal planes. The tape is also a backup medium in case the films are lost.

FUTURE FORMS OF DISPLAY AND STORAGE

Much commercial development money is now being devoted to information storage and retrieval systems. Part of this effort is directed to merging forms of all of diagnostic imaging and radiology display into unified display systems (1). The practical, economical digital radiology department may be relatively far off, but much of the new technology being applied to these comprehensive systems will find its way into systems already based on digital data handling such as CT, sonography, magnetic resonance imaging, digital angiography, and nuclear medicine.

One of the most important aspects of these developments is the use of new mass storage devices, particularly the laser optical disk. These systems store thousands or tens of thousands of images rather than hundreds as with the standard system disk. The space required for storage is reduced manyfold, and even several months of cases are available for immediate retrieval. The disadvantages of these disks are that they cannot be erased and are expensive. Optical disks have already been introduced to the CT market but are not yet widely used.

Another feature is already technically feasible and was even implemented on the old EMI 7000 series CT systems. However, it requires expensive hardware, and CT manufacturers have been reluctant to develop and offer it for fear of limited acceptance in the marketplace. This feature is rapid sequential viewing of CT slices. The purpose of this is to enhance the three-dimensional perception of structures, which is now done tediously by glancing from image to image. Such a capacity could improve detection and characterization of many lesions because they will become more conspicuous when viewed quickly in comparison to adjacent slices. It may also encourage the use of thin-slice, high-detail techniques because filming and viewing examinations with numerous slices will be facilitated.

Such a system is currently available on the Imatron or cine-CT unit, which acquires images in as fast as 50 msec, with several slices acquired simultaneously within this interval. It is virtually essential to view slices rapidly on such a unit because the intent is to view cardiac motion in a film or real-time format. The high cost of the system is incurred by the necessity to have a relatively large memory storage in the display console that can store enough images to permit very rapid changes in display. Units other than the Imatron also offer limited "movie"-style viewing programs.

An alternative to a large memory for rapid sequential display is a videodisk similar to those that were once sold for viewing movies at home. These home systems have now largely surrendered the home market to videocassette recorders. However, videodisks can store and display images at very rapid frame rates. The limitation of such systems is that once the data are transferred to the videodisk for rapid viewing the ability to adjust the window and level and make other measurements is lost.

One of the sore points in many systems is the format camera. Filming is very tedious. CT format cameras with bulk film loading are now available but may not be compatible with all CT units. Bulk loading is similar to angiography systems in which a set of films is loaded into a large cassette and the films are automatically fed into the camera as needed. The advantage of such systems is that handling cassettes is minimized. Busy departments can actually cut personnel hours with these bulk loading cameras, thereby recovering extra costs of the equipment. The disadvantage is that if films are run through the processor less frequently, and there is a malfunction or improper setting, it may not be detected until many films have been exposed.

Another feature that holds great promise is the automated filming of entire scans, with the operator needing only to initiate the process. Because filming is usually so time consuming, this feature may be very attractive, possibly allowing some facilities to reduce personnel coverage. This may be combined with an additional option being developed, namely, bulk loading with automated processing, in which a film is directly connected to a processor and is immediately processed upon completing the film exposure. This would be the same as what is commonly done with plain chest radiographs.

As with many technical innovations, manufacturers are likely to introduce these new features prematurely, before the hardware and software are sufficiently flexible to accommodate future needs. Some features may seem to be unnecessary "bells and whistles." Although it may not be wise to be too early a customer for these developments, such features as rapid sequential viewing, laser cameras, and automated filming should be seriously considered when introduced. As mentioned, each of these developments may superficially seem to have limited use, but all have significant potential to influence the way scans are done and even the types of examinations performed. These new capabilities may in turn stimulate work on new advances in image quality.

REFERENCES

1. Capp, M. P., Seeley, G. W., Ovitt, T. W., Roehrig, H., and Fisher, H. D. (1986): The computerized electronic radiology department. In: *The Computer in Radiology,* edited by T. B. Hunter, pp. 235–254. Aspen Systems, Rockville, MD.
2. Coulam, C. M., and Erickson, J. J. (1981): Equipment considerations in computed tomography. In: *The Physical Basis of Medical Imaging,* edited by C. M. Coulam, J. J. Erickson, F. D. Rollo, and A. E. James, pp. 213–229. Appleton-Century-Crofts, New York.
3. Elliott, D. O. (1981): Data recording and storage. In: *Radiology of the Skull and Brain: Technical Aspects of Computed Tomography,* edited by T. H. Newton and D. G. Potts, pp. 4200–4211. C. V. Mosby, St. Louis.
4. Glenn, V. W., Harlow, C. A., Dwyer, S. J. III, Rhodes, M. L., and Parker, D. L. (1981): Image manipulation and pattern recognition. In: *Radiology of The Skull and Brain: Technical Aspects of Computed Tomography,* edited by T. H. Newton and D. G. Potts, pp. 4326–4354. C. V. Mosby, St. Louis.
5. Lehr, J. L., and Capek, P. (1985): Histogram equalization of CT images. *Radiology,* 154:163–169.
6. Meredith, W. J., and Massey, J. B. (1977): Diagnostic radiology: The properties of the X-ray film. In: *Fundamental Physics of Radiology,* 3rd edition, Chapter XVI, pp. 175–190. Year Book Medical Publishers, Chicago.
7. Schultz, G. W. (1981): Computed tomography displays. In: *Radiology of the Skull and Brain: Technical Aspects of Computed Tomography,* edited by T. H. Newton and D. G. Potts, pp. 4173–4299. C. V. Mosby, St. Louis.
8. Seeley, G. W. (1986): Computer components, peripherals, and other devices. In: *The Computer in Radiology,* edited by T. B. Hunter, pp. 71–92. Aspen System, Rockville, MD.

11

Sources of Artifacts

This chapter reemphasizes the nature and importance of the many artifacts that may affect CT images. Some artifacts may be easily recognized as serious and requiring immediate service from an expert. Other problems are corrected simply. When there is a question, one can often attempt simple solutions before expensive and time-consuming service visits are required.

One should also recognize that each model of scanner has its own idiosyncrasies, and that problems often result from two or more basic physical causes. CT scanners are so complex that multiple malfunctions may occur simultaneously. Many of the artifacts mentioned in this section have already been extensively discussed, and references to the relevant sections are cited. Other artifacts will be discussed more fully.

RINGS AND CHANNEL ERRORS ON CT SLICES

Rings are an inherent problem in third-generation scanners because of the simultaneous circular motion of the tube with the detector array. A single line or ray of X-ray photons from the focal spot to a specific detector forms a tangent to a circle through the field of view as the tube circles the patient (Fig. 11-1). Therefore, if there is a problem with a single detector, it will be represented as a ring on the CT scan. If the detectors are poorly calibrated relative to one another, rings may appear throughout the scan. Therefore, if prominent rings appear, the first step is to check the detector calibration or recalibrate at the factors used (see Chapter 2, p. 24). If this is not the problem, the system is likely to require service. The problem may be in (a) the mechanical aspects of tube-detector rotation, (b) the detector itself, (c) the photodiodes or amplifiers receiving the detectors' signals, (d) the chain of electronics that controls the acquisition of data from the involved channel or channels, (e) the electronics controlling transmission of those data to the computer, or (f) in the back projector, which is the computer hardware that controls the reconstruction process. The solution may be simple, or it may be complex, time consuming, and expensive.

In fourth-generation scanners, errors in single channels affect the overall image subtly, but not as an easily recognizable artifact, because a channel error affects an entire view rather than a single geometrical location in the reconstructed field (see Chapter 7, p. 77). If a single channel is not functioning, and a view is deleted, the overall CT attenuation numbers shift without appreciably affecting image quality. However, as more channels malfunction, noise increases. Thus discontinuities in rays produce more severe artifacts than discontinuities in views, and these ray discontinuities are more likely to arise in third-generation than in fourth-generation scanners. Although unlikely, rings may appear in fourth-generation scanners. These are probably caused by malfunctions in the back projector after the views are constructed from the raw data. If a component assigned to back-project a specific ray in each view is faulty, then third-generation-type rings may appear.

LINES ON SCANOGRAMS

On a third-generation scanner, a faulty channel will cause a straight line artifact on the scanogram, because this represents the direct output of a single channel as the patient passes through the scanning gantry. For a fourth-

A

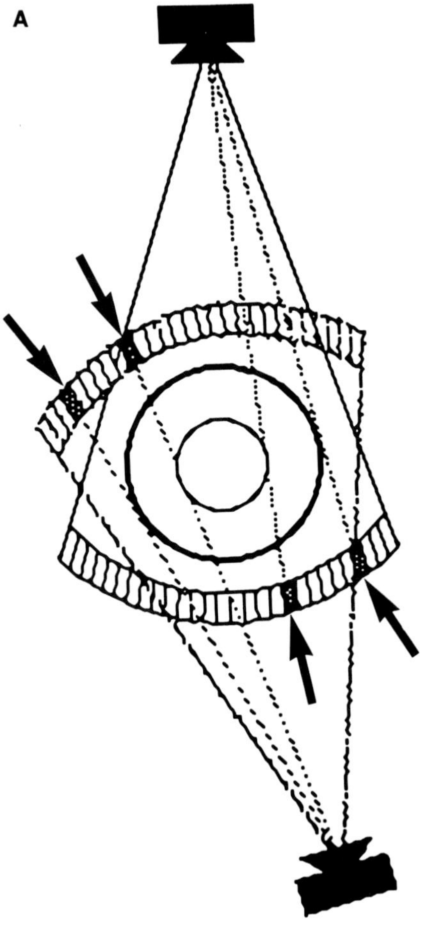

FIG. 11–1. Circular ring artifacts on third-generation CT scans. **A**. Two detectors (arrows) and their associated rays are highlighted. In every position of the X-ray tube and detector array, the rays between the focal spot and a single detector trace a tangent to a circle on the image. Thus, if there is a malfunction in a detector channel, a ring will appear. **B**. Image with a faint ring (arrowheads) visualized in the periphery of the scan from a detector channel imbalance, which was corrected by a recalibration.

B

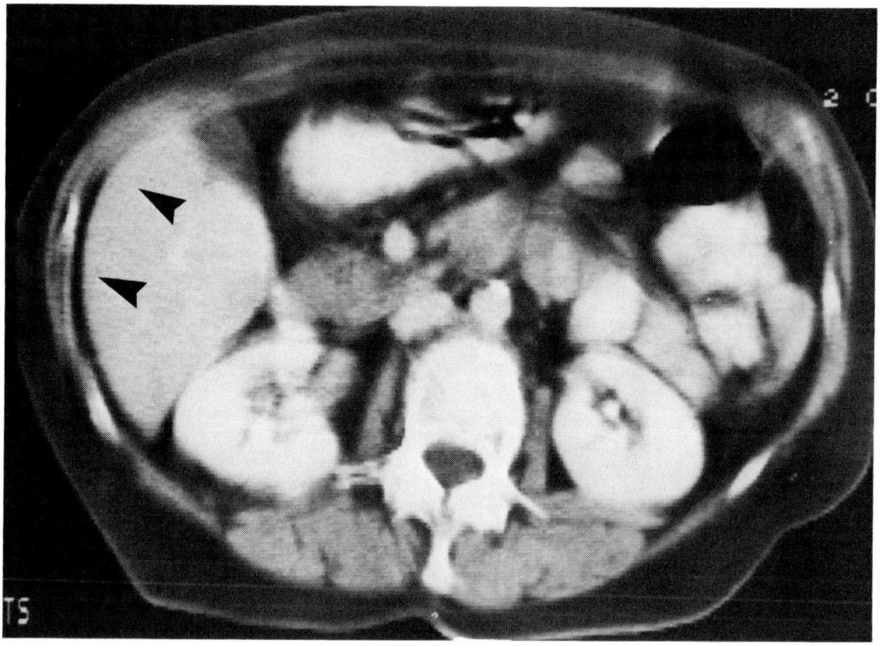

FIG. 11–1. (*cont.*)

generation scanner, if the channel is in the path of the fan beam for t scanogram, it will appear as a straight line as on a third-generation system (Fig. 11-2). If the faulty channel is not used for the scanogram, the problem will not appear on it.

ALIASING AND EDGE GRADIENT EFFECT

Aliasing was discussed in Chapter 5, p. 59, and is the result of an insufficient number of data samples for the spatial frequencies encountered in the body. Infrequent sampling leads to the introduction of false spatial frequencies (alias frequencies) as lines that do not represent real structures (see Figs. 2-12, 2-13). These lines may be very fine and subtle, adding what may be interpreted as noise to the image. Note such images contains streaks, which are more apparent at greater distances from their origin.

Another contributor to fine artifactual streaks is the edge gradient effect. This effect derives from the varying perspective of the X-ray beam with respect to complex structures. If a relatively homogeneous (low spatial frequency) object is viewed within the scanning field, then its attenuation of the X-ray beam is the same no matter from which direction the object is scanned. If the object is dense with abrupt borders (high spatial frequency), the X-ray attenuation will depend on the perspective of view because of the nature of exponential attenuation (Fig. 11-3). Thus the information received by the detectors in different views will appear inconsistent when trying to assign attenuation numbers via the reconstruction algorithm. This is manifested as streaks, which tend to emanate from areas of high spatial frequency, that is, from sharp edges with high density differences. These include the patient support table, gastric air-contrast levels, the thoraco-abdominal junction, and bone–soft-tissue interfaces.

These streaks are less apparent on machines that employ higher data sampling rates and have smaller effective detector apertures. Using a single machine, one may minimize these streaks by first detecting the location from which the lines diverge. One source of objectionable artifacts can be degenerating material within the patient couch needing repair or replacement (see Fig. 2-12). One can move or change the physical source of the artifact, or choose a technique that uses more data samples, which usually requires lengthening scan times. Another technique that will diminish such

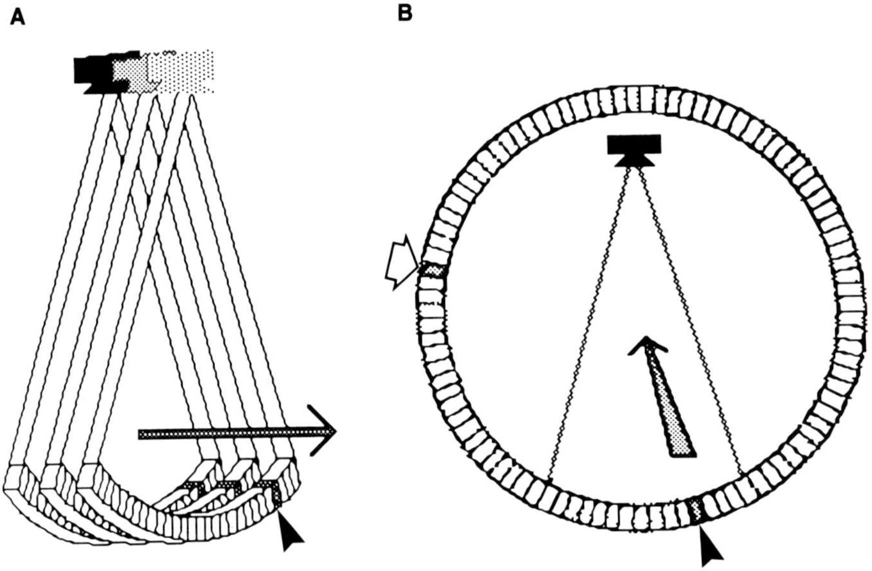

FIG. 11–2. Different effects of detector channel errors between third- and fourth-generation scanners. **A.** A third-generation tube-detector assembly with a faulty detector channel (arrowhead). As the patient table is translated through the scanner for a scanogram, an artifactual vertical line appears on the scanogram at the location of the faulty detector. As in Fig. 11–1, a ring will appear on the CT slice. **B.** In contrast, for a fourth-generation scanner, if the faulty detector is located within the fan angle (arrowhead) of the scanogram projection, a similar line will appear. However, if the faulty detector lies outside the projection (open arrow) for the scanogram, this will have no effect on the scanogram image. **C.** Scanogram from a fourth-generation scanner with two faulty detectors. Two vertical lines are present.

artifacts is to use a thinner slice. This is effective because of the inhomogeneity caused by averaging in tissue above and below the tissue of interest is minimized. However, thinner slice techniques involve many other factors (see Chapter 5, p. 53).

NOISE

Noise is also discussed in Chapter 8, p. 89. The noise level of an image is increased by any factor that decreases the number of photons used to create the image (4). This can be caused by setting too low an mAs, wear on the X-ray tube anode, misalignment of the tube and detectors, pressure loss in gas detectors, and so on. Noise can also be introduced by faulty electronics. Noise is made more visible when using narrow window settings, which increase contrast.

If excess noise is caused by anything other than improper technique selection or filming, service is required. Unfortunately, noise problems are often insidious and not noticed until far advanced. Even then, it is often hard to prove from clinical images that a problem is present, because added noise can be attributable to large patient size or other technical factors. It is impor-

C

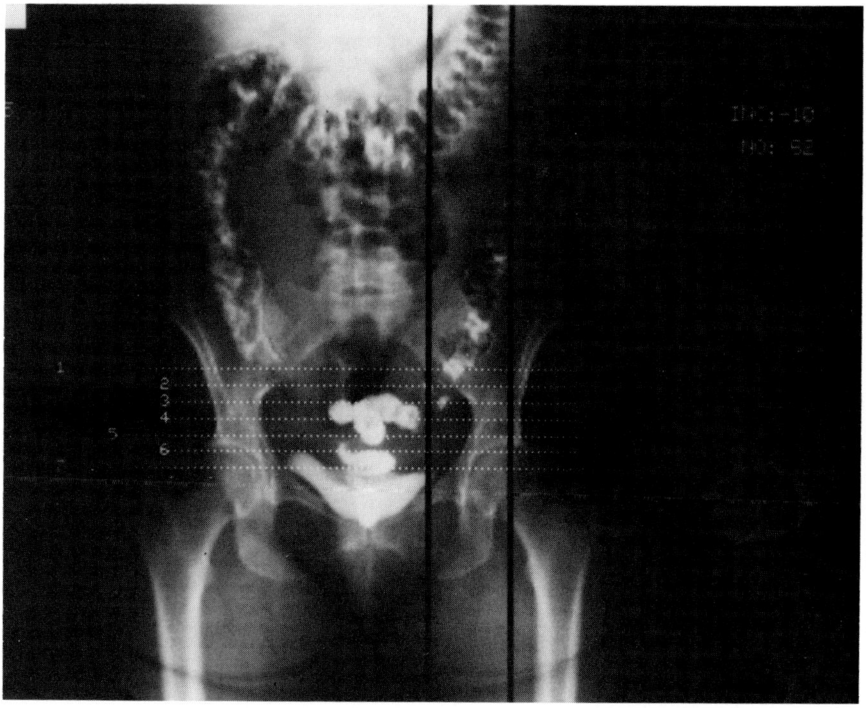

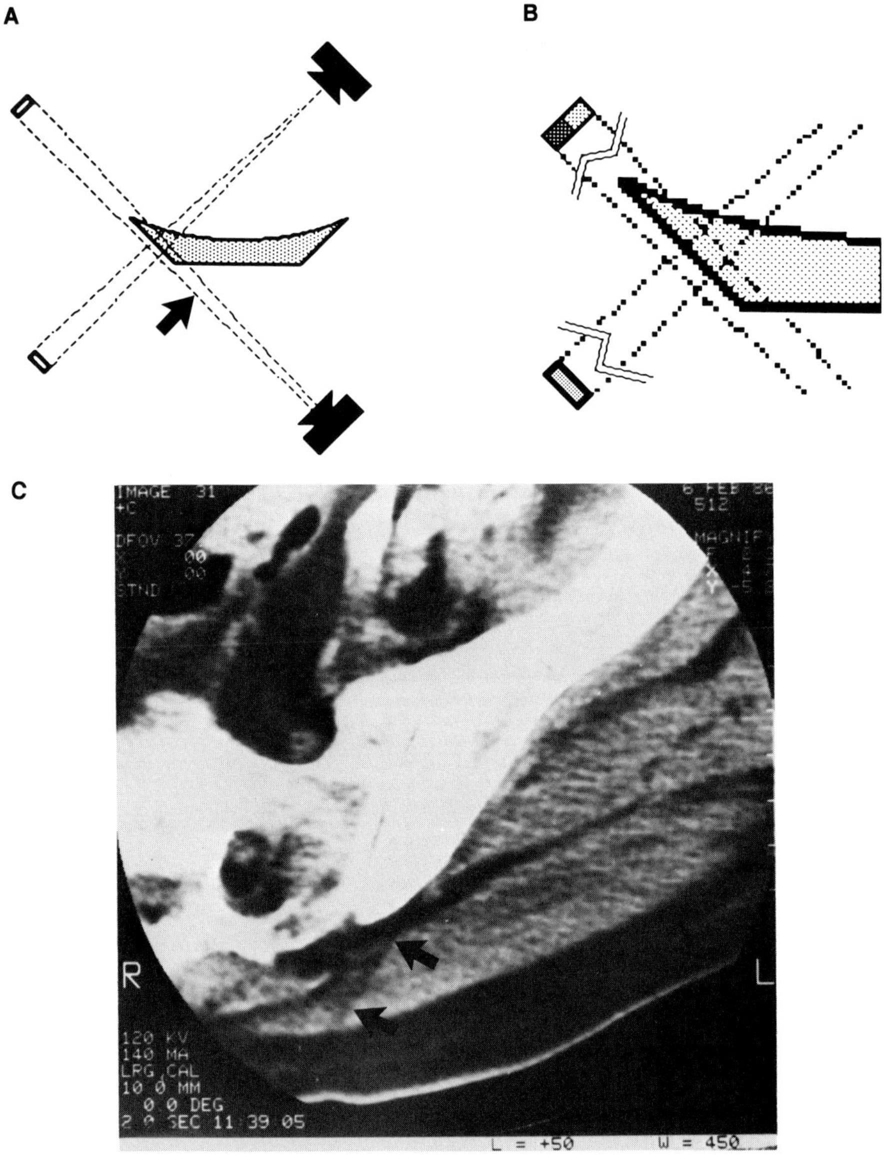

FIG. 11–3. Edge gradient effect. **A**. Two ray projections are illustrated. One projection (arrow) is parallel to the flat, high spatial frequency surface, and the other projection is perpendicular to it. **B**. A close-up of this effect. Because of finite beam width, when the ray is parallel to the flat surface, the detector absorption is the arithmetic average of densities from the less attenuated and more highly attenuated halves of the beam width. When the ray is perpendicular to the surface, attenuation is based on an exponential function rather than an arithmetic average. This inconsistency in data between these two different ray projections creates an artifact (**C**) manifested by a straight line (arrows) radiating from the high spatial frequency interface.

tant for quality control personnel to maintain standard reference films and quantitative data on system performance on test objects under various technical conditions.

BEAM HARDENING

Beam hardening was described in Chapter 8, p. 93. It creates artifacts related to the changes in the spectrum of energies in a polychromatic X-ray beam as it passes through tissues of different thicknesses and compositions (1,6,7). It may be manifested by broad streaks, vague areas of decreased density near bones or through thick body parts (see Figs. 8-6, 10-4), or the cupping artifact (Fig. 11-4). Noticeable areas affected include the interpetrous area on head scans, the shoulders, the ribs, the scapula, the hips (Fig. 11-5), and the spine. Streaks from beam hardening also occur when scanning a body with the arms at the patient's side or in areas with dense contrast such as the bladder or the bowel. Other physical sources such as the nonlinear partial volume effect (see below) and the edge gradient effect (see above) may also contribute to these streaks.

A

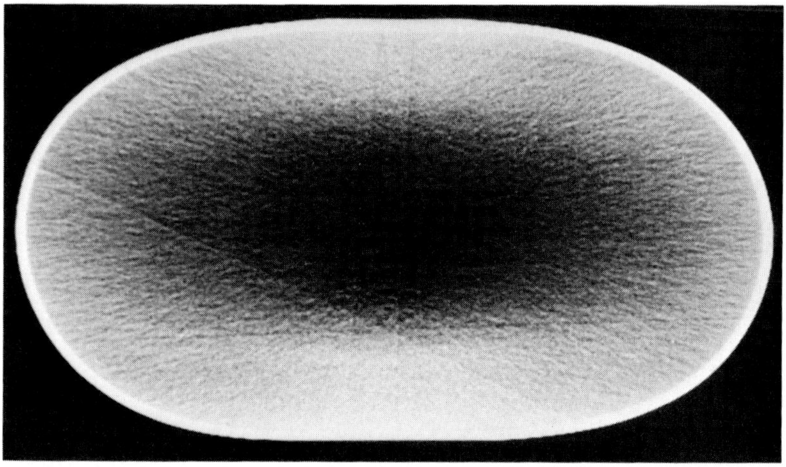

FIG. 11–4. Images of oval water phantoms demonstrating differences in scanner performance. **A**. Scan without correction for beam hardening effect shows cupping. **B**. Scan with proper software corrections on a different scanner shows an even level of noise throughout. However, note the slightly greater noise and the streaks at the periphery because of factors mentioned in the text. **C**. Improper corrections on a third scanner showing prominent low density near the phantom wall. **D**. Scan of a water phantom with pins using the same scanner as in **A**. Severe artifacts originate from these pins, which are used to simulate ribs. **E**. With proper corrections, most artifacts are eliminated. Although these scans are from an older group of scanners, they highlight significant differences between scanners, which cannot be detected from reviewing manufacturers' specifications. (Images courtesy of Dr. Anders Hemmingsson, M.D. Reprinted from ref. 5 by permission.)

B
C

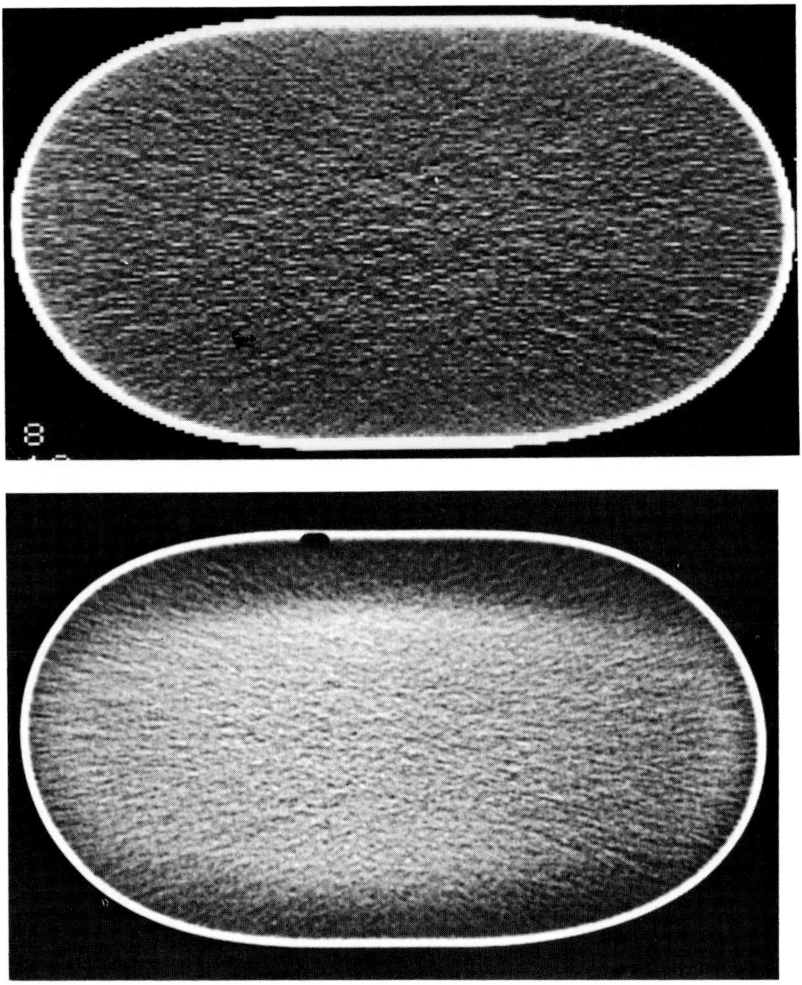

FIG. 11-4. (*cont.*)

There is usually little that can be done to diminish these artifacts for a specific scanner. One can change the kVp, increase the mAs to help suppress noise, change the patient's position to shift the position of vital structures relative to the artifacts, or use thinner slices. Because several physical sources may contribute to what appears to be one artifact, these maneuvers may improve the image without eliminating the artifact. The clinically deleterious effect of beam hardening artifacts causing vague, questionable densities through organs or vessels can often be overcome with adequate quanities of contrast material. The second-order beam hardening corrections discussed in Chapter 8, p. 93, are often done on head scans to correct for characteristic errors at the bone-brain interface, and may also be employed on body scans.

D

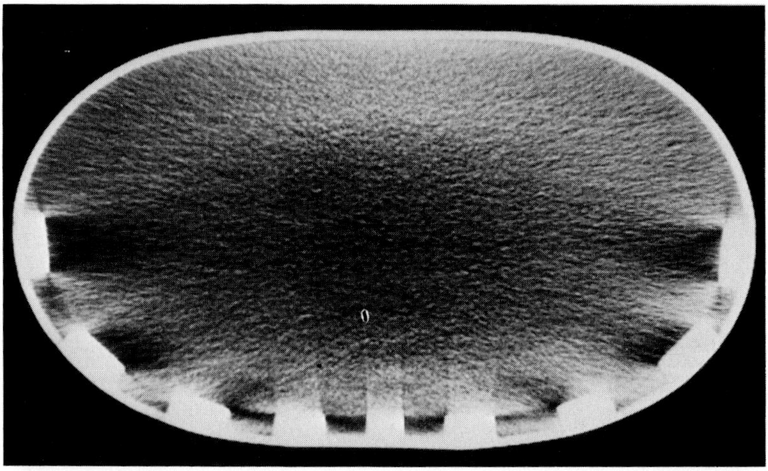

E

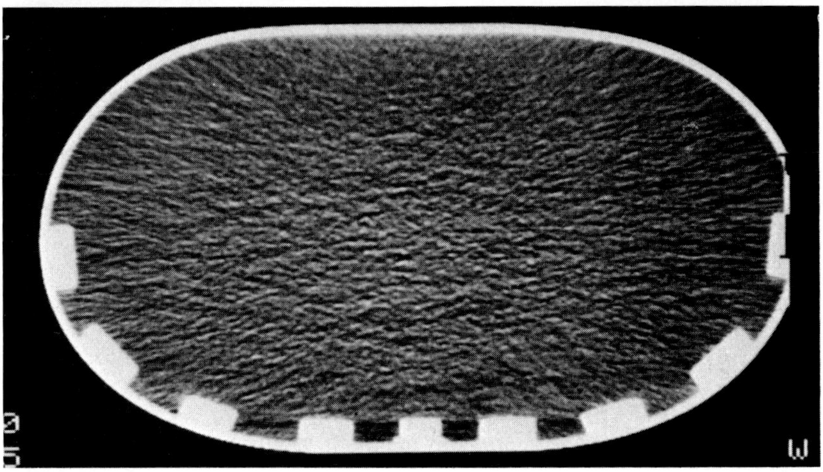

FIG. 11–4. (*cont.*)

OUT-OF-FIELD ARTIFACT

Tissue outside the scanned field of view creates artifacts, the severity of which depends on the amount and density of material outside the field (see Chapter 5, p. 45, and Fig. 5-1). This artifact is partly caused by the presence of tissue obstructing reference detectors. However, tissue and other materials outside the field are also often dense (e.g., arms and thoracotomy tubes), causing the beam harding effect to contribute to the problem. Enlarging the reconstruction field may diminish the artifact. Nothing else can be done easily to correct this problem. In one institution the patient couch was misplaced 3 cm lateral to the proper position at installation, leading to chronically poor patient centering and out-of-field artifacts. Such an unusual

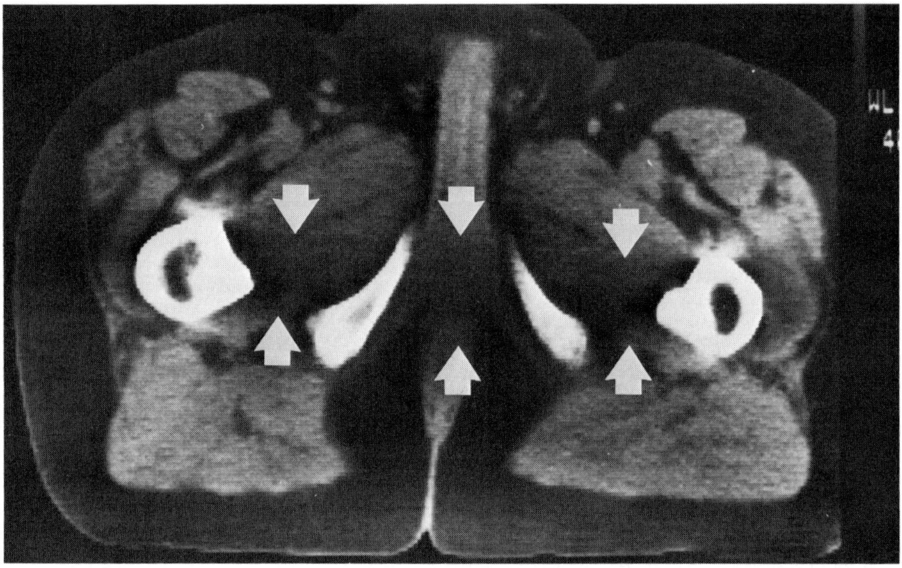

FIG. 11–5. One manifestation of the beam hardening artifact. A region of apparent low density (arrows) between the femurs is caused by beam hardening as the X-rays pass through the dense bone. Although the intensity of the beam (number of photons transmitted) is markedly decreased by bone, the average energy of the beam is shifted upward. Thus, a greater amount of energy is absorbed in the detectors than would be predicted simply by the known path length, and the back projection algorithm thus interprets the attentuation of this region to be lower than it actually is.

problem should be detectable by carefully inspecting the position of the table on routine scans.

METAL

Structures containing metal such as surgical clips, EKG leads, nasogastric tubes, and orthopedic prostheses, as well as other dense objects such as barium, may create severe artifacts. These artifacts are caused by a combination of beam hardening, the nonlinear partial volume effect, the edge gradient effect, and motion. Dense structures and interfaces are difficult enough for the reconstruction process to deal with. Dense structures that are moving are more difficult, and most dense objects do move, even if only slightly, because of respiration and heart pulsation. Surgical clips or wires may also cause tiny, low-density artifacts adjacent to the metal, which may be mistaken for extraluminal gas bubbles (Fig. 11-6).

The best way to minimize these artifacts is to remove as many metallic objects from the scanning field as possible. Nasogastric tubes may be with-

A

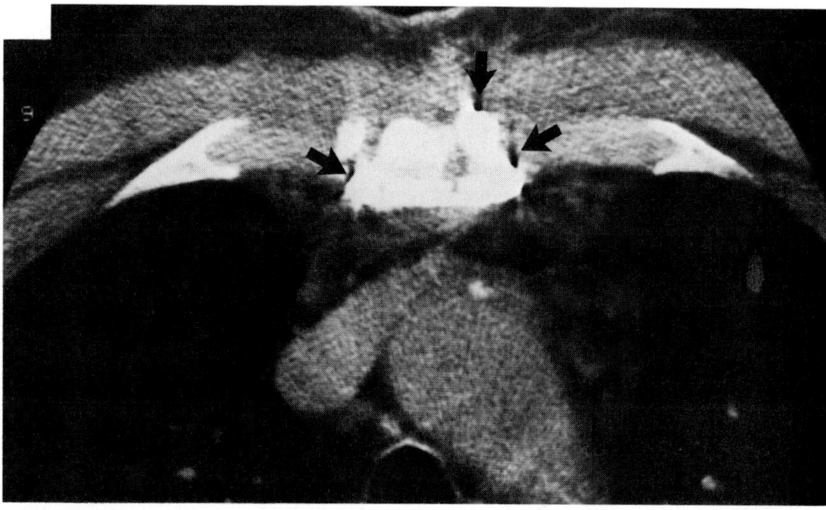

B

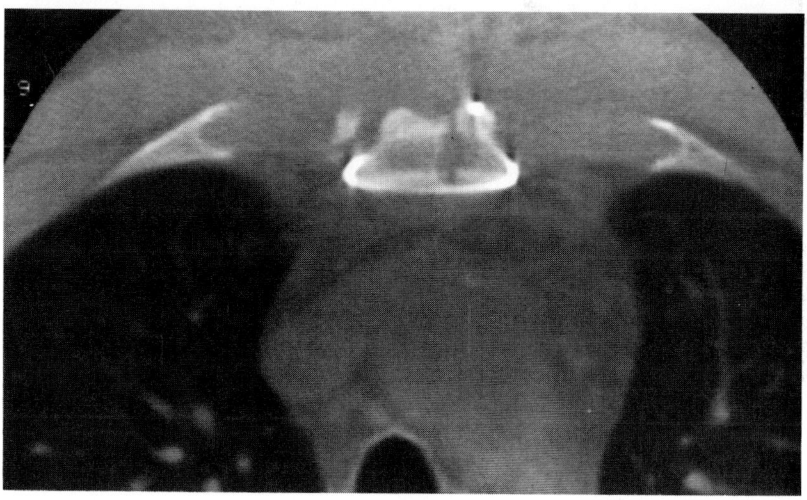

FIG. 11–6. False appearance of gas bubbles caused by wires. **A**. This scan was done because of the suspicion of sternal abscess after sternotomy. At initial interpretation, subcutaneous gas bubbles were suspected (arrows) suggesting infection. **B**. Inspection of the same slice at settings more appropriate for bone shows that these suspected bubbles are simply artifacts adjacent to a sternal wire.

drawn to the midesophagus. Wires may be removed or moved during the scan. Gown snaps should be moved. Inspecting the scanogram for metal is useful to help forestall problems, particularly with seriously ill, bedridden patients, who may come from the intensive care unit with numerous wires and appliances.

A

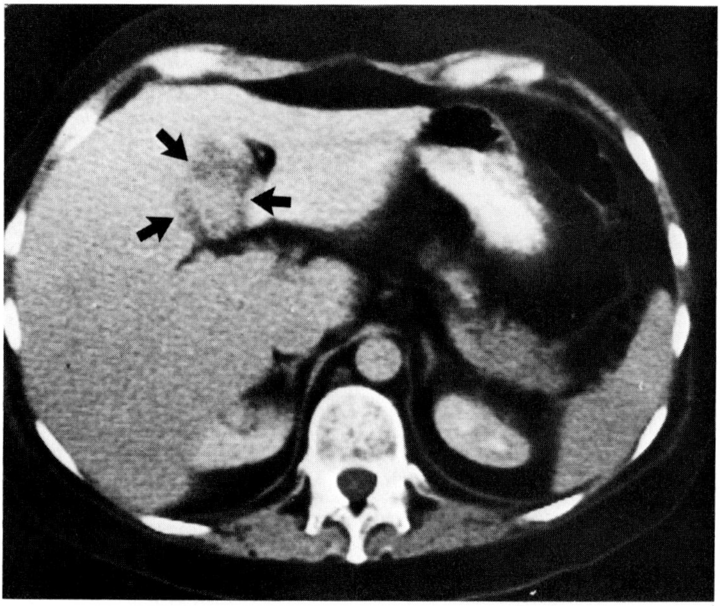

B

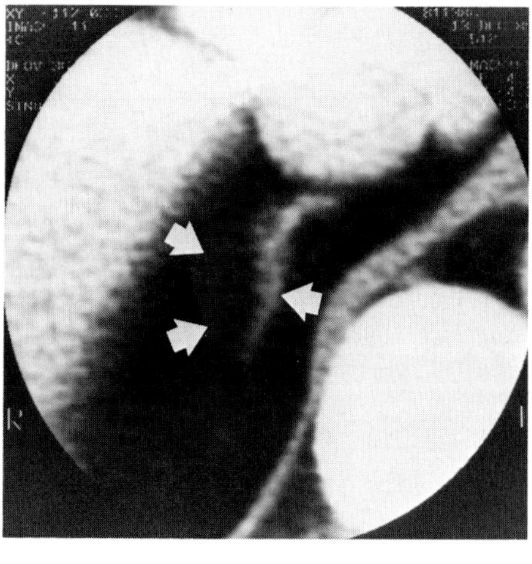

FIG. 11–7. Volume averaging effects or partial volume artifact. **A**. There is suggestion of a 2- to 3-cm lesion in the left hepatic lobe (arrows). However, adjacent slices indicated no such lesion, which would be expected if the lesion were indeed several centimeters in size. This phantom lesion simply represents volume averaging between some of the liver tissue and some of the fat in the fossa beneath the liver. **B** and **C**. False appearance of a fatty adrenal lesion. A standard 10-mm section of an adrenal gland (**B**) suggests a low-attenuation adrenal mass (arrows). However, a thin-section study (**C**) indicates a normal configuration of the adrenal gland. The false appearance of a mass was caused by volume averaging of one adrenal limb with adjacent fat within the thick slice. **D**. Image of a pulmonary nodule, which appears to be traversed by a blood vessel (arrow). This appearance is a volume averaging artifact in which both a portion of the pulmonary nodule and the adjacent vessel were included within the same slice.

C

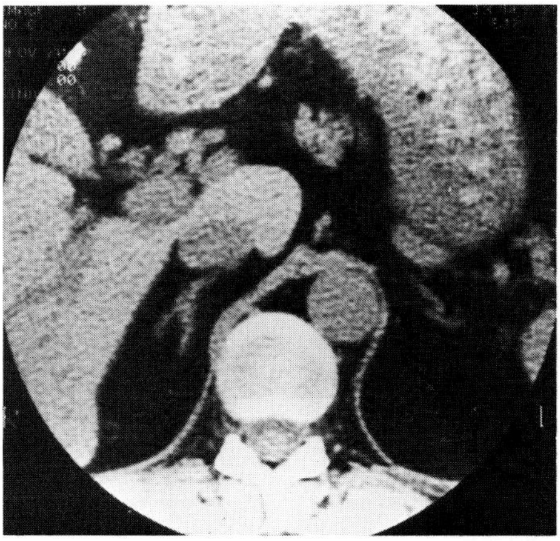

D

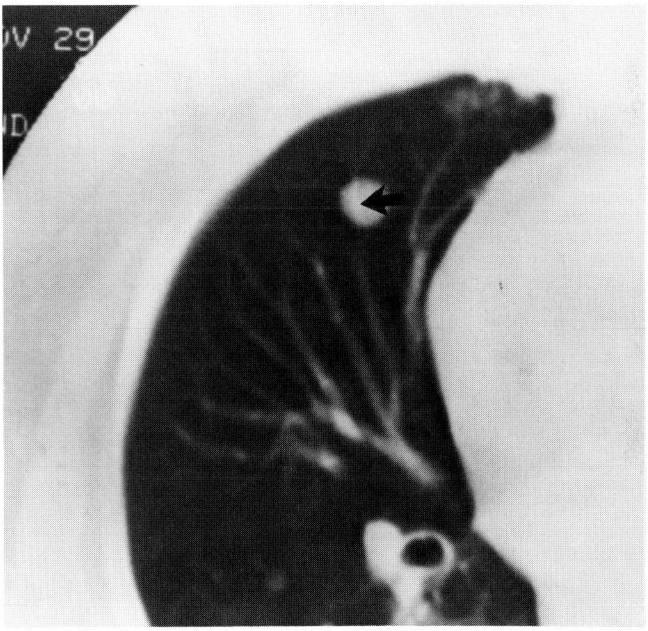

FIG. 11-7. (*cont.*)

PARTIAL VOLUME EFFECT AND VOLUME AVERAGING

Volume averaging is a serious cause of interpretive errors (2,6). Most objects have complex or sloped margins, and volume averaging of adjacent structures is inevitable (Fig. 11-7). Experienced interpreters usually have few problems sorting out most volume averaging artifacts because these observers are accustomed to viewing slices sequentially to resolve questions. For example, a suspected round lesion 3 to 4 cm in diameter must be seen in three to five consecutive slices to be considered genuine. Vague opacities may simply be the top or bottom edges of a rounded structure such as the top of the aortic arch or the diaphragm. Vague margins may simply indicate that the edge is sloping within the thickness of the slice rather than represent infiltration (Fig. 11-8).

However, even experienced observers cannot avoid the confusion caused by the inaccuracy of CT numbers of small lesions. One must also be careful to measure the attenuation of a lesion through its center, rather than the top or bottom (see Chapter 8, p. 93).

There are several ways to minimize the effect of volume averaging artifacts that confuse the interpretation of borders. First, a confusing scan may simply be repeated at the same level. If the structure in question has moved several millimeters, the confusing appearance may resolve. Alternatively, the scan may be repeated, but at a slightly different index, several (3 to 5) millimeters from the first. If the suspected artifact is in an area where consecutive slices have not yet been obtained, the remaining slices can be

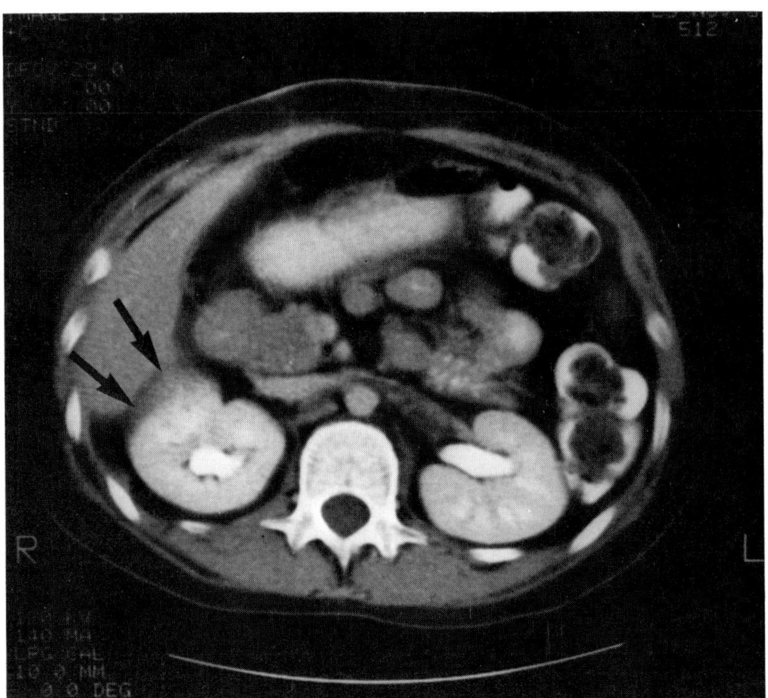

FIG. 11–8. Another manifestation of the volume averaging artifact. The lateral margin of the right kidney (arrows) appears ill defined. This appearance is created by the sloping margin of the kidney within the CT slice. A thin-section study at this level would have demonstrated a sharp renal contour.

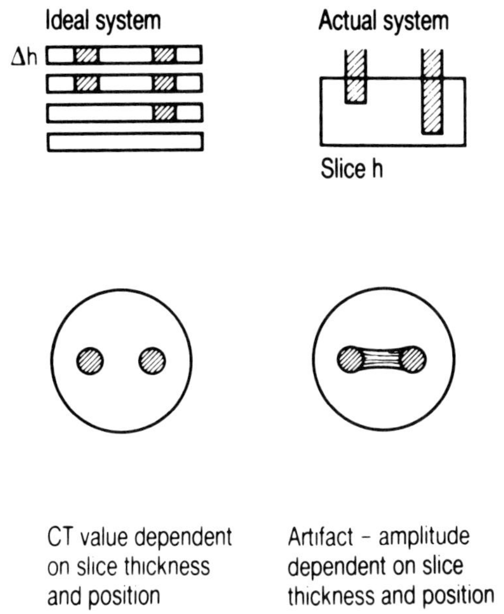

FIG. 11–9. Cause and effects of the nonlinear partial volume effect. The variations of degree of averaging of dense structures into the slice creates streaks between the structures. (Image courtesy of Siemens Medical Systems, Inc.)

acquired. However, the best method is to repeat the scan with a thinner slice. Vague borders will become sharper, and numbers will become more accurate. However, it may be necessary to increase the mAs to compensate for the fewer photons reaching the detectors.

Slices as thick as 12 mm commonly lead to interpretive difficulties caused by volume averaging. In my opinion, slices greater than 10 mm in thickness should not be used.

The volume averaging artifact described above may also be termed the *linear partial volume effect.* It is "linear" because CT numbers that are shifted because a structure is only partly included within the slice may theoretically be recalculated with a simple linear arithmetic equation based on the percentage thickness of the slice occupied by the object.

The nonlinear partial volume effect is one that creates streaks in an image because its effect is not predictable in a straightforward linear fashion (6). Such an artifact may be caused by structures of high spatial frequency and complex shape partly projecting into a slice (Fig. 11-9). If one imagines two cylindrical structures projecting into a slice, one can appreciate that the cylinders averaging with other tissue in the slice will vary considerably depending on the vantage point (view) from which they are seen. This causes an inconsistency in data for back projection, leading to streaks; the problem can be diminished by decreasing slice thickness. As alluded to above, this is part of the cause of the interpetrous streak artifact. However, because beam hardening and the edge gradient effect also contribute to this artifact, decreasing slice thickness improves the image but does not eliminate the streaks (Fig. 11-10).

A

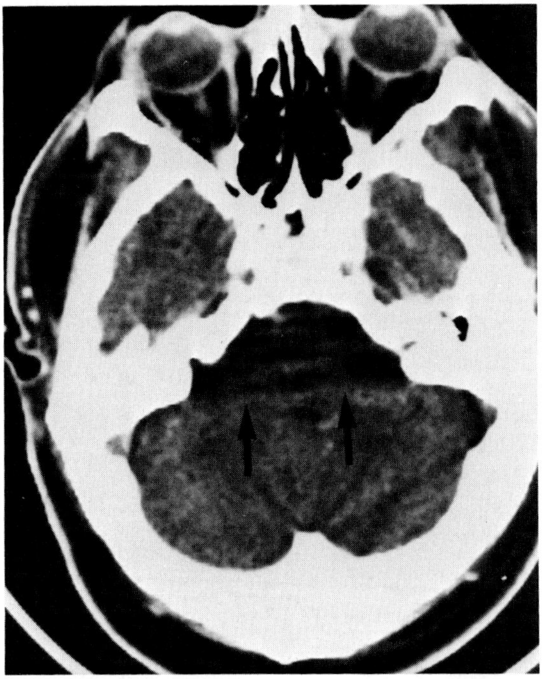

B

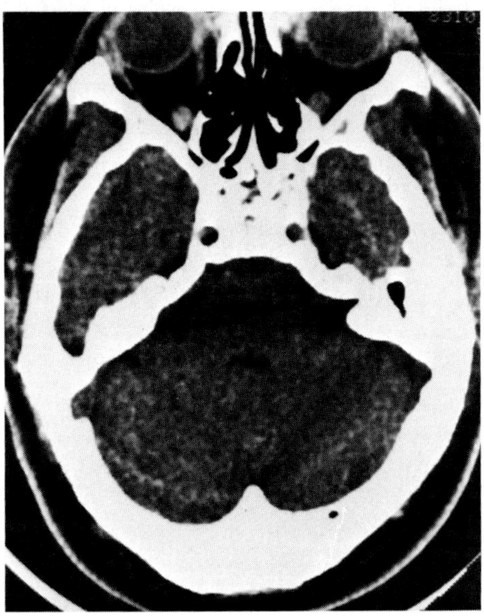

FIG. 11–10. Illustration of a method that improves but does not eliminate the interpetrous artifact. **A**. Standard 10-mm-thick section of the head through the petrous bones. Dark streaks (arrows) obscuring underlying brain detail are seen in the usual location. **B**. A 1.5-mm slice through the same level shows a similar region of streak and low attenuation. However, some underlying brain detail is now seen. Use of a thin slice in this example improved but did not eliminate the artifact because the artifact is due to both beam hardening and the nonlinear partial volume effect. Therefore, the partial volume effect is minimized with a thin slice, but the beam hardening effect is unchanged.

AIR-CONTRAST INTERFACES

The most troublesome consistent air-contrast interface in the abdomen is the gastric air-fluid level. This level often creates streaks through the left hepatic lobe that can obscure even moderate-sized lesions. The streaks are caused by the marked density difference (high spatial frequency) between contrast and air and a small amount of motion of the fluid. This is another manifestation of a combination of the edge gradient effect, the nonlinear partial volume effect, and motion artifact.

The effects of these objectionable artifacts can be alleviated by several maneuvers. First, the amount of fluid in the stomach may be minimized by providing an effervescent solution as the final cup of "contrast" material before scanning. Alternatively, the contrast may be given while the patient lies in the left decubitus position, to allow the gas to pass through the duodenum before scanning. In certain instances one may be able to avoid using oral contrast. Some investigators have attempted to administer a fatty liquid, which then forms a layer on top of the gastric contrast, forming an intermediate-density interface, which causes fewer artifacts by decreasing the attenuation differences at the interfaces. We have not used this technique. It is also important to minimize patient motion because motion will increase the severity of the artifact. A commonly used alternative to the above maneuvers is simply to put the patient into a decubitus or prone position for repeat scans when questions arise from the routine scans.

MOTION

Streaks and blurs come in many varieties and have many causes (9). They are often cited for obscuring areas of abnormality, but such artifacts may be most dangerous to accurate interpretation when they are not recognized as streaks but thought to represent actual lesions. Other than the causes for artifacts mentioned up to now, most artifacts are created by patient or bowel motion. It would be more accurate to say that streaks and blurs emanate from areas where motion occurs, but the effects of that motion on the image relate to the attributes of the individual scanner and the choice of technique. Motion artifacts may be more objectionable on one type of scanner than on another despite identical scanning times, because motion artifacts are actually the result of the several sources of artifact discussed above, including the edge gradient effect, the partial volume effect, and others that depend on scanner design and geometry.

The artifacts that cause the most difficulty with clinical interpretation are those that cause an ill-defined blurring adjacent to a loop of bowel or a rib. The areas are usually of low density, but may have very bright edges. The low-density areas may be confused with ill-defined neoplastic lesions, and the small foci of high-density areas may be mistaken for calcifications. Awareness of these artifacts and experience are the best solutions, because these artifacts are so common that it is impossible to rescan every area brought into question. Before rescanning, supportive evidence of a real abnormality should be searched for. Adjacent areas and slices should be reviewed, and different windows should be examined. Such artifacts also have a multifactorial cause including beam hardening as well as motion.

If repeat scans are deemed necessary, one may wish to use glucagon to suppress bowel motion, although with two-to-five-second scanners we no longer use glucagon. However, those advocating the administration of an oral effervescent material recommend 0.1 mg glucagon i.v. It is also worthwhile to observe carefully the patient's respiration, which may not have been controlled because of improper following of instructions by the technologist or lack of coordination between the timing of the command for breath holding and the initiation of scanning. Some patients take a relatively long time to execute a command to take a breath and hold it. Scanning may then begin prematurely.

Motion artifacts may be suppressed on some scanners by adjusting the scan angle (half, full, or overscan) and the scan time. Paradoxically, sometimes the longer scanning time decreases the motion artifact (see Chapter 5, p. 59). When only half or full scans are used, particularly with fourth-generation scanners, an "underscan" streak artifact appears. This underscan artifact is distinctive because the streaks are oriented in about the same direction for a specific scanner (Fig. 11-11) depending on the position of the tube at the beginning of each scan. For example, in some systems this artifact appears as nearly vertical streaks. In another, the artifact is in an orientation from 10 to 4 o'clock within the scan circle. The streak artifacts emanate from areas of bowel motion but are oriented along the lines between the tube and the detectors at the starting and stopping positions of the tube housing, where the greatest misregistration of rays is present.

Another manifestation of motion may be the appearance of a ghost image (Fig. 11-12; see also Fig. 11-2). This usually occurs because of patient breathing during the scan. It is represented as a faint double margin on organ boundaries. Such artifacts can lead to the false interpretation of perihepatic ascites or bowel wall thickening. Motion is sometimes represented as a blurring and at other times as a ghost image because the imaging process is broken into a series of discrete "views." If the organ is approximately in one position for a series of views, and in another position for another series, then the reconstruction will represent the picture as a superimposition of shadows or "ghosts." If the change is more gradual, the structure will be blurred.

Such ghost artifacts can be minimized by careful patient instruction, but when present, these artifacts can usually be identified by carefully examining

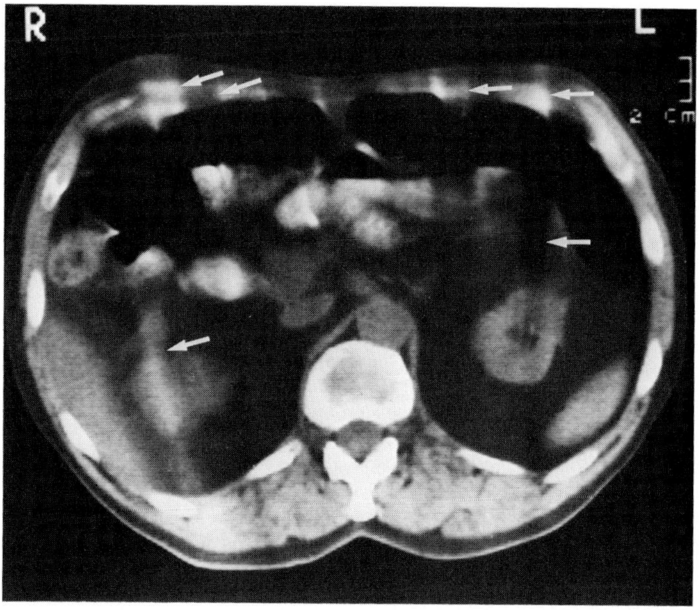

FIG. 11–11. Underscan artifact. Note streaks (arrows) radiating from areas of bowel motion. These streaks are all oriented in the same direction because they represent ray projections from the start and stop points of the X-ray tube and detector assembly. The slight inconsistency in bowel position between the beginning and the end of the scan leads to data inconsistencies, which cause these streaks. Such streaks occur on both third- and fourth-generation scanners and may be minimized by using overscanning.

the entire slice and adjacent slices. A ghost artifact is usually not limited to one organ or region. On abdominal scans, areas to look for ghost artifacts include the renal margins, the liver, the ribs, and the anterior abdominal wall. If an abnormality such as minimal perihepatic ascites is suspected, examining adjacent slices differentiate this finding from a ghost artifact.

DENSITY GRADIENT

Reconstruction algorithms are designed for the average-sized patient. Corrections for beam hardening are based on tissue thickness. However, some machines do not satisfactorily perform these corrections, creating an artifactual attenuation number gradient (the cupping artifact) from the center to the periphery of the reconstruction field. This artifact may be best seen on scans through the liver. The gradient may be complex rather than a

A

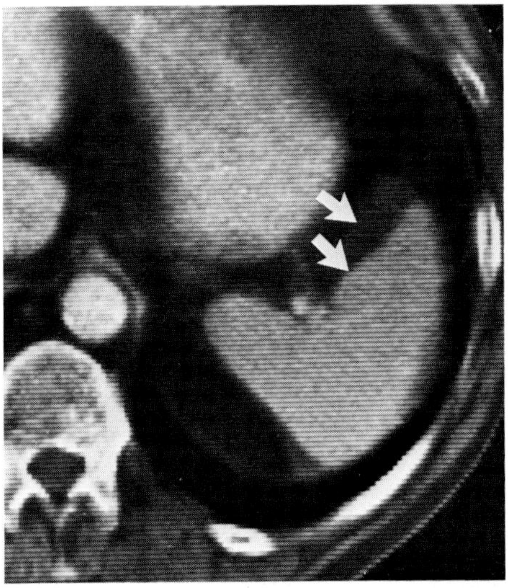

B

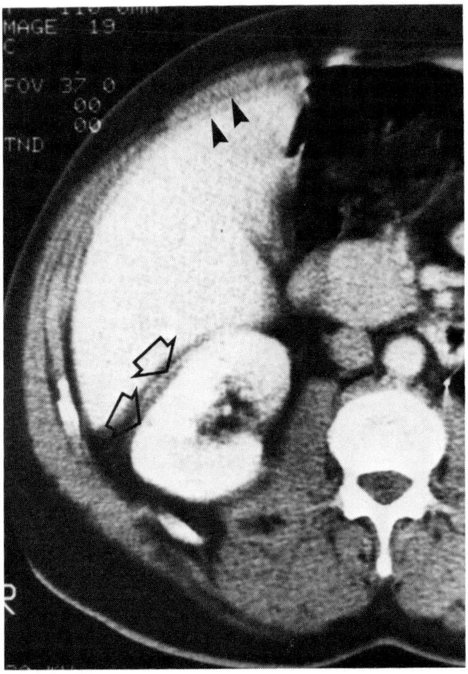

FIG. 11–12. Ghost artifacts caused by patient breathing. **A**. Faint double image of the spleen (arrows) creates the false impression of a small perisplenic fluid collection. **B**. Faint ghost image of the lateral renal outline (open arrows) suggests a small subcapsular fluid collection. The motion can be detected in this image by viewing an associated ghost image in the anterior abdominal wall (arrowheads).

smooth gradation of density, or there may be a point of reversal at which the density gets lighter and then darker again if beam hardening is locally overcorrected. The severity of the gradient depends on the patient's size and the particular scanner.

OVERSHOOT ARTIFACT (GIBBS PHENOMENON)

Early head scanners were plagued by a rim of decreased attenuation inside the calvarium, which was initially misinterpreted as the subarachnoid space or subdural hematoma in some patients. This proved to be an artifact of reconstruction caused by overcorrecting spatial filters in high-density areas. Newer scanners have largely corrected this problem.

CT NUMBERS

The causes for inaccurate CT numbers were discussed in Chapter 8, p. 93 (9). If the CT numbers appear grossly inaccurate, the calibration should be checked. The best method for checking the accuracy of CT numbers is to use a CT number test object containing regions of known density. In a properly calibrated machine, common sources of CT number errors are improper measurement techniques (measuring areas with obvious artifacts, too close to lesion boundaries, or lesions too small to provide accurate numbers because of volume averaging) and measuring lesions in large patients, in whom CT numbers are more affected by beam hardening.

LESION SIZE

Measurements of lesion size are affected by the measurement technique and the window and level settings at which structures are measured (7). These changes are particularly marked when measuring a lesion superimposed on a background of markedly different attenuation. For example, changing the window width and level of a slice containing a liver metastasis will markedly affect its appearance, but the measurement of its size will be relatively unaffected because the densities of the liver and the lesion are quite similar. However, the apparent size of a pulmonary nodule will be different if measured at lung windows rather than soft-tissue windows (Fig. 11-13), because the density of the surrounding lung is much lower than of the nodule. Also, window level settings have much less influence on apparent size than do window width settings. Studies have also shown that the most accurate size measurements for lung nodules are obtained at lung windows.

A

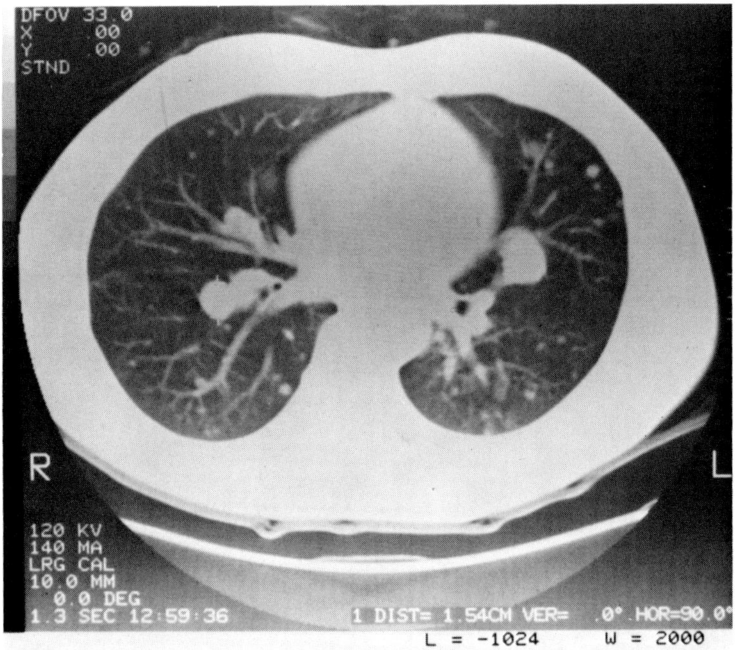
DFOV 33.0
X .00
Y .00
STND
R
L
120 KV
140 MA
LRG CAL
10.0 MM
0.0 DEG
1.3 SEC 12:59:36
1 DIST= 1.54CM VER= .0° HOR=90.0°
L = -1024 W = 2000

B

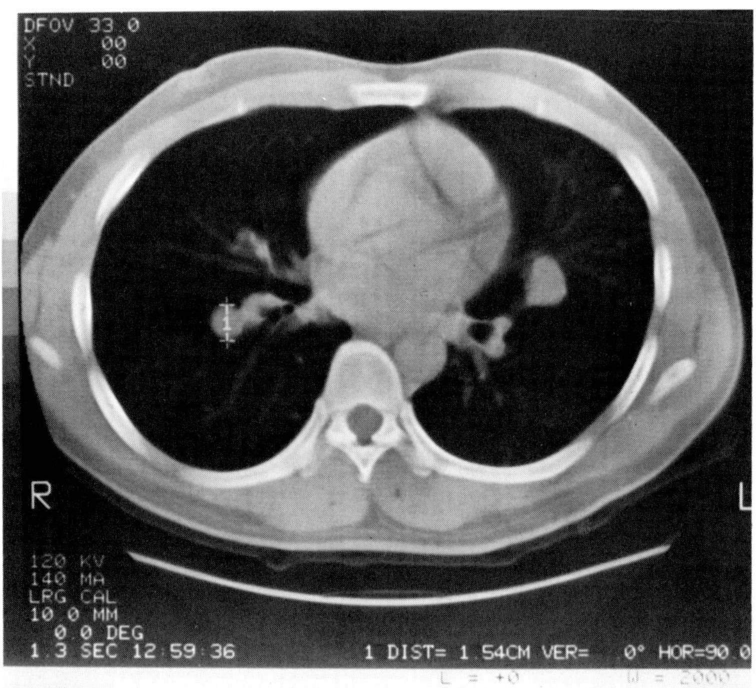
DFOV 33.0
X .00
Y .00
STND
1
R
L
120 KV
140 MA
LRG CAL
10.0 MM
0.0 DEG
1.3 SEC 12:59:36
1 DIST= 1.54CM VER= .0° HOR=90.0
L = +0 W = 2000

C

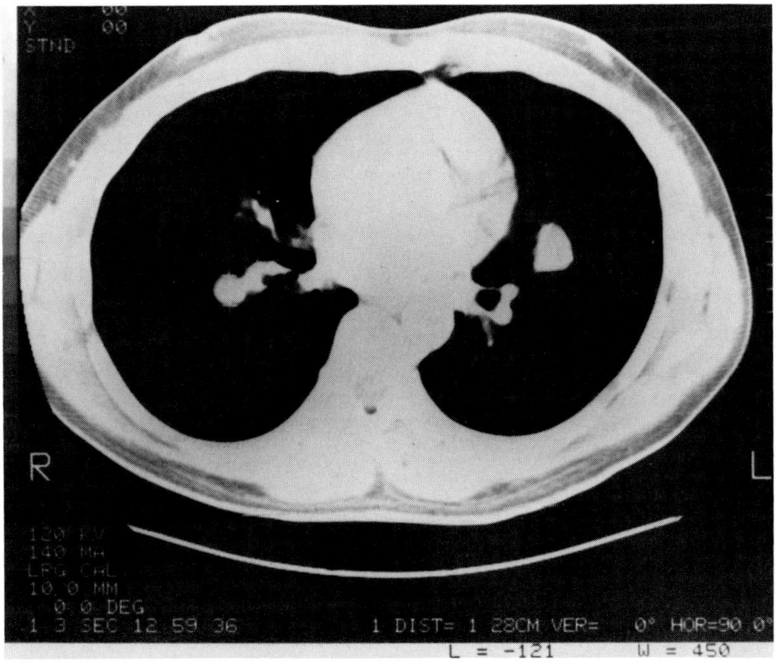

FIG. 11–13. Images showing markedly different size measurements for pulmonary nodules viewed at different window widths. **A**. When viewed at a wide window of 2,000, the nodule measures about 1.5 cm. **B**. At a window of 2,000 and a level of 0, there is no difference in the size measurement. **C**. However, at a window of 450, the lesion measures about 1.3 cm. Measurement differences occur when structures are of markedly different attenuation, such as the pulmonary nodule and the surrounding lung. The gradation of tissue attenuation at the margin of the nodule is obscured on the soft-tissue window. A more nearly accurate measurement of size may be obtained at the lung window. At times, small nodules may be completely obscured at soft-tissue settings. Changing level does not have as significant an effect on apparent nodule size as does changing window width.

The reason for these discrepancies in size measurements is that the boundary of any structure is not as well defined by the computer reconstruction as it appears visually. Even where sharp edges occur in the subject, they are represented on the scan as a gradation of density changes over one or several pixels around the boundary. Thus, when there is a marked density difference between adjacent structures, this gradation occurs over more pixels. The volume averaging artifact also contributes to this effect. This is one reason why thin slices are superior for making nodule measurements.

MISREGISTRATION

Interpretive errors can be caused by misregistration of anatomy from slice to slice. That is, although slices may be intended and annotated as contiguous, they may not represent actual contiguous anatomy. There are several causes of misregistration, both technical and patient related, but the patient-related causes are more common. If the patient takes breaths of slightly different depths on successive scans, or moves slightly between scans, misregistration will occur. Apparent misregistration may result from poor filming technique. If a scan is accidentally skipped during filming, it will appear as a gap in anatomy.

Another form of operator error involves apparent misregistration due to rescanning. On some systems, a new zero reference scan index may be set after every scanogram. Thus, if a series of slices is assigned from an initial scanogram, but the patient is subsequently repositioned and a new scanogram and index are obtained, then the slices and indices may appear incorrect if they are displayed on the wrong scanogram.

The patient table mechanism has a small amount of "play." When the mechanism is worn or functioning improperly, or when heavy patients are being scanned, the table may not move the specified interval. Such problems should be detected in regular preventative maintenance tests. Electronic rather than mechanical malfunctions may also cause misregistration errors.

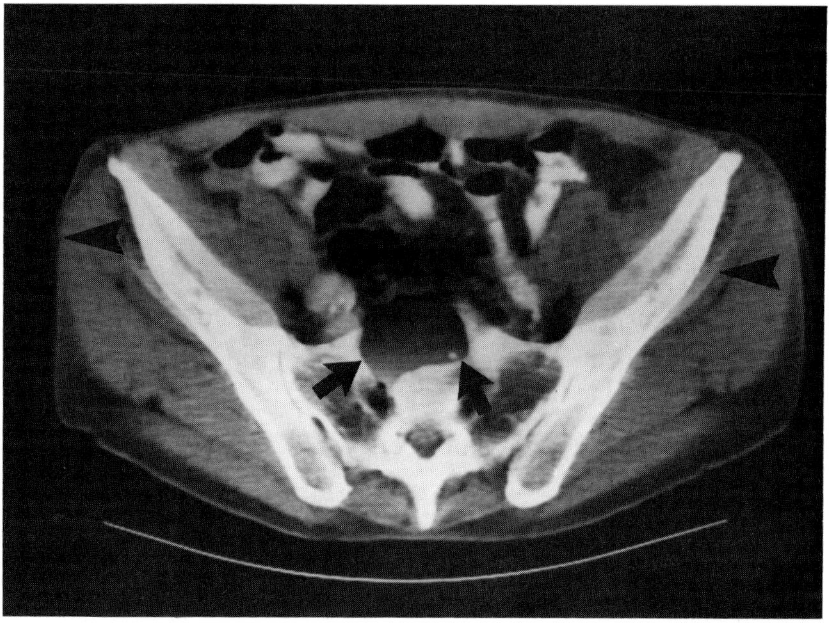

FIG. 11–14. Composite image creating the false appearance of a sacral lesion (arrows). This image was created by accidentally photographing the screen during the painting of one image over another. In this case, rectal gas on the slice being painted is superimposed upon the sacral bone being erased from the previous image. A clue to the nature of this composite image is that the image annotation has not yet been painted on the screen. Careful inspection of the edges of the body contours also reveals slight discontinuities (arrowheads) at the portion of the image being repainted.

Misregistration may affect not only the registration between one slice and another, but also the positioning of a slice on the scanogram. This can cause CT-guided biopsies and radiation therapy treatment planning to fail. One can attempt to assess for such misregistration by carefully examining the scanogram and attempting to correlate the bony landmarks on the scanogram and corresponding slices.

Another form of misregistration occurs only on films. With some systems, it may be possible to photograph an image while a subsequent image is being painted on the screen. This leads to a composite of two separate images, which may be difficult to recognize as such. If this occurs, a false lesion may be interpreted (Fig. 11-14) (8). In such cases, the alphanumeric data are usually not present on the "composite" scan. The absence of these data is one clue to the error.

REFERENCES

1. Coulam, C. M., and Erickson, J. J. (1981): Equipment considerations in computed tomography. In: *The Physical Basis of Medical Imaging,* edited by C. M. Coulam, J. J. Erickson, F. D. Rollo, and A. E. James, pp. 213–229. Appleton-Century-Crofts, New York.
2. Goodenough, D., Weaver, K., Davis, D., and LaFalce, S. (1982): Volume averaging limitations of computed tomography. *AJR,* 138:313–316.
3. Gordon, B. M. (1981): Data acquistion systems. In: *Radiology of the Skull and Brain: Technical Aspects of Computed Tomography,* edited by T. H. Newton and D. G. Potts, pp. 4133–4158. C. V. Mosby, St. Louis.
4. Hanson, K. M. (1981): Noise and contrast discrimination in computed tomography. In: *Radiology of the Skull and Brain: Technical Aspects of Computed Tomography,* edited by T. H. Newton and D. G. Potts, pp. 3941–3955. C. V. Mosby, St. Louis.
5. Hemmingsson, A., Jung, B., and Ytterbergh, C. (1983): Ellipsoidal body phantom for evaluation of CT scanners. *J. Comput. Assist. Tomogr.,* 7(3):503–508.
6. Joseph, P. M. (1981): Artifacts in computed tomography. In: *Radiology of the Skull and Brain: Technical Aspects of Computed Tomography,* edited by T. H. Newton and D. G. Potts, pp. 3956–3992. C. V. Mosby, St. Louis.
7. Koehler, P. R., Anderson, R. E., and Baxter, B. (1979): The effect of computed tomography viewer controls on anatomical measurements. *Radiology,* 130:189–194.
8. Silverman, P. M., Rosen, A., Korobkin, M., and Genkins, S. (1984): The "composite image": A photographic error in computed tomography with a multiformat camera. *AJR,* 142:961–962.
9. Zatz, L. M. (1981): Basic principles of computed tomography scanning. In: *Radiology of the Skull and Brain: Technical Aspects of Computed Tomography,* edited by T. H. Newton and D. G. Potts, pp. 3853–3876. C. V. Mosby, St. Louis.

12

Correcting Common Clinical and Mechanical Causes of Suboptimal Images

I believe that the most common cause of suboptimal image quality is the failure to recognize the potential for better image quality. The availability of good equipment is only the first step to obtaining satisfactory diagnostic examinations. Examinations of strikingly different quality can emanate from the same machine. One of the radiology residents in our institution, recently reviewing examinations from scans done several years before, assumed that the examinations had been done on an older model scanner because of the significantly poorer image quality. In fact, the scans had simply been done on the same scanner prior to the implementation of many of the techniques described in this book.

This chapter will summarize some of the most common problems I have observed leading to less than optimal image quality. It will also outline the means to correct these problems and the findings that indicate the need for mechanical repairs.

CONTRAST MATERIAL

As discussed further in Part 2, rapid injection of contrast material with rapid-sequence scanning significantly improves the enhancement level of both vessels and parenchyma, thereby enhancing contrast between normal and abnormal tissues and providing information about vascular structures (Fig. 12-1). Methods of contrast injection using lower doses of contrast material or slower rates of injection significantly diminish quality. An infusion-type scan for abdominal imaging is probably the worst method of examination, and is even inferior in some respects to noncontrast scanning. A contrast infusion may permit low attenuation lesions within the liver to become isodense with the mildly enhancing liver parenchyma, whereas if scanning were performed prior to the infusion of contrast these lesions would be apparent. One is also exposing the patient to the risks associated with contrast material while actually diminishing the diagnostic value of the scan. Naturally, contrast injections must be performed with knowledge of a possible prior sensitivity to contrast material and knowledge of satisfactory renal function.

It is also important to blend the capabilities for rapid-sequence scanning with the injection technique selected. If, for example, a very rapid sequence

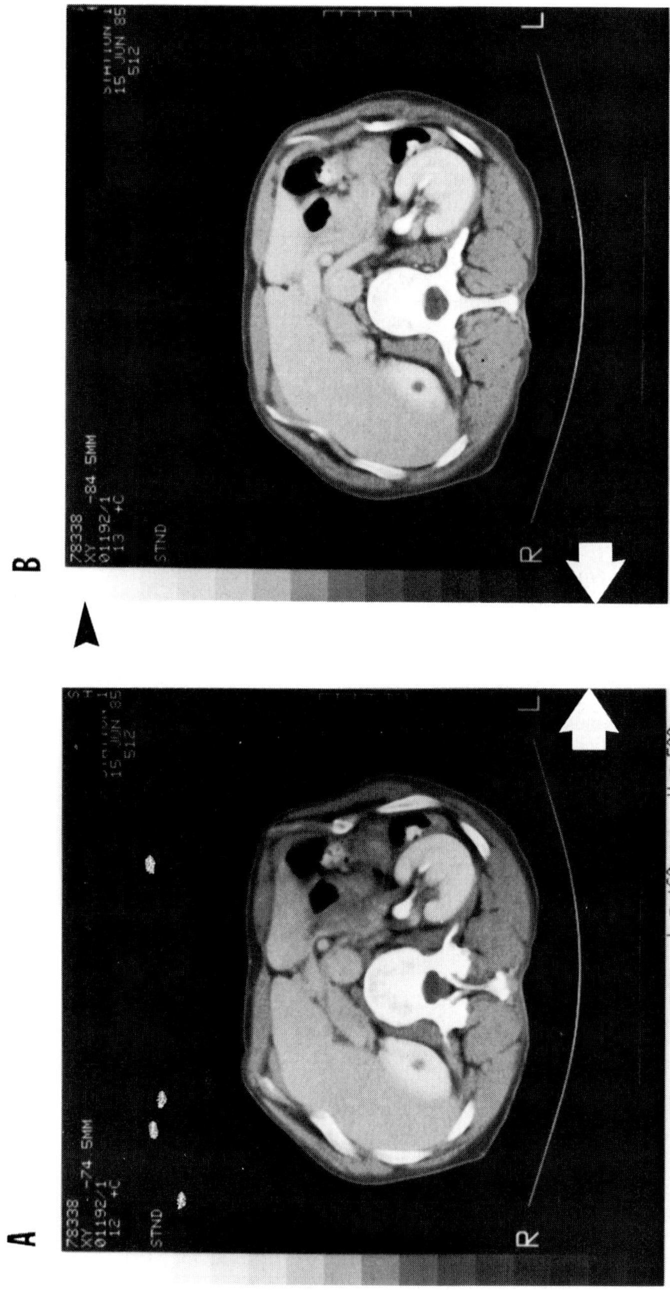

C D

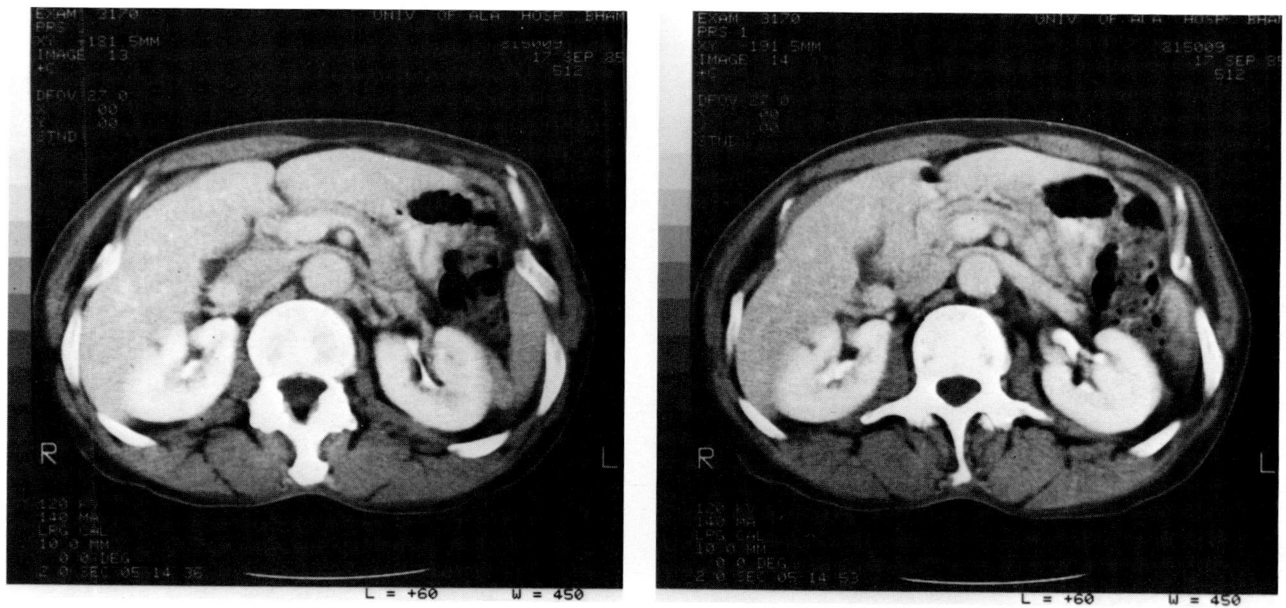

FIG. 12–1. **A**. and **B**. Two images from an examination done on a patient at an outside institution. Several technical problems are present. First, the displayed field-of-view selection is too large, and some wasted space occurs around the body contours. Second, the camera has been adjusted to provide too small a frame on the film. There is a significant white border (arrows) between the images. This decreases the overall frame size and increases the glare between frames. Third, viewing the gray scale reveals that the brightest shade of white (arrowhead) differs slightly from the background film base. It should be adjusted to be identical to the film base. Fourth, contrast material has not been injected optimally, and less than maximum vascular enhancement is obtained. **C**. and **D**. Two comparable images from an examination done on the same patient and the same type of scanner at our institution. The problems have been corrected to provide better image quality.

scan of 10 slices per minute or more is selected, and scanning is begun too soon, then a significant number of slices may be obtained before satisfactory levels of tissue and vessel enhancement are achieved. With slower scanning rates, the same injection time and delay to initiation of scanning may be satisfactory because only one or two slices are obtained before satisfactory levels of enhancement are reached.

We have also found that using more rapid rates of injection of the same volume of contrast material may increase the peak level of tissue enhancement and decrease the time to reach the peak. This may permit a slight reduction in the volume of contrast material used if scanning rates are sufficiently fast.

POOR ATTENTION TO PATIENT SETUP AND COOPERATION

The technologist is responsible for patient positioning and for controlling motion, breathing, and registration from slice to slice. Positioning and other technical factors may be checked by obtaining a preliminary slice.

The patient should be carefully instructed about not moving and about proper techniques for breath holding. We are familiar with one hospital in which patients simply were not instructed to suspend respiration for body scans because the operators felt that the 2-second-scanning time was sufficiently short to avoid motion artifact. This is clearly false, and suspended respiration should be routinely used on any abdominal or chest scan in a cooperative patient.

Even when patients are properly instructed, if the technologist fails to observe whether the patient is adequately holding his or her breath during the initial scan sequence, then an entire examination may be obtained with breathing artifact. A patient who requires an unusually long time to reach the point of breath holding can be reinstructed to do it more quickly, or the interscan delay can be lengthened to compensate.

The technologist should also be careful to remove foreign objects from the scanning field. Whenever possible, the arms should be extended out of the scanning field (Fig. 12-2).

IMPROPER SELECTION OF SCANNING PARAMETERS

Attempts to speed the examination process may be detrimental to the diagnostic quality of the examination. For example, using faster scan speeds or faster reconstruction times than are recommended for the unit may make a potentially diagnostic examination nondiagnostic. Full scans or over-

A

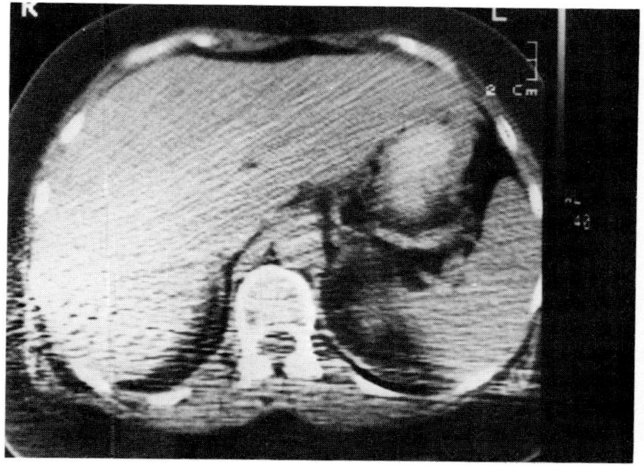

B

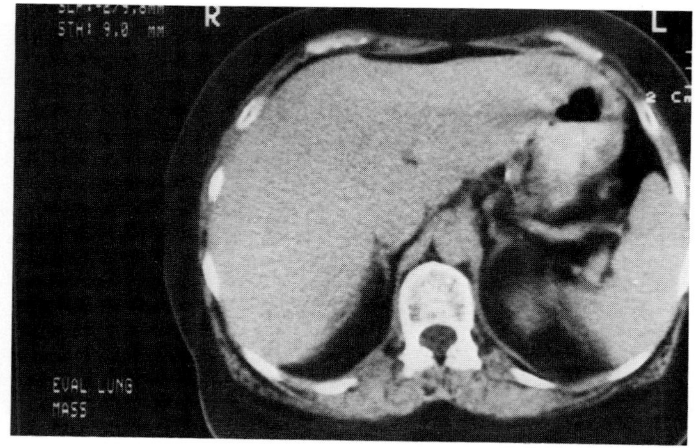

FIG. 12–2. Two consecutive images illustrating the influence of the patient's arms being placed within the scanning aperture. **A**. An uncooperative patient placed his arms at the side, and gross beam hardening and edge gradient artifacts are apparent, as well as the effect of tissue outside the reconstruction circle (out-of-field artifact). Although the arms themselves are not seen, this is a characteristic pattern of artifacts for such an occurrence. **B**. On the next image, the arms have been raised and secured above the head, and image quality is remarkably improved.

A

B

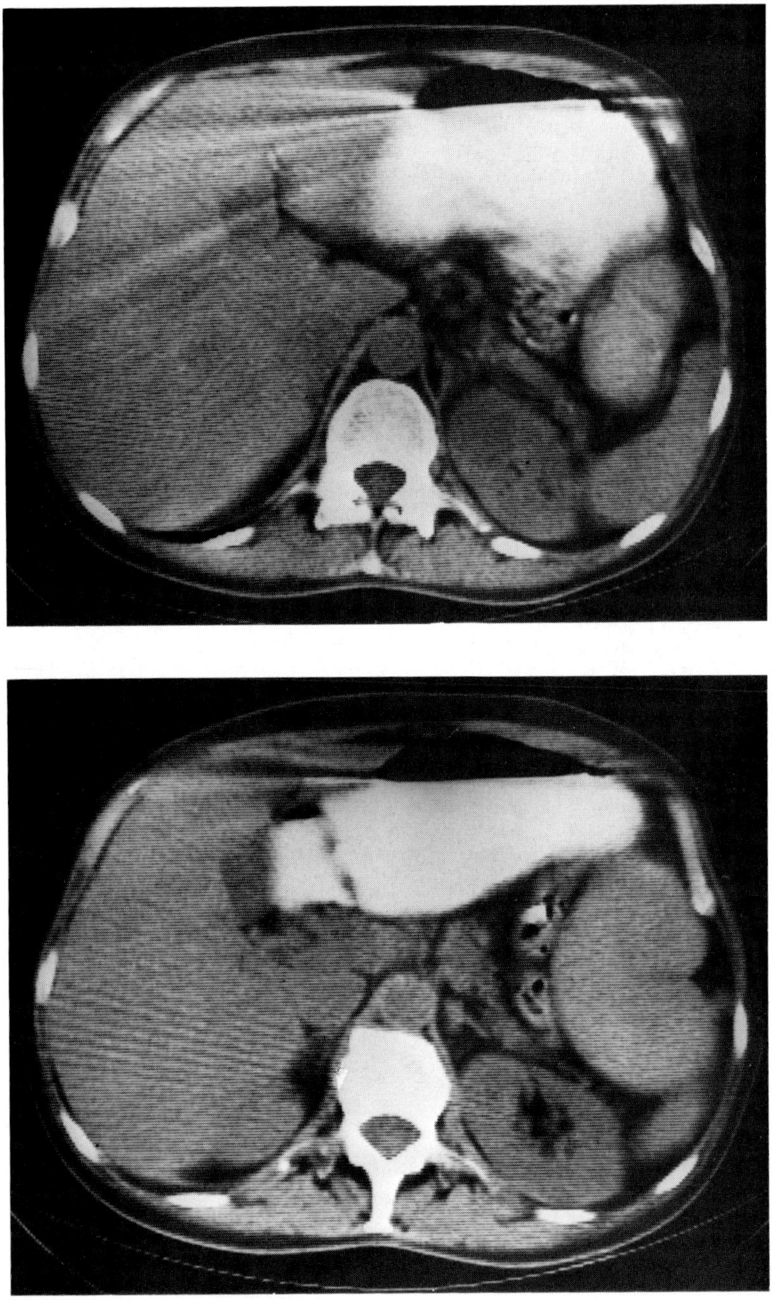

FIG. 12–3. Several images from an examination done on a patient at an outside institution are compared to scans on the same patient done at our institution. **A.** and **B.** Images from the scan done elsewhere demonstrate prominent gastric air-fluid interface artifacts caused by motion, beam hardening, and the edge gradient effect. Intravenous contrast has not been given.

C

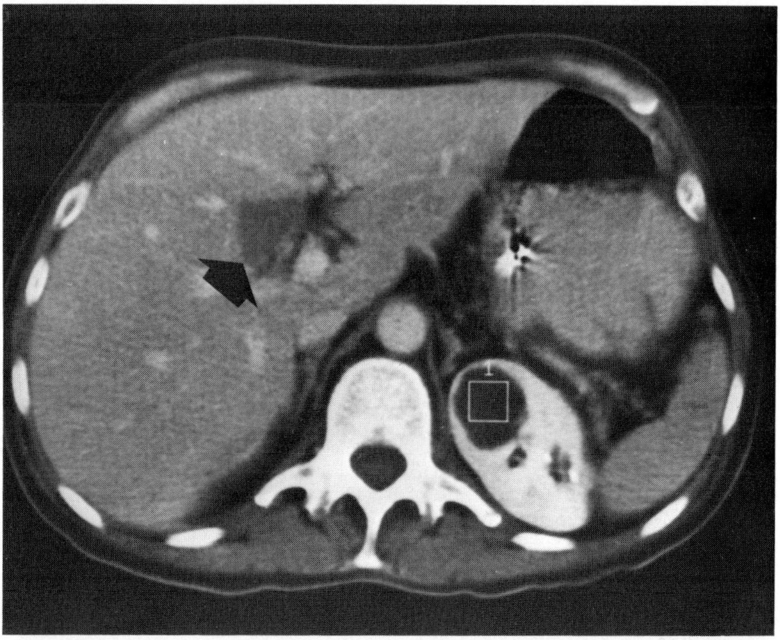

D

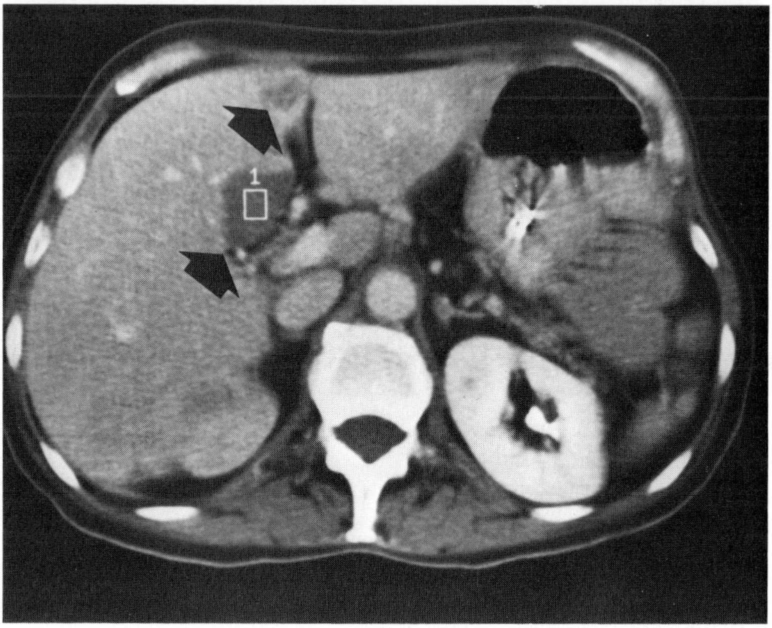

FIG. 12–3. (*cont.*) **C** and **D**. Scan done on the same patient on a newer model scanner at our institution. Use of the newer scanner and intravenous contrast has improved anatomic detail. Also, two low-attenuation lesions (arrows) are now apparent that were not easily detectable on the prior examination. In retrospect, the larger lesion was present on the outside scan. However, because those scans were done with 10-mm collimation at 15-mm intervals rather than at 10-mm intervals, the lesion appeared simply to be a prominent gallbladder neck. On our scan using 10-mm collimation with contiguous slices, this lesion was apparent as a discrete intrahepatic abnormality. The other lesion was detectable because intravenous contrast was used and the gastric air-contrast level did not obscure this region.

scans are recommended for most applications, and the use of fast reconstruction options may diminish contrast resolution or introduce aliasing artifacts.

Whenever attention is directed to a particular area of interest, contiguous slice examination is usually required. We virtually always employ contiguous sections through the upper abdomen rather than alternately scanning and skipping 4-to-10-mm intervals as some facilities do. The use of noncontiguous slices not only decreases the ability to detect small lesions, but also hinders the appreciation of the shape of lesions that are detected and hinders the comparison of sequential examinations because of the likelihood that the same slice registration will not be present on successive studies (Fig. 12-3).

Perhaps the most common single technical error I have observed is the inappropriate selection of the displayed field of view. There seems to be a strong tendency among technologists to select a larger than optimal field of view, which permits the display of the patient's entire body contour. Although in some respects this makes the image more aesthetically pleasing and requires less care in positioning by the technologist, it diminishes perceptibility of detail, as discussed earlier.

Specialized reconstruction filters or algorithms are often useful for neurological and orthopedic applications. Bone detail algorithms can significantly improve the depiction of small fracture framents within the hip or joint discontinuities in the feet, for example.

IMAGE DISPLAY

Even institutions that take great care to achieve good-quality computed tomograms may have difficulties maintaining consistent film quality. The use of the appropriate film size has been discussed in Chapter 10, p. 131. Although one can decrease film costs by placing a greater number of images on a film, I have observed several instances in which small lesions went unnoticed simply because of small image size.

Window width and window level settings are usually easily standardized. As discussed in Chapter 10, p. 123, as the window width narrows, the choice of window level becomes more critical, and inappropriate choice is often a cause of poor image quality. The standards set forth in Part 2 are useful for standard protocol filming by technologists. However, if the radiologist is performing the filming, slightly narrower windows may be desirable. The radiologist is likely to be more sensitive to the need for readjusting the window level and can then take full advantage of the added contrast offered by this narrower window.

Every format camera is subject to drift in contrast and brightness and deterioration with age. Using the techniques of readjusting brightness and contrast (see Chapter 10, p. 128) when film quality deteriorates can literally save months of suffering with poor images. Periodically and frequently cleaning the camera monitor face can also eliminate frustrating artifacts.

Most institutions have some need to create copies of X-ray films. If care is taken to instruct those creating copied films about the need to place the two single emulsions in contact and about the need to properly adjust the copier timer, consistently good copies can be easily obtained.

Although not directly related to the quality of the display, improper performance and use of CT attenuation measurements may be a significant clinical problem. Care must be taken to properly place the ROI cursor in an area free of streak artifact and away from areas that may lead to volume averaging errors. As discussed in Chapter 11, p. 167, even if measurements are done properly, the value of CT attenuation numbers is extremely limited and should be used only as a last resort with conventional scanners to confirm or refute a clinical impresssion.

FAILURE TO RECOGNIZE THE NEED FOR SERVICE

The development of artifacts such as increased noise or subtle rings on third-generation scanners may be insidious. It is useful to keep films on file to use for a baseline comparison of image quality.

Few institutions may recognize more than one or several of the above factors as recurring problems. However, correcting even one of these systematic errors can often lead to a marked improvement in overall examination quality. Figs. 12-1 and 12-3 illustrate examinations done on two patients each on two scanners, and demonstrate how attention to several of these factors can improve examination quality.

MALFUNCTIONS AND ARTIFACTS COMMONLY REQUIRING SERVICE

When a CT scanner is not functioning, the need for service is usually obvious to the operator (although even then an experienced technologist may be knowledgeable enough to restart the system). However, when image quality begins to deteriorate, it is often the radiologist who first identifies the problem. The following are several of the most common technical problems that call for a service engineer's assistance.

Rings on Slices or Lines on Scanograms

Such artifacts are often caused only by improper calibration, but may be caused by malfunctions anywhere in the chain of electronics related to a detector channel (see Chapter 11, p. 147).

Excessive Noise

Poor technique or an obese patient can cause excessive noise, but a worn X-ray tube, malalignment of the tube-detector system, or failure of other electronic components can also. Failure of multiple detector channels in a fourth-generation instrument can increase noise (see Chapter 8, p. 89).

Excessive Aliasing or Streak Artifacts

There are often technique factors involved in aliasing, including the selection of scan techniques with too few views (see Chapter 5, p. 59). However, excessive streak artifacts may also be caused by systematic introduction of high-frequency areas within the CT gantry such as cracks or defects in the patient couch. Malalignment of the tube and detector arrays can also create such artifacts.

Large Bands or Bizarre Patterns Obscuring Part of an Image

Large metallic appliances or retained barium may lead to such artifacts (see Chapter 11, p. 156). However, other causes include electrical tube arcing or abnormal discharge (sometimes called a tube spit) of a faulty X-ray tube, software bugs, or damaged tapes.

We have recently encountered two other mechanical problems that led to severe image artifacts. In one case, improperly functioning slice thickness collimators led to bright rings obscuring the entire image. The collimators were intermittently moving into position during the actual scan, rather than in preparation prior to the scan. In the other instance, a coarse fan pattern of streaks obscured the image (Fig. 12-4). This was eventually traced to a damaged, misshapen reel which takes up the power cable to the X-ray tube as it turns around the gantry. On occasional scans, as the reel reached a specific point, it jarred the tube-detector assembly. Tracing the streaks to the convergent point of origin led to the suspicion that the problem was a mechanical one originating near the tube.

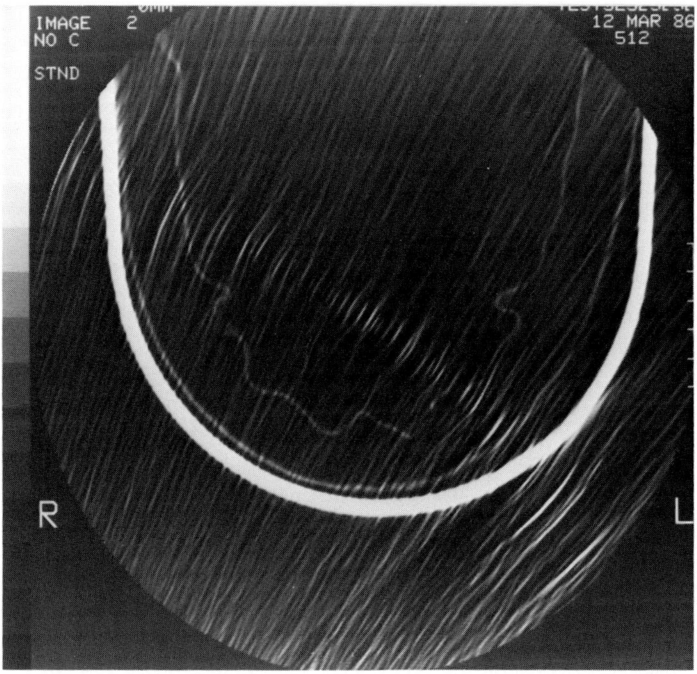

FIG. 12–4. Bizarre, irregular pattern of oblique streaks caused by a mechanical malfunction on a third-generation scanner. These streaks can be roughly traced to a converging point approximately at the level of the X-ray focal spot. This artifact proved to be caused by a mechanical malfunction of the reel that takes up the power cables to the X-ray tube. A deformity in the reel periodically caused a vibration at one point in the rotation cycle on occasional scans and created data discontinuities.

Improper Contrast or Brightness on Film

The most easily corrected problem causing bad films is improper contrast and brightness control settings. The other possible causes include a dirty camera lens or monitor, monitor or shutter malfunction, film fogging, or processing problems including improper temperature settings or replenishment malfunction (see Chapter 10, p. 138).

13

Criteria for Selecting Equipment

This chapter provides guidelines and a checklist for selecting CT equipment and options. Some commonly used sales techniques will be cited with an assessment of their validity. The points discussed will follow the order of the book to this point to facilitate reference back to the original chapters for more in-depth discussions.

Naturally, these guidelines represent the personal opinions and advice of the author. Although the specific recommendations often reflect what is currently available in the marketplace, it is hoped and believed that these standards will be valid for several years. The more specialized software and hardware options are dealt with less thoroughly because they are more likely to change and are better discussed in other texts or by the manufacturers themselves.

One way in which this checklist may be used is to find which specifications the manufacturer chooses *not* to include in the specification sheet. Such information is likely to represent the features that the manufacturer believes relate to the weaknesses of the product.

These guidelines also reflect the assumption that the customer wishes to purchase a full-purpose, top-of-the-line scanner. Many high-quality CT scanners now available cannot meet most of the stringent specifications set forth below, but fully meet the purposes of a small or specialized facility, or one that needs an inexpensive additional scanner. Such units can be obtained at a much lower price with surprisingly little sacrifice in image quality or flexibility. The types of sacrifices that must be made to purchase a lower priced unit include (a) image quality, (b) reconstruction time, (c) system disk memory capacity, (d) maximum scanned field of view size, and/or (e) dynamic scanning capability. One must identify which features are unavailable to determine if this hinders the scanner's usability in its chosen environment.

CT GENERATIONS

There is no clear-cut superiority inherent in either the third- or the fourth-generation design. Image quality, examination flexibility, and consistency depend on numerous design features. I emphasize that some of these observations are conjectural and are based on personal experience and anecdotal observations. The intent of including these speculations is to allow the reader to evaluate these possibilities firsthand when selecting equipment.

First, third-generation scanners appear to have somewhat more difficulty than fourth-generation scanners in maintaining good image quality when the patient is larger than the scanned field of view. Second, fourth-generation scanners appear to have somewhat degraded image quality compared to third-generation units when patient motion is a problem even when the scan time is the same (see Chapter 5, p. 59).

CT generations are discussed in detail in Chapter 2, p. 9.

DETECTORS

Neither the number of detectors, detector composition, nor detector array geometry alone should strongly influence equipment selection. Although gas ionization detectors (xenon) have lower sensitivity, numerous other design features affect overall patient dose and image noise. Currently manufactured third-generation scanners have between 270 and 1,035 detectors, and current fixed-detector scanners have between 1,200 and 2,304 detectors. Modulation transfer function and contrast-detail curves are much more valuable in estimating potential scanner image quality than are specifications of the effective detector aperture. However, even these factors provide an insufficient gauge of image quality, because images are strongly affected by the quality of scatter suppression, beam hardening and scatter corrections, and display systems.

Detectors are discussed in Chapter 2, p. 16.

RADIOGRAPHIC MAGNIFICATION FACTOR

As discussed earlier, the radiographic magnification factor does not refer to the magnification of the image on the monitor, but rather to the tube-object-detector geometry. This factor will relate to but not directly specify the spatial resolution. Again, this factor should not be a significant criterion for selecting equipment, but it is interesting to compare one unit with another produced by the same manufacturer. If the magnification factor is variable, one should also learn how limited the reconstructed field of view becomes when using the higher magnification factors. Lower mA and longer scan times with smaller focal spots must be used in these variable geometry units.

Radiographic magnification is discussed in Chapter 2, p. 17.

CALIBRATION

The calibration procedure may be time consuming with some units. One should learn both the frequency with which calibration is required and the time necessary to perform the standard calibration sequences. For example, with one scanner, about 8 hrs of calibration must follow every X-ray tube replacement. Another manufacturer requires a 2-min calibration sequence every 2 hrs, whereas a third recommends a 2-hr calibration every 2 weeks.

If one attempts to perform a specialized procedure with unusual scan factors, a calibration sequence may be required immediately prior to the examination. It is useful to know how long such a calibration procedure might require. If it is time consuming, it is likely that specialized examinations requiring such calibrations simply would not be done.

Calibration is discussed in Chapter 2, p. 24.

PATIENT TABLE

A rating should be indicated for a maximum weight for a patient. Determine whether the maintenance contract is voided if the scanner is broken by a patient weighing over that limit. Also, the maximum and minimum heights to which a table may move should be specified. This varies greatly and may be a significant ease-of-use factor in a hospital with many patients who are transported by bed or cart.

Patient table characteristics are discussed in Chapter 2, p. 25.

GANTRY

The physical gantry aperture dimensions should be specified. Larger openings with the plane of section further to the front of the gantry generally provide better patient comfort and convenience. A small gantry aperture may limit patient size when the weight limit does not. Gantry openings vary in size from 52 to 85 cm, and maximum scanned field-of-view sizes vary from 40 to 52 cm.

Gantry characteristics are discussed in Chapter 2, p. 28.

SCANOGRAM

The representative quality of scanogram images should be inspected. In general, scanograms from third-generation units are superior to those from fourth-generation units because many more detectors are used for the scanogram in the third-generation unit, and therefore there is a smaller detector-to-detector spacing. The maximum length of the scanogram also varies from scanner to scanner.

Scanograms are discussed in Chapter 3, p. 31.

RADIATION EXPOSURE TO THE PATIENT

Figures provided may be somewhat deceiving. Radiation figures strongly depend on recommended examination techniques. It is useful to evaluate the difference in radiation exposure between standard and high-resolution studies in the same patient. Marked differences may occur in some units because of the geometric methods used to improve resolution.

Radiation exposure is discussed in Chapter 4, p. 39.

FIELD OF VIEW

One should find out the largest displayed field of view available and the flexibility of choices. A state-of-the-art scanner should permit choices of the displayed field of view in small increments and may permit choosing the field of view either by selecting a specific field size or by displaying a cursor box on an image. Centered and off-centered fields should be available.

Field of view is discussed in Chapter 5, pp. 45 and 47.

MATRIX SIZE

A 512×512 matrix choice should be available. Although a somewhat smaller matrix may be acceptable for most applications, we prefer not to use a 256 matrix. Some older scanners used a 512 matrix, but the information was simply interpolated from data reconstructed to a 256 matrix. This should not be the case with modern scanners.

Matrix size is discussed in Chapter 5, p. 49.

SLICE THICKNESS

A modern, top-of-the-line scanner should have at least four thickness choices between 1 and 10 mm. A slice thickness between the 1-to-1.5-mm and 5-to-6-mm ranges, such as 3-to-4.5 mm, has significant clinical applications. Some scanners permit slice thickness changes in increments of 1 mm from 1-to-10, providing the greatest flexibility. However, four slice thickness choices are usually satisfactory. I do not believe that a slice thickness above 10 mm is clinically useful, because significant volume averaging artifacts are introduced by slice thicknesses of about 12-to-13 mm. One scanner selects a slice thickness upper limit of 8 mm, which is satisfactory, if not indeed preferable.

Slice thickness selection is discussed in Chapter 5, p. 53.

SCAN TIME

Since most standard scans will be done with full scans or overscans of 360° or more, scan times corresponding to these should be noted. Short scan times such as 1 sec may be cited, but these may represent half scans and have limited clinical applicability. One must also determine the scan time of the full scan, which is used for the majority of examinations. Therefore, even if short scan times are available with full or overscans, they should not simply be available but be the practical standard for that particular unit.

For reasons already cited, the standard scan time for a third-generation scanner should be for a full scan or an overscan. For a fourth-generation unit, the overscan will be the standard scan time. Several scanners now provide a scan time on the order of 3 sec or better, which is usable for the majority of examinations. This is a reasonable standard against which to judge machines.

Scan time is discussed in Chapter 5, p. 59.

SAMPLES AND VIEWS

A sufficient number of views and samples is required to minimize the introduction of fine artifactual streaks throughout an image. A rough minimum is 400 views. Good image quality is created with the 600 to 1,200 views or samples used in most newer scanners. Another interesting figure is the number of individual detector readings (data values) used to create an image. This varies from about 300,000 to over 8,000,000! This value depends on the scanner and selection of scan factors, but is again only one of the many factors that affect image quality. This value also helps to account for the marked difference in reconstruction times among different scanners.

Samples and views are discussed in Chapter 5, p. 59.

DYNAMIC SCANNING

The use of dynamic scanning is strongly advised, and close attention to specifications for dynamic scanning is recommended. Features to consider include the number of scans possible per minute, the interscan delay, the potential number of scans in a dynamic sequence, and X-ray tube heat limits. One should be able to determine whether mA settings must be decreased significantly to achieve a standard dynamic series.

Most incremented dynamic scans can be performed with a minimum of about 15 slices. The mAs should have to be lowered to no less than about one-half to two-thirds of the standard recommended mAs to achieve a satisfactory 15-scan dynamic sequence.

Although the above is a minimum requirement, the ability to perform a greater number of scans at a higher mAs is preferable. One should also be aware of whether the number of scans in a dynamic sequence will be limited by the computer's ability to retain the raw data. Because scans are obtained so rapidly, the information must be stored as raw data during the performance of the dynamic scan and can only be reconstructed afterward. For example, if the computer can accumulate only 10 or 15 scans before having to stop to reconstruct an image, this will seriously hamper the use of dynamic scanning. This specification may vary widely even in modern scanners. Different scanners or scanner options offer limits of 10, 25, or over 60 dynamic scans before memory is saturated.

A 3-sec interscan delay for an incremented dynamic scan is a liberal standard that most modern scanners should meet. This would permit as many as 12 scans per min, which is usually faster than necessary or even desirable. One may be able to achieve higher mA settings by increasing the interscan delay, and one will achieve better patient cooperation because of the ability to breathe between scans.

Dynamic scanning is discussed in Chapter 6.

RECONSTRUCTION FILTERS

One should become familiar with the flexibility of choices for reconstruction algorithms or filters. A minimum of two choices should be available, one for high-resolution bone detail and one for standard detail.

Reconstruction filters are discussed in Chapter 7, p. 79.

TARGETED RECONSTRUCTIONS

Targeted reconstructions should be available at a variety of choices of fields of view and centering. They should also be able to be done as the first method of reconstructing the raw data or as a secondary choice subsequent to an initial standard reconstruction.

Targeted reconstructions are discussed in Chapter 7, p. 81.

RECONSTRUCTION SPEED

Reconstruction speed is the single most important factor limiting "throughput," or the number of examinations that can be done in a specific period of time. However, fast reconstruction speed is important not only to those with busy schedules. Fast reconstruction can facilitate immediate review of examinations to determine if repeat scans or further maneuvers are required for the best diagnosis.

One should learn the reconstruction times of scanners being considered for purchase. The best value to compare is the reconstruction time for an image fully using the data from a full or overscan. Faster reconstructions may be available at the sacrifice of image quality for any given unit because averaging and approximation programs may be used. Wide ranges of reconstruction speeds are available in the industry. As long as the full scan data are used and the other criteria discussed here (such as the number of data points contributing to the image) are fulfilled, faster is clearly better when comparing scanners. Not only does faster reconstruction speed increase the number of examinations that can be done in a period of time, but it improves the smooth functioning of patient set up and filming.

Patient filming is facilitated with fast-reconstruction scanners because filming may proceed immediately as the scans are done and reconstructed. When reconstruction time creates a computer backlog, filming may become more disorderly and haphazard. Placing the next patient in the scanner may be delayed while reconstruction is completed. An acceptable value for reconstruction speed is very subjective. However, it is my opinion that reconstruction speeds much longer than about 30 sec may significantly hamper examination efficiency.

Reconstruction speed is discussed in Chapter 7, p. 85.

IMAGE QUALITY

The usefulness of a scanner is closely related to the quality of the images it produces. Improved diagnostic accuracy and confidence lead to increased utilization. Unfortunately, image quality is one of the most difficult features of a scanner to assess. I believe that the most important test of a scanner is its ability to produce images of *consistently* high quality. Factors to evaluate when inspecting images include the sharpness of edges and the overall level of noise. However, one should appreciate that these two factors will be inversely related. That is, for any given unit, sharpness may be improved at the sacrifice of increased noise, and vice versa.

When viewing individual images, specific artifacts should be searched for. These include the effect of bones such as ribs creating areas of altered density, the effect of air-contrast levels such as occur in the stomach, the presence of rings, the bone-brain interface, the effect of surgical clips, and the effect of bowel motion.

Other important criteria for evaluating a scanner are its performance under adverse circumstances and when operating at the limits of its capabilities. Such adverse circumstances include (a) pediatric scanning (because of the fine detail required and patient motion), (b) uncooperative (moving and breathing) patients, (c) obese patients (to test the severity of out-of-field artifacts and quantum noise), (d) chest scans (because of cardiac motion), and (e) scans through shoulders or hips (to test the severity of beam hardening and scatter artifacts, and dynamic range limitation effects). Scanners operate at the limits of their performance with (a) thin sections through low-contrast areas, (b) dynamic scanning, (c) bone detail algorithm reconstructions, and (d) scans requiring high detail at the periphery of the scanned field of view.

One should ask not only to inspect individual images, but also to view entire examinations. Although all manufacturers can produce images of extremely high quality in certain circumstances, some fail to provide a high level of consistency from image to image.

Image quality is discussed in Chapter 8, p. 89.

BASIC AND COMMON PROGRAM FEATURES

Priority reconstruction is an important feature in scanners with longer reconstruction times. The ability to select specific slices for early reconstruction to determine if the area of interest has been thoroughly scanned will significantly shorten examination time in many cases. However, when reconstruction times are short, priority reconstruction is not necessary because all slices are completed quickly and may be reviewed immediately.

The speed with which an image is painted on the screen and can be recalled from computer memory significantly affects the filming process, which is highly labor intensive with most manual cameras. Long paint times on the order of 7-to-10 sec may add several minutes to filming any examination. It may also make reviewing scans at the console so frustratingly slow that it is not done when it might be advantageous to do so.

Window level controls may also contribute to how user friendly a console is, but taken alone should probably not be a significant factor influencing a purchase decision.

All scanners have methods for making linear and attenuation measurements. However, some systems are considerably easier to use than others.

Many institutions heavily utilize reformatting capabilities, whereas others do not use reformatting at all. If reformatting is to be used, the method implemented may materially affect the usability of the system. A cumbersome program will not be properly utilized in day-to-day practice.

Methods for displaying multiple images on a single screen may be important where examinations with large numbers of slices are done. In our own institution, this fairly simple software feature has significantly influenced which scanner is selected for certain types of examinations.

Basic and common program features are discussed in Chapter 9, pp. 105, 111.

SPECIAL PROGRAM FEATURES

The availability and nature of specialized hardware and software features are local considerations. Specialized programs include three-dimensional reformatting, bone densitometry, dual-energy scanning, gated cardiac imaging, dynamic scan segmentation, xenon blood flow imaging, radiation therapy treatment planning, stereotactic biopsy, and correlative annotation of scanograms from CT slices. If one wishes to maximize use of a scanner, certain of these specialized applications can account for a significant number of procedures. The availability and features of these specialized programs continue to evolve.

Special program features are discussed in Chapter 9, p. 113.

CAMERAS

Filming is a critical link in the diagnostic process because films are the primary method of diagnosis in most institutions. Features to evaluate include whether multiple formats are available, and the available image size. We prefer a format that requires no more than 12 images on a 14 × 17 film or 6 images on an 11 × 14 film. We do not use 8 × 10 inch film. Unfortunately, scanners offering a rectangular format image may use a standard 15-on-1 format on a 14 × 17 film. This diminishes the perceptibility of detail by making images small, and a prospective purchaser must determine whether this is an acceptable sacrifice.

A camera option worth considering is bulk or auto loading, in which films are automatically fed into the camera rather than individually loaded by cassette. Because filming requires a great deal of technologist or physician time, the use of a bulk-loaded system can significantly decrease personnel overtime or even eliminate the need for a part- or full-time position in a busy institution.

Camera systems are now also available that film and process automatically. In such systems, a standard filming protocol can be programmed, and filming and possibly even film processing proceed without further user interaction. Laser cameras are another new technology that provides improved image quality. Such cameras can also be combined with automated filming and processing. These systems are not yet fully developed at this writing and should be thoroughly evaluated before purchase, although they are promising.

Camera systems are discussed in Chapter 10, p. 134.

IMAGE STORAGE

Flexibility of information storage can have a significant effect on efficient operations. If too few images are storable on the magnetic disk from which images may be immediately retrieved, this can seriously hamper the scanning process, because if filming cannot proceed rapidly enough, one may have to complete filming an examination so that the information is deleted before another patient can be scanned. Also, one wishes to retain the flexibility to reload cases on the disk for later review.

Laser optical disks on which thousands of images may be stored are now becoming available for some model scanners, although once written to the disk these images cannot be erased nor can the disk be reused. Such options should become widely available as technology improves.

Also, especially if dynamic scanning is to be done routinely, a sufficient number of images should be savable in raw data form. This permits the rapid accumulation of slices sufficient to complete an examination prior to the need for reconstruction. Because most abdominal examinations require about 30 slices or more, this may be a reasonable minimum requirement.

Image storage is discussed in Chapter 10, p. 141.

SERVICE SUPPORT AND RELIABILITY

The availability of prompt and good-quality service is essential. The mention of this factor late in this chapter should not be construed as an implication that it is of secondary importance. One should inquire about the quality of service available to other CT users in your area using the types of equipment being considered.

Personal experience has taught that the availability of a knowledgeable service engineer can make the difference between repairing a nonfunctioning scanner literally in a matter of minutes versus days. Repeated periods of lengthy downtime are sometimes attributable to a service engineer's failure to diagnose a problem completely even though he or she may be able to repair it for partial or intermittent operation. Lengthy periods of downtime are often inappropriately attributed to poor scanner design rather than inadequate service. However, faulty designs certainly can also account for repeated scanner failures.

All manufacturers claim high reliability, but some are indeed more reliable than others. It is helpful to ask people who currently use scanners you are considering for purchase about reliability. However, it may not be satisfactory to ask only one or two users, because people can get "lemons," older models may have more problems than the newer ones, and reliability may be difficult to separate from the quality of service. You may wish to ask the local sales representative to find several users in your service district who already have one of the models being considered for purchase.

Service and reliability considerations are discussed in Chapter 13.

SITE CONSTRUCTION

Although not specifically dealt with in this book, two issues regarding site construction are of paramount importance and worth paying personal attention to during planning for installation. These items are air conditioning capacity and power supply.

Major chronic difficulties may be caused by inadequate air conditioning capacity. Most CT scanners' computers produce a great deal of heat and are very sensitive to elevated temperatures. Problems caused by overheating are often very difficult to diagnose and correct. If air conditioning capacity is well planned in advance, these problems should be entirely avoidable. Some newer scanners claim satisfactory operation at room temperature.

The complicated components of the CT system, including the computers and tubes, also require both an adequate amount and a satisfactory stability of the power supply. In hospitals in which power supplies are interconnected or poorly shielded, fluctuations in voltage may cause serious system malfunction or damage. Adequate power supplies with voltage regulation should be ensured before scanner installation.

It is hoped that, with the above checklist in hand and a healthy dose of skepticism regarding manufacturers' claims, equipment selections can be made without later regrets.

Part 2
Practical CT Techniques

14

General Examination Techniques

PREPARING TO SCAN

Patient Preparation

Abdominal

Patients to be scanned in the morning should have nothing to eat or drink after midnight the night before the examination except for important oral medications. If the scan is to be done in the afternoon, the patient may have a clear liquid breakfast to avoid dehydration, which may accentuate the toxic effects of contrast material. However, most patients receive a large volume of oral contrast material, which helps to rehydrate the patient. When possible, diabetic patients should be scanned early in the morning so that their diet and insulin schedules are minimally disrupted. One should consider withholding or delaying insulin injections if meals are withheld.

The reasons to avoid full meals prior to scanning are (a) to minimize vomiting and potential aspiration if patients are to receive intravenous contrast injections, (b) to make it easier for the patient to consume the oral contrast material, (c) to avoid diagnostic confusion among intragastric masses, recently ingested food, and retained food due to poor gastric emptying, and (d) to decrease the chances of rapid bladder filling leading to patient discomfort during scanning.

Pelvis

In addition to the above, 300 ml of oral contrast material may be administered 2 to 3 hr prior to scanning or the night before scanning to fill the colon.

Neck, Thorax, and Extremities

No preparation is required for these examinations if no intravenous contrast is to be given. However, if intravenous contrast is injected, it is wise to limit the patient to liquid meals to minimize vomiting and aspiration.

It is preferable not to scan both the chest and the abdomen, the chest and the pelvis, or the neck and the abdomen or pelvis on the same day when intravenous contrast is to be used, because each examination is optimized by using the proper volume of contrast material and timing of scanning. However, for medical urgency or patient convenience, exceptions are frequently made to this policy. Newer scanners with rapid scanning rates may also permit scanning multiple body regions within a period of significant enhancement. However, programming such studies may be complex, and satisfactorily high levels of enhancement may not be maintained throughout the entire scan. Therefore, we do not currently recommend it.

Nonvascular Contrast Materials

Oral Contrast

We prefer water-soluble agents such as Gastrografin (Winthrop), Gastroview (Mallinckrodt, Inc.), and Hypaque (Squibb) for oral contrast. Of these, we prefer the liquids because they are easier to mix than the powdered forms. Preflavored agents are available, or flavoring may be added to soften the bad taste of these agents. Alternative oral contrast preparations use barium and are available as E-Z-CAT (E-Z-EM Company, Inc.) or a similar preparation named TomoCat (Lafayette Pharmacal). However, our previous experience with TomoCat suggested that it is inferior to E-Z-CAT because the barium does not consistently remain in suspension. We prefer the water-soluble preparations because they seem to lead to better bowel filling and do not settle out of suspension. Other centers use mixtures of water-soluble and barium agents, or administer water-soluble agents followed by barium. There does not appear to be sufficient scientific evidence to determine the best of any of these approaches.

Adequate bowel opacification is essential for accurately interpreting CT examinations of the abdomen. Yet sufficient bowel filling is useful only if the correct concentration of oral contrast material is given. The optimal density of oral contrast preparations is much less than that used for conventional radiography. For CT, Gastrografin should be diluted to an approximately 3% solution by mixing 3 ml of Gastrografin in 100 ml of water or 9 to 10 ml in 300 ml of water. E-Z-CAT containers include instructions for proper dilution.

The density of contrast material should be monitored. Excessive density will create streak artifacts. Insufficient density leads to inadequate bowel opacification and potential misinterpretation of bowel loops as masses and vice versa.

Other errors that may occur in administering oral contrast include inadequate stirring or mixing and administering inadequate quantities to the patient. Technologists or aides may estimate rather than measure the quantities of contrast to add to water. Thus, periodic supervision is helpful.

To be effective, contrast must be given at the proper time. When given too soon, contrast will be found only in the distal bowel. If given too late, the contrast may not have the opportunity to complete bowel transit. When scanning the abdomen, a total of 300 to 1,000 ml of contrast material should be given, depending on the reasons for and the extent of the examination. A first dose of 300 to 500 ml may be given 30 to 60 min prior to routine abdominal scanning. A second volume of approximately 300 to 500 ml may be given just before scanning because this leads to better gastric filling, which minimizes false interpretations of abnormal gastric wall thickness. An alternative to a final cup of contrast immediately before scanning has been advocated by the radiologists at New York University Medical Center. They administer a cup of contrast mixed with a packet of E-Z-Gas granules (E-Z-EM Company, Inc.). This distends the stomach better than liquid contrast alone and has led to the detection of gastric tumors that would otherwise have been missed. They also administer 0.1 mg glucagon i.v. with the intravenous contrast injection, to inhibit gastric peristalsis caused by the rapid gastric distention.

One may wish to give extra oral contrast after scanning has begun if there is some confusion about the nature of a structure. The timing and volume of contrast administration will vary depending upon the area studied. For example, a smaller volume of oral contrast may be given if the area of interest is the pancreas, since only the stomach, duodenum, and proximal jejunum need to be opacified. If the lower abdomen and pelvis are to be studied, a larger volume is needed. Air-contrast levels in the stomach may create streak artifacts within the adjacent liver, but despite this limitation we do not usually withhold oral contrast for this reason alone. If patients are unable to ingest oral contrast, it may be injected through a nasogastric tube. More detailed descriptions of oral contrast administration are presented in Chapter 15.

Colon

Enemas of about 300 to 500 ml should be given whenever scanning the pelvis. This is usually sufficient to opacify the rectosigmoid and portions of the descending colon. We also instill 10 to 15 puffs of air through the type of pump used for air-contrast enemas. The amount of air depends on patient tolerance, and enemas should not be given when there are medical contraindications. Enemas are not usually helpful when scanning only the abdomen.

It is helpful to have the patient begin to drink contrast material 1 to 2 hr before scanning or the night before scanning in patients who are undergoing pelvic CT. This allows opacification of the colon without using enemas.

However, as a practical routine, we usually give oral contrast on the patient's first arrival in the CT area and begin scanning about 45 to 60 min later.

Bladder

For most studies, the patient should be instructed to void before the start of the examination. However, urine may act as a natural contrast agent to outline bladder lesions, and masses are often better defined when the bladder is distended rather than collapsed. Thus, if one intends to scan the pelvis at the beginning of an examination, one may wish not to have the patient void before intravenous contrast has induced a diuresis. Alternatively, when scanning the pelvis alone with particular attention to the bladder, about 30 ml of intravenous contrast may be injected 5 to 10 min before scanning to induce a contrast diuresis.

SCANNING

Scanogram

Each current manufacturer offers a scanogram feature (see Chapter 3). This provides an image analogous to a plain radiograph for determining the limits of the region to be scanned. These views may be obtained in lateral, frontal, and oblique projections, and frontal views are used routinely in body scanning.

Before selecting the levels of the axial slices to be performed, patient positioning should be evaluated. Lack of centering or rotation may be evident. Metallic objects visible on the scanogram should be removed from the scan field. These include EKG wires, gown snaps, belts, and the like. When practical, nasogastric tubes should be withdrawn to the midesophagus for abdominal scans. If dense barium is present at the area of interest, the scan should be postponed unless it is medically urgent. Surgical clips will create artifacts but are not a contraindication to scanning.

Respiration

Communicating with the patient is one of the most important prerequisites to obtaining a satisfactory study. This is particularly important if rapid-sequence scanning is used, because cooperation with breathing instructions is more difficult than for scans done at a routine rate. The physician performing the injection or the technologist should indicate the following to the patient:

1. The length of time for breath holding (2 to 10 sec per scan).
2. The need to avoid shifting or moving the body during scanning and why this is important.
3. The breath for each scan should be the same depth.
4. Relaxed expiration is preferred for abdominal scans. Patients should be told not to *blow* their breath out forcefully, but to *let* it out. The patient should be told that the reason for this breathing technique is to find the most reproducible point in the breathing cycle. One may even demonstrate this form of breathing to the patient. Deep inspiration is preferred for most chest scans to expand the lungs and mediastinum. If doing both a chest and an abdominal scan on the same day, the operator must appreciate that they are done with different breathing instructions. Therefore, the positions of organs will differ, and scan levels must be prescribed from separate scanograms.
5. The patient should be told that the technologist can be heard through the intercom to instruct the patient about breathing.

If rapid-sequence (dynamic) scanning is to be done, the following additional points should be discussed:

1. Before breath holding, the technologist may have the patient take several deep breaths to hyperventilate to improve breath holding ability during scanning.
2. The patient should be told that the scans will occur in rapid sequence with only a short time to breathe between scans.
3. If the patient has difficulty holding the breath in the midst of a series, he or she should be told to take slow, shallow breaths rather than fast or deep breaths.
4. The number of scans or the length of the sequence should be mentioned.
5. The patient should be informed that the contrast material may cause a feeling of warmth or flushing and has a metallic taste.

With faster scan rates, some centers do two or three scans per breathhold. We obtain more consistent results with one scan per breathhold.

Particularly with an anxious or otherwise difficult patient, it may be advisable to rehearse a sequence before actually scanning. Less-anxious patients vomit less frequently during contrast injections.

Discretion should be used with difficult patients. One may wish to do scans in inspiration rather than expiration if patients are short of breath. With anxious patients it may be better to perform scans during quiet respirations rather than risk agitating the patient by insisting on breath holding.

Once scanning begins, the technologist should closely observe breathing patterns and modify the breathing technique and timing if necessary. It is preferable to extend the interscan delay slightly on a dynamic scan rather than have image quality seriously degraded.

One cannot overemphasize the importance of discussing these points with the patient. It provides reassurance and a better understanding of what difficulties might be encountered during scanning.

Patient Positioning

It has been reported that scanning patients in the prone position may decrease bowel motion artifacts because of displacement and compression of bowel gas. Scanning in the decubitus or prone position may also be helpful for other reasons in patients with confusing findings. For example, scanning in the right decubitus position after the patient ingests extra oral contrast may lead to better opacification of the duodenum and better definition of the pancreatic head than may be available from supine scanning. Decubitus and prone scanning may be helpful to determine whether pleural fluid collections are free or loculated and may uncover underlying parenchymal abnormalities. However, we prefer not to move the patient unless absolutely necessary because such maneuvers may greatly lengthen examination time.

SCANNING WITH VASCULAR CONTRAST

Inserting the Intravenous Catheter

Whenever possible, an 18 to 21 gauge Angiocath, Jelco, or comparable short, plastic catheter is inserted in a forearm or antecubital vein for contrast. The antecubital or medial (basilic) vein is preferred because the lateral vein may lead into a cephalic vein, which tends to occlude when the arms are raised. Good blood return should be confirmed before beginning a rapid hand or power injection.

Plastic-sheathed needle-catheter combinations have several advantages over 19 or 21 gauge "scalp veins." The large bore of the 18 gauge catheter allows easy hand injection of 60% contrast media up to a rate of about 6 ml/sec. An advantage of the catheter is that the antecubital vein may be used and there is a lower risk of infiltration or extravasation even with arm bending, provided the catheter is well seated and taped. We currently use 60% contrast material (about 30% iodine) by weight exclusively. Some centers use only meglumine salts because of the observation that they cause less pain than sodium salts when extravasated subcutaneously. They may also cause slightly fewer systemic side effects. However, with careful technique, significant extravasation should not occur, and the differing incidence of side effects is difficult to confirm. Newer nonionic and hyposmolar contrast agents may cause somewhat fewer contrast reactions, but evidence is still inconclusive and the agents are many times more expensive.

The person performing the injection must closely monitor the injection site. Injection should cease immediately upon any indication of a problem such as palpable extravasation or localized pain. **The person injecting must always observe and feel the site of the catheter tip within the vein (not the insertion point of the needle) during the first few seconds of the injection.** There is virtually no chance for a significant extravasation if this is done. The person injecting is not exposed to any radiation during this observation period because one can stop observing the site before scanning begins.

Power injectors have recently been designed for use in CT. We now prefer the use of these injectors over hand injections because of the consistent reproducibility of enhancement. Observing the injection site is even more critical because of the large volumes of contrast that may extravasate. The operator may stand with one hand on the injection site to palpate for extravasation and the other hand on the injector disarming button ready to cease injection promptly upon detecting a problem. Lawsuits have resulted from failure to follow this procedure because it is unfailingly evident to an alert patient that major extravasations are not supposed to happen.

Rationale

The reason for intravenous contrast injection is to opacify the blood vessels, the organs, and the surrounding structures and increase contrast between normal parenchyma and intraparenchymal lesions. By improving image contrast, contrast media help to define organ boundaries and to minimize the effects of streak artifacts. Thus, intravenous contrast improves the sensitivity and specificity of diagnoses provided that the contrast material is not so dense that it creates artifacts.

Injection Techniques

The advantages of contrast material have been amply demonstrated in the literature for numerous body regions. Nevertheless, contrast administration for certain examinations such as the chest is somewhat controversial. If a patient has an increased risk for contrast toxicity, contrast should be used only when the diagnosis is uncertain after precontrast scans. However, this approach entails a thorough review of all scans before releasing the patient and requires that some patients be scanned with and without contrast, thus increasing examination time and radiation exposure.

We perform most body scans only with contrast enhancement because it improves our diagnostic confidence and accuracy. Some types of examinations are done before contrast only, and others are done both before and after contrast injections. Precontrast scans help to detect acute hemorrhage or calcifications. Pre- and postcontrast scans are used to maximize sensitivity to lesions that may become isodense with surrounding tissue after contrast administration. A technique of delayed scanning is also useful to study some hepatic lesions. About 4 to 6 hr after a large dose of intravenous contrast, the liver becomes mildly enhanced from excretion, causing lesions to stand out as negative defects.

Dynamic Scanning Versus Drip Infusion

To maximize the effect of intravenous contrast, it should be given at a high dose, and scans should be done in rapid succession (dynamically). This takes advantage of the phase of maximal opacification of both vessels and parenchyma. It leads to the best definition of arterial and venous vascularity of neoplasms and to the least likelihood of lesions becoming isodense because of slow accumulation of contrast material within them. Theoretically, the best examination is obtained when scanning is completed before significant interstitial diffusion of contrast media, which occurs within about 2 to 4 min after beginning the injection.

Rapid-sequence scanning requires some compromises. Because of tube heat loading limits, one may not be able to perform a rapid-sequence scan and still obtain a tube output that provides satisfactory image quality. As the tube output or mA setting is decreased, graininess or noise is introduced into the image. Also, such dynamic sequences put stress on the X-ray tube, which may lead to earlier tube failure. One must pay attention to detail, because if one factor is programmed improperly it will affect an entire sequence of scans. For example, the technologist may inadvertently program the wrong direction for table movement, leading to a dynamic scan upward from the diaphragm when a liver scan was actually intended.

If nondynamic scanning suffices, such as for retroperitoneal nodal surveys, contrast may be administered as a loading dose of 30 to 50 ml of 60% solution followed by a rapid drip of up to 300 ml of a 30% solution or of up to 150 ml of a 60% solution, depending upon body size and renal function. **However, there is no diagnostic advantage to using a drip infusion whether dynamic scanning is used or not.** The only minor advantage is that there is no need for someone to be present in the room to perform the injection during scanning or start the injector. Drip infusions are significantly more difficult to monitor. One may complete an entire scan sequence only to find that the infusion was so slow that only a small percentage of the contrast entered the vein, or that because the patient changed the position of his or her arm the drip stopped. Under these circumstances, the advantages of contrast material are eliminated although the patient is still exposed to the risk of injection. Furthermore, in many cases, diagnostic quality is actually diminished by drip infusion because of the tendency of parenchymal lesions to become isodense with surrounding tissue. **Because of this, a drip infusion is the worst way to examine the liver, being inferior even to a noncontrast technique.** Yet this remains a common technique for CT examination. Therefore, we never use a gravity drip infusion.

When hand injections are done for nondynamic scans, the selected volume of contrast material should be injected over a period of 2 min or more. **Whenever possible, hand or power injections should be used for both dynamic and nondynamic scans.** One possibly acceptable alternative is the use of a pressurized drip infusion in which air is instilled within the bottle to speed the drip rate. However, one must inject less air than the original volume of fluid in the bottle to avoid air embolism.

General Dynamic Scanning Techniques

Choice of a dynamic scanning method depends on the purpose of the scan and the limitations of the particular CT unit. Each of our scanners has a different capacity for dynamic (rapid-sequence) scanning. Newer model scanners often permit routine scanning at a rate of about 3 to 4 scans per min. The dynamic scanning program may permit over 12 scans per min. For most applications, about 8 to 10 scans per min is optimal. To perform a rapid-sequence scan, a dynamic scanning program separate from the routine program may be used. Other scanners may allow up to about 6 scans per min in a nondynamic mode until tube cooling delays are encountered. Special dynamic scanning programs may provide more rapid repetition rates but may not be practical because of tube loading limits.

There are two basic types of dynamic scanning: rapid sequential scanning with table incrementation between each scan (survey or incremental dynamic scanning) and rapid sequential scanning at a single level (single-level dynamic scanning).

Survey Dynamic Scans

Survey dynamic scans are used for routine examinations. This technique surveys a body region or organ during a period of maximum vascular and parenchymal enhancement. In most abdominal studies for liver, pancreas, or kidneys we usually perform a dynamic sequence of contiguous dynamic slices from the diaphragm to below the liver, pancreas, or kidneys. This is followed by nondynamic, noncontiguous (interval of 18 to 20 mm) slices to the iliac crest. The length of the dynamic portion of the examination depends on the scanner's capabilities. Specialized thin-section techniques are discussed below.

Both the scanogram and preliminary CT slices may be used for localizing organs. The liver is usually well seen on the scanogram; however, preliminary slices may be required to determine the upper and lower limits of the kidneys and the pancreas. A plane in the midbody of the first lumbar vertebral segment almost invariably shows some pancreatic parenchyma, but for thin-section studies a preliminary precontrast series of scans from near the diaphragm to below the pancreas should be done so that the scan limits can be determined prior to contrast injection. These preliminary precontrast slices are valuable not only to locate the organ, but also to evaluate patient positioning, cooperation, and technique settings.

Single-sequence Survey Scan

If the superior and inferior limits of the region or a lesion to be studied are well established by the preliminary scanogram, by preliminary precontrast CT images, or by prior CT examinations, a single scan sequence may be established. The choice of slice thickness and other scan factors depends upon the area to be examined. One usually wishes to use the highest resolution technique available, understanding that compromises are necessary between tube heat loading and the number of scans in a sequence. For example, with pancreatic scans, contiguous 3- to 6-mm sections may be used for optimal detection of ducts and small lesions. However, such optimum resolution factors are not usually appropriate for encompassing the liver, which might require 30 or more 5-mm sections. Sections 9 to 10 mm thick are used instead, so that scans can be completed during the phase of maximum contrast enhancement. However, with some of the newer scanners, a large number of scans may be completed in less than 10 min.

The smallest displayed field of view should be used that is compatible with the patient's size. If too small a field of view is selected, the patient's external contours will fall outside the field of view (reconstruction circle), and artifacts may degrade the image. If too large a field of view is selected, the image will be too small and more difficult to interpret. The proper field of view displays the smallest reasonable volume of tissue per pixel (picture element) and thus provides the highest potential spatial detail. However, you should also recall the difference between the scanned field of view and the reconstructed field of view (see Chapter 5, p. 47).

The highest tube output or mA setting allowable for a complete scan sequence should be chosen. Output may be decreased somewhat to permit a longer scanning sequence if the number of scans is limited by tube heat capacity. However, if the choice of mAs is too low, images may contain objectionable quantum noise or be "photon poor." There is virtually always a need to perform further scans to finish scanning a body region after an incremental dynamic sequence is completed. The two most important points to consider are: (a) One may increase the mAs for the nondynamic sequence because there is more time between scans for the tube to cool, and (b) the standard sequence should be programmed and performed as quickly as possible to take advantage of persisting contrast enhancement.

Contrast Dose and Timing

For a single scan sequence, 100 to 180 ml of 60% iodinated contrast medium may be given. We usually give up to 150 ml for people weighing about 150 lb or more. For adults under 150 lb we give about 1 ml/lb. The length of the injection and the delay between initiating injection and scanning depend upon the area being examined. For example, an injection for a mediastinal scan may be given over a period of about 1 min. Scans of the liver and pancreas may have injections prolonged over 2 min. The delay after initiating scanning may be only about 10 to 20 sec for the chest, 20 to 30 sec for the pancreas, and 45 to 60 sec for the liver. The reasons for these variable delays depend upon the time of arrival of the contrast in the structures of interest. A 45-sec delay is used for the liver because of the desire to obtain scans only after contrast material is in the portal vein. The long, high-dose injection prolongs vascular and parenchymal enhancement to encompass the complete time of scanning. Using such high doses of contrast medium demands that the patient be well hydrated and nondiabetic and have a serum creatinine level of less than about 1.5 mg/dl. This technique uses up to 55 g of iodine, and doses up to 80 g have been given safely under the clinical conditions described, but toxicity is dose related and discretion should be used in patients with impaired renal function. Our policy is usually to give one-half of the ordinary dose in patients with moderately elevated creatinine or patients on dialysis. No contrast is given to patients with severely elevated creatinine who are not on dialysis.

Modified Dynamic Scan

If a scan rate of more than 4 scans per min is unavailable, the advantages of bolus injection of contrast medium may still be exploited by using multiple boluses of 25 to 30 ml followed by one or two successive scans per bolus timed to coincide with maximum vascular filling. For example, if scans can be taken 30 sec apart, this may permit the bolus to be viewed first in the arterial and then in the portal venous phase on successive scans.

A more commonly used technique involves giving a loading bolus of 30 to 50 ml followed by a rapid, controlled drip infusion of 60% contrast. The use of a pressurized bottle, or a drip combined with a large-bore (19 gauge or larger) catheter helps to ensure a satisfactory drip rate. Scans should be obtained at the fastest rate allowable on a machine without dynamic scanning capabilities.

Single-Level Dynamic Scan

If vascular patency, intravascular thrombus or tumor, or aortic dissection is a clinical consideration, a single-level dynamic scan may be helpful. Precontrast scans should be done to locate the vessel of interest. A series of scans at a single level may then be done after a rapid 50-ml bolus of 60% contrast medium.

DYNAMIC SCANNING WITH THIN SECTIONS

The newer varieties of scanners are much better suited to thin-section dynamic scanning techniques than the older, 5-to-10-sec scanners, because thin sections can be obtained at fast scan times (2 sec) and standard tube output, without sacrificing excellent depiction of anatomic detail. A dynamic series of 20 to 30 slices 3 or 5 mm thick may be obtained without encountering tube heat capacity limits.

To prepare for a thin-section dynamic scan of the upper abdomen, a series of contiguous 8-to-10-mm precontrast scans is usually done. This allows one to select a limited area for thin-section scanning. Thin-section scans of the neck, pelvis, and limbs may be prescribed from the scanogram alone. The thin-section series should be confined to the area of maximum interest and should usually include fewer than 30 slices. When the dynamic series is completed, the unit should be reprogrammed as quickly as possible to complete the remainder of the body region to be studied, usually with 8-to-10-mm slices.

The thin-section scans may be done with 1.5-to-6-mm slices, and the displayed field of view should be optimized for the area of interest as described elsewhere. Most patients can be scanned with a 2-to-3-sec scan even if 3-mm slices are used. The timing of contrast enhancement can be the same as for the standard incremental dynamic scan.

The following is a formal protocol for thin-section dynamic scanning:

1. In many cases (see below for exceptions), a series of low-dose, low-resolution precontrast slices will be done first to localize a small area of interest for the thin-section, high-resolution study:

Matrix size:	Set to provide fastest reconstruction
Scan time:	2 to 3 sec (or fastest available)
mA:	Low, perhaps one-third or less of routine
Slice thickness:	8 to 10 mm, contiguous
Scanned field of view (if applicable):	To include skin contours
Displayed field of view:	To include skin contours

These images will be used to select the area of interest and displayed field of view, to check patient centering, and to help select mA and scan time.

2. Then a *single* precontrast slice should be done through the middle of the newly selected area at the techniques selected for the high-resolution, thin-section series:

Matrix size:	512, standard reconstruction kernel

Scan time:	2 to 3 sec
mA:	Moderate to high, satisfactory for diagnosis
Slice thickness:	1.5 to 6 mm
Scanned field of view (if applicable):	To include skin contours
Displayed field of view:	20 to 35 cm, depending on organs of interest

3. The resident or attending radiologist should view this slice (with image annotation to confirm proper factor selection) to approve the technique for the dynamic sequence. The standard dose of contrast material and timing should be used as selected for the dynamic sequence. Scans should be done in contiguous sections except in special circumstances.
4. Upon completing the dynamic sequence, the scanner should be **reprogrammed as quickly as possible** to complete the nondynamic part of the examination before diffusion and excretion of contrast.

Specific applications of this technique include:

1.5 to 2 mm:	Chest (lung and bronchi) Hands and feet
3 to 4.5 mm:	Chest (mediastinum, trachea) Neck (parathyroid, larynx) Pancreas and biliary system Renal hilum for renal tumors Pelvis (acetabulum, femoral head)
5 to 6 mm:	Adrenals Pelvis (pelvic tumors) Limbs

In cases where the thin slices may be satisfactorily prescribed from the scanogram or previous CT examinations, the precontrast series need not be done. **However, the single precontrast slice through the area of interest at the thin-section technique is still necessary to check technique.**

Scans not requiring low-resolution precontrast series include:

Previous scan available from which slices can be prescribed from the scanogram
Chest
Neck
Pelvis

Although this section emphasizes the combination of thin sections with dynamic scans, the above thin-section protocol may be applied with slight modifications to nondynamic, noncontrast studies.

Scans not requiring intravenous contrast or dynamic scan include:

Chest (pulmonary nodules, bronchi)
Pelvis (acetabulum, femoral head)
Feet

Scans that may be done in noncontiguous sections (e.g., 1.5 mm at 3-mm intervals or 5 mm at 10-mm intervals) include:

Chest (selected)
Limbs
Feet

Scans to be done with bone detail algorithm include:

Chest (selected bronchial cases)
Pelvis (acetabulum, femoral heads)
Feet

In summary, reasons to use thin-section scanning include:

Small area of interest
Complex anatomy
Determination of tumor resectability by subtle anatomic signs
Small bone fragment or foreign body

FILMING

Standardizing the filming of body scans is important to facilitate interpretation. Each scanner has a different method of displaying information about the technical factors selected for each scan, but accounting for these variations, the following should be filmed in a group of images at either the beginning or the end of the scan:

1. Patient labeling information
2. Slice listing information (usually including the timing and technique factors for each slice)
3. Scanogram both with and without slice annotations, filmed on adjacent frames for easy comparison
4. One nonmagnified image with a grid or some form of measurement annotation.

The slices should be filmed according to the following guidelines:

1. Slices in anatomic sequence from cephalad to caudad, whether or not obtained in that order
2. Slices at different window and level settings, for example, for viewing the mediastinum and the lung
3. Slices with special magnification or measurements.

Guidelines for filming of various body areas are as follows:

Standard filming of noncontrast body scans (many contrast-enhanced scans provide only mild levels of tissue enhancement and should also be filmed at these settings):

Window	350 to 500
Level	0

Scans with marked contrast enhancement:

Window	350 to 500
Level	40 to 80

Lung scans:

Window	1,600 to 2,000
Level	−600 to 750

Very thin patients (narrowing the window improves the appreciation of organ boundaries, which are difficult to see in thin patients):

Window	250 to 400
Level	0 to 60

Bones:

Window	1,200 to 2,000
Level	100 to 200

These suggested window and level settings will vary depending upon the scanner and the camera settings, and all settings should be monitored and readjusted accordingly. A single case should be viewed at one or two defined sets of window width and level settings (e.g., at soft-tissue and lung settings). It may be quite confusing to view slices of one patient at multiple soft-tissue settings, unless this is done deliberately to highlight findings on selected images, for example, using additional narrow windows to accentuate liver metastases.

It is important to view lungs at a window of 1,600 to 2,000 because some small pleural metastases are obscured at a window of 1,000. In selected cases, scans of patients with malignancies should be viewed at both bone settings and soft-tissue settings to evaluate areas suspicious for bone metastases. However, filming all images at bone settings is not done routinely. Also, scans of the abdomen including the lung bases should be filmed with lung settings in addition to standard tissue settings.

Scanners with square frames have a standard 12 images on a 14 × 17 film. Other scanners with rectangular frames use cameras that allow a choice of several formats on an 11 × 14 film, or a 15-on-1 format on a 14 × 17 film. We prefer the 6-on-1 format on the 11 × 14 film. Larger images in 2-on-1, or 4-on-1, or 6-on-1 format may be used for displaying in conference rooms.

With some systems, the software and camera permit a convenient format for filming chest scans at both mediastinal and lung settings. The two settings can be switched back and forth instantly by pushing a button. This allows filming each image at the lung setting with the mediastinal setting immediately above or below it on the 12-on-1 format. This leads to a film with alternating rows of lung and mediastinal windows and avoids having to repaint the image on the monitor to film at the second window and level setting.

Dual window capabilities are also available on some machines so that lung and soft tissue can be viewed superimposed on the same image. However, we find these images objectionable because of the distracting edges that appear between structures. The term *dual window* may also apply to placing two images on the same screen and selecting window width and level settings independently. This may save film if the two images fit satisfactorily on one frame.

15

Specific Examination Techniques

This chapter describes protocols for most CT examinations excluding CT of the spine and head, and pediatric CT. Detailed technical parameters for each type of examination for most scanners are not given; rather, the discussions of scan factors are descriptive, with ranges of values suggested. Alternative techniques are often provided with the rationale for their use. Also, scans performed to further investigate previously identified abnormalities may be done differently from those intended to provide new diagnostic information.

It is beyond the purpose of these guidelines to cover exhaustively the reasons for selecting each factor; however, three of the most crucial selectable factors affecting image quality are slice thickness, scan time, and tube output. With most modern scanners, selection of slice thickness usually depends more on the body part being examined and the size of the patient than on which scanner is being used. That is, one approximate slice thickness is likely to be chosen no matter which scanner is used. Exceptions to this rule occur if a scanner cannot obtain good image quality with thin slices. Also, reconstruction time is longer with the older scanners, making the acquisition of more numerous thin slices cumbersome.

Scan time choices are more dependent on the scanner than on the patient. However, scan time choice does require a compromise between the need to minimize motion artifacts and the need to obtain a satisfactory tube output (which can increase proportional to scan time). These considerations vary greatly from scanner to scanner. For example, on older, five-to-ten-second scanners, decreasing scan time may improve image quality with uncooperative patients. With new one-to-four-second scanners, scan time may make little difference for patient motion, although longer scans are needed for high resolution. Because of these differences, specific scan times are not indicated in these guidelines.

Tube output (mAs) selection is the third important selectable factor and depends greatly on the scanner's capabilities. The tube capacity will affect image quality and the ability to perform scans in rapid sequence because tube heat loading units may limit the number of scans obtainable at a specific tube output. Therefore, specific tube output guidelines are also avoided in this chapter.

In the "Scan Factors" section, the term *high-detail technique* is used to refer to a combination of higher than ordinary tube output and/or longer scan time, depending on the scanner.

HEAD AND NECK: NASOPHARYNX

Oral contrast:	None.
Respiration:	Quite respiration.
Scanogram:	Lateral scanogram of the base of the skull and the upper neck. The orbitomeatal line should be perpendicular to the tabletop. The sternal notch may be used as an external landmark.
Slice factors:	3- to 10-mm contiguous scans depending upon the clinical history and the reason for the scan.
Scan factors:	High-detail technique should be used. Motion is not usually a limiting consideration.
Scan extent:	From the hard palate through the temporal bone at the base of the middle cranial fossa.
Intravenous contrast:	Discretionary, but contrast to define tumor texture or nodal metastasis may be helpful.
Comments:	Direct coronal scans are often necessary. A head-holding device or taping the patient's head to the table may be helpful to ensure good examination quality. Because bone metastasis or invasion is often a consideration in nasopharyngeal lesions, one should view the scans at bone and soft-tissue window settings. Some scans of this region overlap with head scanning, which is not covered in this book. Specialized texts should be consulted (1).
Reference:	1. Silver, A. J., Sane, P., and Hilal, S. K. (1984): CT of the nasopharyngeal region: Normal and pathologic anatomy. *Radiol. Clin. North Am.* 22:161–176.

HEAD AND NECK: LARYNX

Oral contrast:	None.
Respiration:	Depends upon the scanner used. With slower scanners, quiet respiration. With faster (2 to 3 sec) scanning, slow inspiration. Other techniques with the faster scanners include phonation of the letter "E" for definition of cord mobility, the modified Valsalva maneuver for distending the pyriform sinus,

and the reverse or inspiratory "E" for distending laryngeal ventricles. The patient should be instructed not to swallow during scanning. A reasonable routine consists of one series in quiet respiration during contrast injection, with a second during phonation when using 3-sec or faster scans.

Scanogram: Lateral.

Slice factors: 3-mm contiguous scans (preferred) or 5-mm scans overlapping every 3 mm.

Scan factors: High-detail technique, favoring shorter scan times. The patient's cervical spine and consequently the larynx should be parallel to the scanning table and the head extended to remove the mandible from the field. If this positioning cannot be accomplished, then the gantry should be angled so that the CT section is perpendicular to the larynx. The smallest reasonable displayed field of view should be used for maximum spatial detail, and the patient should be well centered. This may cause some problems if the patient has a short neck and the shoulders are included in the lowest scans. One may ask the patient to hold his or her shoulders down.

Scan extent: Base of the tongue proximally to below the anterior cricoid cartilage. It is particularly important to monitor the highest and lowest slices of these scans to be certain that the area of suspected involvement has been completely encompassed and to scan farther if one needs to include lymph node groups, which may be involved with tumor.

Intravenous contrast: The policy varies from one imaging center to another. We use contrast routinely, 100 to 130 ml with dynamic scanning. Others reserve it for confusing cases in which it is important to define the exact extent of tumor infiltration and identify small cervical nodes. Contrast should be used when attempting to define stomal recurrence after laryngectomy. Small lesions are more easily defined. Metallic tracheostomy tubes should be removed when this is feasible.

Comments: CT is valuable in defining areas difficult to assess by laryngoscopy, and CT is more accurate than laryngography (1–3). CT may also be helpful for laryngeal trauma. In patients with carcinoma of the throat or larynx, it is particularly important to evaluate the pre-epiglottic fat, the thyroid cartilage, the vertical extent of tumor including the subglottic space, and the presence of tumor crossing the midline. One should film phonation scans at the level of the true cords at lung settings to see the cords themselves.

References:

1. Gamsu, G., Webb, W. R., Shallit, J. B., and Moss, A. A. (1981): CT in carcinoma of the larynx and pyriform sinus: Value of phonation scans. *AJR* 136:577–584.
2. Horowitz, B. L., Woodson, G. E., and Bryan, R. N. (1984): CT of laryngeal tumors. *Radiol. Clin. North Am.* 22:265–279.
3. Mafee, M. F. (1984): CT of the normal larynx. *Radiol. Clin. North Am.* 22:251–264.

HEAD AND NECK: PAROTID OR SUBMANDIBULAR GLANDS

Oral contrast: None.

Respiration: Quiet respiration.

Scanogram: Lateral head.

Slice factors: 3 to 6 mm, contiguous.

Scan factors: High resolution with moderate to high mAs. Minimum displayed field of view to encompass the glands. Head positioning and gantry angulation should be adjusted to avoid dental fillings.

Scan extent: For parotid glands done with axial scans, from the zygomatic arches to below the mandibular angle. For submandibular glands, from the mandibular angle to the hyoid bone. If there is a question about neck adenopathy, continue the scan caudad with 8-to-10-mm sections.

Intravenous contrast: Several investigators believe that scans without intravenous contrast are usually adequate, although contrast almost always helps define tissue detail. We favor its routine use with a dynamic scan with 100 ml of 60% contrast material. This is particularly important if neck nodes are being looked for.

Comments: Parotid CT sialography offers few advantages over routine CT except for difficult cases (1–4). Submandibular sialography may be helpful, and a low-concentration water-soluble agent may be used. Palpable masses may be marked using a small radiopaque device such as a section of thin catheter tubing taped to the skin.

References:

1. Larsson, S. G., Mancuso, A., and Hanafee, W. (1982): Computed tomography of the tongue and floor of the mouth. *Radiology* 143:493–500.
2. McGahan, J. P., Walter, J. P., and Bernstein, L. (1984): Evaluation of the parotid gland: Comparison of sialography, non-contrast computed tomography, and CT sialography. *Radiology* 152:453–458.
3. Rabinov, K., Kell, T. Jr., and Gordon, P. H. (1984): CT of the salivary glands. *Radiol. Clin. North Am.* 22:145–159, 1984.
4. Som, P. M., and Biller, H. F. (1980): The combined CT-sialogram. *Radiology* 135:387–390.

HEAD AND NECK: TEMPOROMANDIBULAR JOINTS

Oral contrast: None.

Respiration: Quiet respiration.

Scanogram: Several types of positioning have been described (1–4). If standard head positioning has been used with images to be reformatted, then a lateral scanogram can be used. If direct sagittal scanning is done, then a scanogram may not be possible because the patient may not be lying on the table. Reference to the cited articles may permit a selection most appropriate for a specific scanner or facility. We prefer not to use the reformatting technique and have used a position in which the patient is placed in a decubitus position with the head against a wedge sponge and angled maximally to lie as close to parallel to the gantry plane as possible. The gantry is also maximally angled with the top of the gantry away from the patient.

Slice factors: High-detail, high-resolution technique with a small field of view centered on the joints.

Scan extent: Through both temporomandibular joints. Scan with mouth closed and open to a point prior to the click. The mouth should be propped open to minimize motion.

Intravenous contrast: None.

Comments: Some centers have used this technique extensively. However, we have done only a small number of such CT examinations. The radiation dose is high, and the setup and examination time are long if not done routinely in the institution; temporomandibular joint arthrography is an excellent alternative study.

References:

1. Manco, L. G., Messing, S. G., Busino, L. J., Fasulo, C. P., and Sordill, W. C. (1985): Internal derangements of the temporomandibular joint evaluated with direct sagittal CT: A prospective study. *Radiology* 157:407–412.
2. Sartoris, D. J., Neumann, C. H., and Riley, R. W. (1984): The temporomandibular joint: True sagittal computed tomography with meniscus visualization. *Radiology* 150:250–254.
3. Simon, D. C., Hess, M. L., Smilak, M. S., and Beltran, J. (1985): Direct sagittal CT of the temporomandibular joint. *Radiology* 157:545.
4. Thompson, J. R., Christiansen, E., Hasso, A. N., and Hinshaw, D. B. Jr. (1984): Temporomandibular joints: High-resolution computed tomographic evaluation. *Radiology* 150:105–110.

HEAD AND NECK: BRACHIAL PLEXUS

Oral contrast:	None.
Respiration:	Suspended inspiration.
Scanogram:	Frontal of the neck from the base of skull to the carina. Arms at the sides.
Slice factors:	5 to 10 mm, contiguous.
Scan factors:	Full or overscans and moderate- to high-detail technique. Large enough scanned field of view to encompass the shoulders. This technique should minimize out-of-field artifacts and other effects that degrade images through the shoulders.
Scan extent:	From C4 to T4 (1). Although scanning with the arms above the head at the level of the shoulders and at the sides below the shoulders may diminish artifacts, but changing from an arms-down position for the neck to an arms-up position for the upper thorax may be confusing.
Intravenous contrast:	Dynamic scan with up to 120 ml of 60% contrast material. Because the dense contrast causes artifacts near the area of suspicion, a contralateral arm injection is preferred. One may also use a 1-min injection and begin scanning from the neck caudad immediately upon completing the injection. By the time the opacified veins are reached, they should be clear of undiluted contrast material.
Comments:	Film upper chest scans at lung windows. Review the scans at bone windows for possible tumor involvement.
References:	1. Gebarski, K. S., Glazer, G. M., and Gebarski, S. S. (1982): Brachial plexus: Anatomic, radiologic, and pathologic correlation using computed tomography. *J Comput. Assist. Tomogr.* 6:1058–1063.

HEAD AND NECK: PARATHYROID AND THYROID

Oral contrast:	None.
Respiration:	Suspended in inspiration. Inspiration is used in these types of scans because the upper

mediastinum is better distended during chest expansion and thus improves visualization of mediastinal masses.

Scanogram: A frontal scout film should be used encompassing the region from above the thyroid cartilage to the hila. It may be necessary to magnify the scanogram or to perform an additional lateral scanogram to better define the superior extent of scanning.

Slice factors: Contiguous scans 3 (preferred) to 6 mm in thickness or overlapping 5-mm scans every 3 mm for the neck; 5- or 10-mm scans for the mediastinum from the sternal notch.

Scan factors: High-detail technique should be used because one is searching for small soft-tissue structures. However, one may degrade views of the mediastinum with longer scanning times. Scans should be reconstructed on a small field of view to optimize resolution. Shoulders are likely to cause artifacts in the area of interest. The patient may be positioned supine in hyperextension with a head holder (1). However, standard supine positioning will detect most adenomas.

Scan extent: For the parathyroid, from the top of the thyroid cartilage to the carina. One may keep the arms at the side for the neck scans and move the arms over the head for mediastinal scans. For the thyroid, from the top of thyroid cartilage to the sternal notch or below if there is a substernal thyroid.

Intravenous contrast: At the radiologist's discretion. We use it routinely. The iodine-containing thyroid is already increased in density over other tissues. However, intravenous contrast may help differentiate blood vessels from small lesions. Use 150 ml, with adjustments as necessary for smaller patients.

Comments: Injecting contrast will disrupt thyroid function studies. Some articles have indicated that the preoperative localization of parathyroid adenomas is clinically useful. This contention is not accepted by many surgeons, however. This test is probably most useful for postoperative cases with recurrent or persistent hyperparathyroidism. Recent work with a radionuclide specifically localized in the parathyroid glands suggests that CT may more convincingly isolate the lesion after the radionuclide scan locates its approximate position. High-frequency sonography is cheaper, easier, and nearly as accurate as CT for detecting parathyroid lesions (1). CT should be reserved for patients with inconclusive or negative parathyroid sonograms.

Reference:

1. Stark, D. D., Gooding, G. A. W., Moss, A. A., Clark, O. H., and Ovenfors, C. O. (1983): Parathyroid imaging: Comparison of high-resolution CT and high-resolution sonography. *Radiology* 148:297–299.

CHEST: MEDIASTINUM, HILUM, LUNG

Oral contrast: None.

Respiration: Suspended inspiration. Inspiration is used because mediastinal structures are better depicted with chest expansion than with contraction during expiration.

Scanogram: Frontal chest.

Slice factors: Routinely, 8-to 10-mm contiguous slices; 1.5-to 6-mm slices for special cases such as to define bronchial lesions (1.5 to 3 mm) or to clarify an equivocal finding of mediastinal, hilar, or aortopulmonary window adenopathy (3-to 6-mm slices).

Scan factors: Short scan times are usually best for the mediastinum to minimize motion artifact.

Scan extent: From the sternal notch to a lower limit depending on the indication. In cases of lung carcinoma, scans should be extended caudad to include the adrenal glands. One may consider extending the scan through the liver because liver metastases are about as common as adrenal metastases from lung cancer. However, if one extends the scan through the liver, it may be scanned after the optimum peak of enhancement and lesions may be obscured. One also may then be obligated to consider such an examination as covering two complete body regions. For esophageal carcinoma, scans should include the celiac axis to detect adenopathy.

Intravenous contrast: Depends upon the reason for the scan and is somewhat controversial. Many feel that scans should be performed prior to contrast administration and contrast given only if there is diagnostic uncertainty after the precontrast examination. However, we believe that contrast should be administered routinely to obtain the best information from the outset. We use a dynamic sequence of up to 150 ml of 60% contrast medium injected over 1 to 2 min. Scanning may begin with a delay of only about 15 sec depending on the patient's cardiac status. Longer delays are better for patients with long circulation times. The dynamic sequence need only be obtained through the mediastinum and the hila, and nondynamic scanning suffices for further slices if the unit will not permit a larger scanning series. A half scan selection may permit a longer dynamic sequence. Lower mAs is permissible in the chest because of the intrinsically high contrast between tissue, air, and fat and because of the decreased absorption by lung.

Comments: Film scans at soft-tissue settings and separately with lung settings with a wide window of 1,600 to 2,000. When scans are requested to detect suspected metastatic disease to the lungs or the mediastinum, a contrast-only technique may still be preferable. As mentioned in the protocol for lung nodule evaluation, there is only a small chance of modifying the interpretation of calcification of a lung nodule because of intravenous contrast. Patients with equivocal results can be rescanned. Nodules will be detected even if not precisely characterized, and the mediastinum and hila will be better evaluated with contrast.

CHEST: LOCALIZED LUNG LESION

Oral contrast:	None.
Respiration:	Relaxed expiration (end tidal volume).
Scanogram:	Frontal chest.
Slice factors:	Contiguous or overlapping thin sections depending upon the scanner and the size of the nodule. A guideline is that the slice thickness should be no more than about one-fourth of the diameter of the nodule or, if the nodule is less than about 5 mm in diameter, the thinnest slice available (1 or 1.5 mm).
Scan factors:	Favoring faster scan speeds. The scanned field of view should attempt to include the patient's body contour so that CT numbers are not artifactually disturbed by tissue outside the reconstruction circle. However, the displayed field of view may be smaller to encompass only the relevant area.
Scan extent:	Images should be monitored closely to determine that lesions have been satisfactorily encompassed without volume averaging or other artifact.
Intravenous contrast:	None. If pulmonary arteriovenous malformation is suspected, this may be diagnosable from the standard incremented dynamic scan. If not, a single-level dynamic scan with 50 to 75 ml of contrast material and rapid scanning should be diagnostic.
Comments:	For analyzing CT numbers of pulmonary nodules see reference 1. However, this is a controversial area. We do not do these types of scans, and others also question the value of the technique. The examination requires control of numerous variables, and most centers successfully diagnose most nodules properly with other techniques or conventional CT (see Chapter 8, p. 93). Another technique that has been developed involves the use of a phantom to simulate nodules. Also, if doing CT for pulmonary nodule attenuation, do not hesitate to study the nodules with thin-section techniques just because a patient has received intravenous contrast. Although the density of the nodule

may be increased, it probably will not be altered enough to change it from the indeterminate to the definitely calcified category. Questionable cases may be rescanned later.

Reference:

1. Siegelman, S. S., Zerhouni, E. A., Leo, F. P., Khouri, N. F., and Stitik, F. P. (1980): CT of the solitary pulmonary nodule. *AJR* 135:1–13.

CHEST: WHOLE LUNG

Oral contrast: None.

Respiration: Relaxed expiration (end tidal volume). This is used because it is the most reproducible point in the respiratory cycle. Thus consistent registration of each slice is more likely than with inspiration scans.

Scanogram: Frontal chest.

Slice factors: Preliminary contiguous 8-to-10-mm sections. Because the lungs are an area of intrinsically high contrast, a lower mAs may be used for the survey sections through the lungs without sacrificing significant diagnostic information.

Scan extent: From the pulmonary apices to the costophrenic sulcus. Care should be taken to examine the entire lungs including the posterior costophrenic sulcus. One of the advantages of CT is its ability to clearly define this area, which is difficult to evaluate on plain films and conventional tomography.

Intravenous contrast: If the sole purpose of the study is to detect and characterize pulmonary nodules, then no intravenous contrast is necessary.

Comments: Reviewing chest films is important prior to beginning the examination. Satisfactory rehearsal and observation of breath holding are more important than the scanning factors selected. The indications for whole-lung CT are somewhat controversial. The yield in patients who are being screened for pulmonary metastases but have a normal chest X-ray is low. The study is valuable for patients believed to have a solitary metastasis. Some of these patients will have small lesions elsewhere, which would eliminate the value of a surgical resection for a presumed solitary lesion. Lungs should be filmed at a window of 1,600 to 2,000. We have seen several cases in which tiny subpleural deposits are seen only on wide-window films. Many of our whole-lung scans are currently done for patients being staged for soft-tissue or bone tumors or for patients with melanoma.

CHEST: AORTA FOR DISSECTION

Oral contrast:	None.
Respiration:	Suspended inspiration. Inspiration is used because breath holding may be required for up to 40 sec.
Scanogram:	Frontal chest.
Slice factors:	8-to-10-mm sections as described below.
Scan factors:	Fast scans are required.
Scan extent:	Two levels should be selected: one section at the aortic root and descending aorta and one at the arch. Preliminary precontrast scans should be obtained to check technique and confirm the location. Dynamic scans should follow as described below.
Intravenous contrast:	Fifty milliliters of 60% contrast should be injected at about 6 to 8 ml/sec, which can be achieved with a rapid hand injection or power injector through a short intravenous 18 gauge catheter. Six scans at each level in rapid sequence should be obtained after the injection. Scanning may begin at or within a few seconds after the beginning of injection. The six scans should be prolonged over a period of about 40 sec. **Bolus injection must be used because dissection may be easily missed with inadequate contrast enhancement.** If the patient has congestive heart failure or another slow-flow state, then the beginning of the scanning sequence may

be delayed. The results of the first scan sequence may be used to check the timing for the subsequent sequences. Following the two dynamic scans at the preselected level, a third sequence of scans with more intravenous contrast incremented through the thoracic aorta should be done to improve detection and map out the intimal flap, if present. Also, new information from the Mayo Clinic indicates that perforated, ulcerated atherosclerotic plaques may clinically mimic dissections and might present with a localized extravasation of contrast outside the intimal layer. Thus the entire thoracic aorta should be scanned to maximize detection.

Comments: If one is simply attempting to define the extent of an aneurysm rather than a dissection, then a simple incremented dynamic scan or a bolus infusion with incrementation may suffice.

ABDOMEN: LIVER, SPLEEN, ROUTINE ABDOMEN

Oral contrast: Oral contrast should be given for most scans unless only a limited area of the liver is being studied to evaluate a change in the size of a known lesion. Give 300 to 500 ml 15 to 30 min prior to examination and 300 to 500 ml immediately prior to positioning the patient on the table.

Respiration: Suspended expiration (see Chapter 15, p. 226).

Scanogram: Frontal abdomen.

Slice factors: Contiguous 8-to 10-mm slices. Thin slices are occasionally used to determine the CT numbers of small lesions suspected to be cysts. However, ultrasound is usually preferred over thin-section CT of the liver.

Scan factors: Tend toward longer scanning times if necessary, depending on the scanner, to allow potential detection of small lesions.

Scan extent: Diaphragm to the inferior tip of the right hepatic lobe. Start exactly at the apex of the diaphragm to include the entire span of the liver. Continue with 8-to 10-mm scans at 8-to

20-mm intervals to the iliac crest for a routine abdominal scan.

Intravenous contrast: Should be tailored to the patient. Dynamic scanning is more sensitive than precontrast or infusion scans. Dynamic scans may be performed as follows:

1. Begin injection of 150 to 180 ml of 60% contrast. Injection should be prolonged for a 2-min period with the first 30 to 50 ml injected rapidly. This volume of contrast is appropriate for an average-sized patient. Reduce the volume for a small patient. A guideline is 1 ml/lb up to 150 lb. We use a CT power injector with settings of 2.5 ml/sec for 50 ml followed by 1 ml/sec for the remaining 100 ml.
2. Begin scanning 45 sec to 1 min from the beginning of injection with the *longer* delay for faster scanners. This permits contrast to reach the portal system prior to scanning. With faster dynamic scan rates of 8 or more scans per min, if scanning is begun too early, then the sequence may be completed even before the peak of enhancement and the early scans may show poor enhancement.
3. Use incremental dynamic scanning beginning cephalad and moving caudad.
4. Allow satisfactory time for breathing between scans. In a normal patient this is 6 to 8 sec; it is longer in a less cooperative patient.
5. After completion of the dynamic component of the examination, complete the study as quickly as possible at a routine scan rate.

For maximum sensitivity both pre- and postcontrast scans may be performed. However, we routinely do only postcontrast scans. If a patient is being scanned in follow-up, and prior precontrast scans have shown a lesion well, then a follow-up precontrast examination may suffice. It is difficult to compare pre- and postcontrast scans because the apparent size of lesions may change.

When liver lesions are suspected but not seen on the images filmed at standard window and level settings, the films should be repeated at narrow windows. Which narrow window width to use depends on the scanner and the size of the patient because too narrow a window will create a noisy image. The range of narrow window widths to use is about 80 to 250.

A tailored dynamic scanning technique is often satisfactory to diagnose hepatic hemangiomata. For examinations specifically designed to determine the nature of a liver mass, a precontrast series of slices may be done with a smaller matrix, fast scan times, and low mAs to speed reconstruction and minimize patient radiation and tube heating.

The lesion thus localized may then be studied with a single-level dynamic scan. At least 75 ml of 60% contrast should be injected in a rapid bolus. Scans may then begin within about 15 sec from the beginning of the injection. Six scans should be done at the selected level over a 45-to-60 sec period. This should be followed by a series of scans every 30 sec for the next 2 min, and more scans every minute for another 2 min. If two lesions are seen at different levels and the computer permits it, one may scan the two levels rapidly in alternation after the injection of a single bolus.

The characteristic pattern of enhancement for benign hemangiomata is the early appearance of a bright, nodular, enhancing border followed by a gradual filling in of the lesion from the periphery. The lesion then usually remains of greater attenuation than the normal surrounding liver until the end of the sequence. In some cases the center of the lesion may never opacify.

Although CT may be satisfactory in most patients with this suspected abnormality, angiography or radionuclide flow studies are good alternatives. Good results have been found in some centers with blood pool imaging with single photon emission computed tomography (SPECT) scanning. The best candidates for CT are those who have solitary, moderate-sized lesions. Small and large lesions may be difficult to interpret.

The ability of the patient to cooperate with breathing instructions is also absolutely necessary. We usually also do another single precontrast slice immediately before we begin the single-level dynamic scan at the level selected from the precontrast series. This is done to check that the patient is not breathing differently or did not move after the first series or when the intravenous catheter was inserted.

Another aid for diagnosing focal liver lesions is the delayed iodine scan. If patients are rescanned 4 to 6 hr following administration of a full dose of intravenous contrast, lesions may be better detected because the liver remains enhanced by hepatic excretion, while the lesions return to normal density (1). This method may be used for questionable cases from the original dynamic scan or may be done after giving additional contrast the day following an examination.

Reference:

1. Bernardino, M. E., Erwin, B. C., Steinberg, H. V., Baumgartner, B. R., Torres, W. E., and Gedgaudas-McClees, R. K. (1986): Delayed hepatic CT scanning: Increased confidence and improved detection of hepatic metastases. *Radiology* 159:71–74.

ABDOMEN: PANCREAS, BILE DUCTS

Oral contrast: From 300 to 500 ml is given 15 to 30 min prior to examination and 300 to 500 ml immediately prior to the study. The contrast dose may be given as the patient enters the room in an effort to have contrast within the duodenum during scanning of the pancreatic head. Additional oral contrast may be given during the examination to attempt to refill the duodenum.

Respiration: Suspended expiration (see Chapter 15, p. 226).

Scanogram: Frontal scan.

Slice factors: For a study to diagnose small masses or abnormalities of the ducts use 3-to-6-mm contiguous slices. For follow-up of known or large lesions, 8-to-10-mm slices suffice, and the entire scan may be done as would a routine liver-abdomen scan.

Scan factors: (See Chapter 14, p. 210). To optimize the use of thin cuts, high-detail technique should be used with longer scanning times if necessary. If maximum resolution is desirable, a small displayed field of view may be used. If this technique is used prospectively (before scanning), one will not be able to evaluate peripheral portions of the liver, spleen, etc. If done retrospectively (after standard reconstruction), one must be careful to save the raw data, which are ordinarily erased. One may need to instruct the computer prior to scanning to save the raw data. Retrospective reconstructions may be time consuming.

Scan extent: Through the entire pancreatic tissue as defined by preliminary precontrast slices or by previous CT scan. These preliminary scans to localize the pancreas may be done with a low radiation exposure of 10% to 30% of normal depending on the scanner. Faster scanning and image reconstruction times may be used. The poorer image quality is usually satisfactory for localizing the pancreas, if not for diagnosing disease. We use a series of precontrast contiguous 10-mm slices through the upper abdomen (see Chapter 14, p. 210). If one would rather attempt to localize the pancreas with fewer slices, the following rules are helpful: Some pancreatic tissue is usually seen at the mid-L1 level. Levels about 3 cm below the left hemidiaphragm and at the L2–3 interspace are often good estimates of the top and bottom of the pancreas, respectively.

Intravenous contrast: Dynamic scanning should be selected as the routine for detecting small lesions or ductal lesions, using up to 150 ml of 60% contrast.

	Scanning may begin 30 sec after the beginning of injection (see Chapter 14, p. 204).
Comments:	Be careful to check the scans at the cephalad and caudad ends. It is common to incorrectly estimate from the scanogram, or, even after scans are viewed, incorrectly assess the lowest position of the pancreatic head, which is usually lower than the novice believes. Thin cuts are particularly important to help define ducts within the pancreatic head. The dynamic sequence can be followed with a standard contiguous 8-to-10-mm scan through the areas not covered by the thin-section study. This should proceed as rapidly as possible after the dynamic scan is completed to take maximum advantage of the contrast injection. The thin-section technique has been valuable for detecting choledocholithiasis as well as small pancreatic or ampullary lesions.

ABDOMEN: AORTA, ILIAC ARTERIES

Oral contrast:	As for a standard abdomen. Rectal contrast if the pelvis is included.
Respiration:	Suspended expiration.
Scanogram:	Frontal view from the diaphragm to the symphysis pubis.
Slice factors:	8-to 10-mm slices at 15-to 20-mm intervals.
Scan factors:	May use a slightly smaller field of view. Otherwise standard abdominal technique.
Scan extent:	Depends on the area of interest. May extend from the diaphragm to the symphysis pubis or from above the aortic hiatus to the iliac crest if scanning a thoracoabdominal aneurysm.
Intravenous contrast:	May use standard abdominal dynamic scan routine, but extending injection time to 3 min may prolong vascular enhancement. Use about a 15-sec delay from the beginning of injection to scanning.

Comments: If an aortic leak is suspected, precontrast scans will help to define fresh hemorrhage by its increased attenuation. CT is usually done for suspected hemorrhage, dissection, or graft infection (1).

Reference:
1. Goodwin, J. D., and Korobkin, M. (1983): Acute disease of the aorta. Diagnosis by computed tomography and ultrasonography. *Radiol. Clin. North Am.* 21:551–574.

RETROPERITONEUM: ADRENALS

Oral contrast: 600 ml (see Chapter 15, p. 231).

Respiration: Suspended expiration (see Chapter 15, p. 226).

Scanogram: Frontal abdomen.

Slice factors: Discretionary and depends on the reason for the examination. Contiguous 3-to-6-mm sections provide better resolution and sensitivity than 8-to-10-mm scans. Thin sections are necessary in a search for small tumors such as aldosteronomas. Most pheochromocytomas and other functional adenomas are large enough to be seen with 10-mm sections. For a pheochromocytoma evaluation, begin with a series of 10-mm sections and follow with 5-mm sections if questions remain.

Scan factors: High-detail technique with longer scanning times if needed, depending on the scanner.

Scan extent: May be difficult to estimate. If 10-mm slices are used, scanning may begin near the diaphragm. For pheochromocytoma evaluation, scans should be extended to below the aortic bifurcation to search for a lesion in the retroperitoneum or organ of Zuckerkandl at the aortic bifurcation.

For lesions likely to be isolated to the adrenals, scans should be monitored to determine the lower extent of the gland. If the kidneys are visible, begin scanning about 2 cm above the upper pole of the left kidney.

For scans limited to the adrenals, such as

aldosteronoma, the glands should be localized with preliminary scans to minimize the number of thin, high-resolution slices. These preliminary scans should be done with a reduced radiation exposure (10% to 30% of normal) and fast reconstruction.

Intravenous contrast: We have decided to use intravenous contrast routinely with our standard dynamic scan technique of injecting up to 150 ml of 60% contrast, unless the patient has had a prior contrast reaction. However, elevation of norepinephrine levels has been reported in patients with pheochromocytoma who receive contrast material (1). Many doubt the clinical significance of this laboratory finding. Occasionally a suspected adrenal mass is a venous varix. Intravenous contrast is helpful to diagnose such cases. Also, other possible lesions will be better detected and characterized with intravenous contrast.

Comments: Do not use glucagon in patients suspected of having a pheochromocytoma. In patients with unequivocally positive chemistries for pheochromocytoma and normal abdominal scans, further scans of the chest or pelvis may locate the lesion.

Reference:

1. Radin, D. R., Ralls, P. W., Boswell, W. D. Jr., Colletti, P. M., Lapin, S. A., and Halls, J. M. (1986): Pheochromocytoma: Detection by unenhanced CT. *AJR* 146:741–744.

RETROPERITONEUM: KIDNEYS

Oral contrast: 600 ml (see Chapter 15, p. 231).

Respiration: Suspended expiration (see Chapter 15, p. 226).

Slice factors: Contiguous 8-to-10-mm slices; 3-to-6-mm slices for small lesions.

Scan factors: High-detail technique for some renal lesions. Standard technique may be adequate for single-level dynamic scanning to determine renal vein patency. However, if possible, high detail is preferred as described below (see Chapter 14, p. 210).

Scan extent: From above the upper poles to below the lower poles for a series of precontrast scans. From the diaphragm to the iliac crest for the dynamic scan. Be careful to monitor superior and inferior scans to ensure that the examination is complete. Also monitor the adequacy of suspended respiration so that areas are not missed.

Intravenous contrast: When attention is directed specifically to the kidney, a series of precontrast scans through the kidney is often helpful. This should be followed by a standard abdominal dynamic scan beginning at the diaphragm with contiguous 8-to 10-mm slices extended through the kidneys. The liver should be included to search for metastases in the lung bases and the liver itself.

When there is a moderate to high likelihood of renal neoplasm, the following sequence is suggested: First, a precontrast series. Second, a thin-section study using 3-to-6-mm contiguous, dynamic incremental scans with contrast enhancement. This may be limited to the area of the renal vein and include fewer than 10 slices. Third, a sequence of contiguous 10-mm sections through the liver and kidneys to follow the thin sections as quickly as possible. If the renal vein has been satisfactorily assessed by ultrasound or inferior vena cavogram, the thin-section series may be eliminated.

Comments: When filming cases in an attempt to differentiate cystic from solid masses, measure the CT numbers of the masses carefully. Attenuation numbers should be obtained from as large an area as possible that is relatively free from artifacts. Use a slice through the center of the lesion. Be cautious when interpreting CT numbers because of the many technical and biological variables that may affect these values. The absolute CT attenuation number is usually the *last* factor to consider in diagnosing a cystic versus a solid lesion.

ONCOLOGIC SURVEY: LYMPHOMA

Oral contrast:	Begin 600 ml 60 min prior to the study and an additional 300 ml immediately prior to the study.
Respiration:	Suspended expiration (see Chapter 15, p. 226).
Scanogram:	Frontal view to include the pelvis to the pubic symphysis, 8 to 10 mm in thickness.
Slice factors:	Intervals of 15 to 20 mm may be used for an initial survey. Scans should be monitored to determine if contiguous slices or more intravenous contrast is required to define questionable areas.
Scan factors:	Standard technique.
Scan extent:	Dome of the diaphragm to the pubic symphysis. If local extent is the only consideration, then only the pelvis may be scanned from the iliac crest down to the pubic symphysis. May need a chest scan.
Intravenous contrast:	Dynamic scan recommended (see Chapter 15, p. 228). We do a contrast-only technique for the initial staging examination. Follow-up studies may be done without contrast if there is a sufficient amount of retroperitoneal fat.
Comments:	Rectal contrast should also be administered. Use 300 to 500 ml of the same solution used for oral contrast. Also, use 10 to 15 puffs of air unless the patient experiences significant pain. A dynamic scan of the abdomen may be followed immediately by a nondynamic scan of the pelvis. On some scanners, slices may be obtained sufficiently quickly that the entire scan may be completed within about 5 to 7 min and visible enhancement of the pelvic vessels remains. If minimal pelvic adenopathy is an important clinical question, one may wish to begin the examination with a dynamic scan of the pelvis. Our technique would simply be a standard dynamic injection with a long (about 1 min) delay before scanning begins using 5-to 10-mm contiguous slices. However, an alternative has been described

as follows: Scans should extend from the aortic bifurcation to the top of the acetabulum in contiguous 8-to 10-mm slices. A rapid bolus of approximately 80 ml of 60% contrast is given, followed by a 90-sec delay. Then a second injection of 100 ml is started, and scanning is begun 30 sec after the beginning of this injection. This leads to satisfactory opacification of both the arteries and the veins.

ONCOLOGIC SURVEY: ABDOMINAL MALIGNANCY

Oral contrast:	600 to 1,000 ml (see Chapter 15, p. 231).
Respiration:	Suspended expiration (see Chapter 15, p. 226).
Scanogram:	Frontal view.
Slice factors:	Depends upon the type of disease. Usually contiguous 10-mm slices through the abdomen to below the kidneys if the site of the primary tumor is unknown.
Scan factors:	Intermediate- to high-detail technique.
Scan extent:	Dome of the diaphragm to below the aortic bifurcation. Depends upon the suspected primary site.
Intravenous contrast:	Dynamic hepatic scanning as described for study of the liver is preferred. Scans may be continued in a nondynamic mode through the remainder of the region to be studied. If any clinical indicators are available to direct attention to a specific organ system, one may wish to optimize the study for that system and survey the remainder of the abdomen with 10-mm slices.

This type of scan is essentially the same as a standard abdomen examination and is used to survey for a primary tumor when malignancy is suspected or when metastases are present from an unknown primary tumor.

ONCOLOGIC SURVEY: PELVIC MALIGNANCY

Oral contrast:	600 ml 60 min prior to scanning and 300 ml immediately prior to scanning.
Respiration:	Suspended expiration (see Chapter 15, p. 226).
Scanogram:	Frontal view to include the abdomen and pelvis to below the pubic symphysis.
Slice factors:	Usually 8-to-10-mm thickness. For pelvic malignancies, which are at high risk to metastasize to the liver, use contiguous slices through the liver and pelvis and 20-mm intervals for the remainder of the abdomen. In an effort to decrease patient charges, we are now doing pelvic malignancy surveys in which we scan the entire abdomen with 10-mm scans at 20-mm intervals, followed by a pelvic scan with 5- or 10-mm contiguous slices.
Scan factors:	When asked to scan the abdomen and pelvis for staging or suspected recurrence of a primary pelvic malignancy, we do dynamic contiguous 10-mm slices through the liver, 10-mm slices at 20-mm intervals through the retroperitoneum and iliac crests, and 5-mm slices through the pelvis from the true pelvic inlet to the bottom of the pubic symphysis. If the abdominal and pelvic scan is for follow-up of a known tumor, we use essentially the same routine, but change to 10-mm rather than 5-mm slices through the pelvis.
Scan extent:	Diaphragm to the pubic symphysis. If local extent is the only consideration, then only the pelvis may be scanned from the top of the iliac crest to the pubic symphysis.
Intravenous contrast:	Dynamic scanning is preferred (see Chapter 15, p. 228). Dynamic scan of the liver and continued routine scanning of the remaining abdomen and pelvis are suggested. The best definition of local disease extent and local adenopathy may be afforded by dynamic scanning of the pelvis with 5- or 3-mm slices. If we are asked to scan the pelvis alone for primary tumor or suspected recurrence, a full

bladder with unopacified urine will decrease artifacts and better define the bladder wall. Therefore, one should not have the patient void prior to the study. If the bladder is empty, begin with a 30-ml i.v. contrast injection prior to scanning, and then wait 5 or more min to provide some contrast filling of the bladder before proceeding with the scan. The scan then consists of a dynamic injection of the remaining available contrast (120 to 150 ml), a delay of 1 min before scanning begins, and scanning from caudad to cephalad using 5-mm contiguous slices through the true pelvis, followed by 10-mm slices through the remaining pelvis up to the iliac crest. (See Chapter 15, p. 237).

Comments: This protocol applies to gynecologic malignancies and bladder and prostate carcinoma. The details of technique should be adapted to the needs of the scan.

About 300 to 500 ml of rectal contrast should be given to patients capable of tolerating it. We also instill about 10 to 15 puffs of air through the type of hand pump used for air-contrast enemas. The amount of air given depends on patient tolerance.

Pelvic and abdominal malignancies may metastasize to bone, and one should view or film scans at bone window settings if there is a strong suspicion (see Chapter 15, p. 237).

MUSCULOSKELETAL: EXTREMITIES, PELVIS, HIPS, SHOULDERS

Oral contrast: None.

Respiration: Normal respiration.

Scanogram: Region of interest.

Slice factors: Determined by the clinical problem. Over large areas, 10-mm slices every 20 mm are satisfactory. Other areas may require contiguous 1.5-mm sections. Adjust slice thickness to the necessity for anatomic detail.

Scan factors: Motion is not a problem, so high-detail

technique can be used. Be careful to include the entire bony area within the field of view to avoid artifacts. When examining bone only, lower radiation exposure can be used because bone has intrinsically high radiographic contrast.

Scan extent: Since many of these examinations are done to determine the extent of lesions, care should be taken to monitor the most cephalad and caudad slices to confirm complete inclusion of lesions.

Intravenous contrast: Depends on the clinical problem, but contrast may be helpful in soft-tissue lesions to better define their extent and any involvement of vessels. Vascular lesions may require injection of intravenous contrast. Dynamic scanning technique may be used.

Comment: When scanning the limbs, usually include both sides so that symmetry may be evaluated. One may wish to attempt unusual positions for coronal and sagittal views of various body parts. Depending on clinical need, film or view slices at both bone and soft-tissue settings to appreciate bony and medullary involvement of soft-tissue lesions and fine calcifications in soft tissues. One may also perform bone detail reconstructions if there is a suspicion of bony involvement.

MUSCULOSKELETAL: SACROILIAC JOINTS

Oral contrast: None.

Respiration: Normal respiration.

Scanogram: Lateral view of the lumbosacral spine.

Slice factors: Contiguous 3-to 6-mm sections. Angle the gantry as close as possible to the long axis of the sacrum.

Scan factors: Motion is not a problem, so high-detail technique may be used such as may be obtained with a bone reconstruction algorithm. However, low radiation exposure suffices because bone has intrinsically high contrast.

Scan extent: Through the synovial portions of the sacroiliac joints as determined by scans. The first scan should be obtained at the midpoint of the sacral axis at the midpoint between the anterior and posterior borders of the sacrum. Scan caudally from this point. This covers the synovial component of the sacroiliac joint. The fibrous component is more cephalad and is normally irregular and wider. The sacroiliac joints usually extend over about 4 cm.

Intravenous contrast: None.

Comments: CT of the sacroiliac joints has been shown to be the most sensitive technique for detecting early joint narrowing and erosions. It is more sensitive than plain films of the sacroiliac joints.

MUSCULOSKELETAL: HANDS AND WRISTS

Oral contrast: None.

Respiration: Normal respiration.

Scanogram: Patient positioning depends on the patient's mobility and the area of interest. The patient may be seated next to the gantry with the hand taped to the table, or may lie supine with the hands over the head. It is often too uncomfortable to lie prone with the arms extended above the head. The hands should be secured with tape to the table and bolstered with sponges to maximize comfort and minimize motion. Depending on the reason, both hands may be scanned simultaneously. For discrete, palpable lesions, generally only one hand needs to be scanned, and this is usually more comfortable. The scanogram should extend through the area of interest, usually in a frontal projection. One may also wish to scan with the hand flexed within the scanning plane. Then the scanogram should be lateral.

Slice factors: Usually 1.5-mm or 3-mm contiguous scans, depending on the size of the lesion or the area of interest.

Scan factors:	Limited displayed field of view. High detail.
Scan extent:	Area of interest.
Intravenous contrast:	Usually a dynamic scan to highlight soft-tissue features. Depends on the reason for the scan.
Comments:	Film at soft-tissue and bone windows. We use this technique particularly to determine the nature and extent of palpable masses. Bone detail reconstructions may be helpful, depending on the reason for the scan.

MUSCULOSKELETAL: ACETABULUM, FEMORAL HEADS

Oral contrast:	None.
Respiration:	Normal respiration.
Scanogram:	Frontal pelvis.
Slice factors:	Contiguous 5 mm. Consider 3 mm or even 1.5 mm in special circumstances, looking for fine detail such as subtle changes from aseptic necrosis or tiny bone fragments. No gantry angulation.
Scan factors:	Limited displayed field of view to include the femoral heads. A preliminary, low-dose, fast-reconstruction scan through the middle of the area of interest helps to check positioning and establish the field of view. Use a bone detail algorithm.
Scan extent:	From just above the roof of the acetabulum to the greater trochanters.
Intravenous contrast:	None.
Comments:	This scan is most often used to detect the position of major fracture fragments and to detect intraarticular bodies.

MUSCULOSKELETAL: FEET

Oral contrast:	None.
Respiration:	Normal respiration.
Scanogram:	The initial series should be done with the patient supine and the feet together and extended, taped to a wedge sponge. A lateral scanogram should be done. A second series should be done with the involved foot studied alone. With this series, the patient

should be lying in the decubitus position on the side of the foot to be studied. The foot should be positioned in passive plantar flexion with slices to be taken parallel to the long axis of the calcaneus. The scanogram should be lateral.

Slice factors: Contiguous 2-to-3-mm scans, depending on the scanner. For supine series, angle the gantry as close to perpendicular to the plantar surface as possible. For the decubitus series, use no gantry angulation.

Scan factors: High detail. Limited displayed field of view. Bone detail algorithm.

Scan extent: For both series, through the relevant tarsal joints. Attempt to use close margins to minimize the number of slices.

Intravenous contrast: None.

Comments: These examinations are usually for tarsal coalition, other congenital deformity, or posttraumatic degenerative changes that cannot be seen with plain films (1,2). Under these conditions, one may film only at bone windows. Reformatted images or three-dimensional reformations may also be useful.

References:

1. Goiney, R. C., Connell, D. G., and Nichols, D. M. (1985): CT evaluation of tarsometatarsal fracture-dislocation injuries. *AJR* 144:985–990.
2. Sarno, R. C., Carter, B. L., Bankoff, M. S., and Semine, M. C. (1984): Computed tomography in tarsal coalition. *J Comput. Assist. Tomogr.* 8:1155–1160.

SPECIAL STUDIES: RADIATION THERAPY TREATMENT PLANNING

Oral contrast: At the discretion of the radiologist. As appropriate for a diagnostic scan if diagnosis is required. None if planning therapy only.

Respiration: Quiet respiration.

Scanogram: Center on the radiation therapy treatment field. The scanogram should also be done in quiet

	respiration. May need both frontal and lateral scans.
Slice factors:	10 mm at intervals designated depending on the region.
Scan factors:	No gantry angulation. Use an adequately large field of view to include the entire body contours.
Scan extent:	To include the radiation therapy field.
Intravenous contrast:	As required for diagnosis.
Comments:	Patients should be positioned on the specially designed radiation therapy treatment planning cushions with a flat surface or on a flat table. The position of the patient during radiation therapy should be duplicated for the CT scan. That is, if the patient is treated prone or supine or with the arms above the head or at the side, this should be reproduced for the CT scan for radiation planning. Inclusion of the entire body contours is important for therapy planning. Most patients will require a separate diagnostic and radiation therapy treatment planning scan. Treatment planning scans are best carried out with the cooperation of and communication with the radiation therapist. We use a brief questionnaire, which is filled out by the therapist regarding the desired positions, extent of the scan, and other factors as noted above. If the scanner is equipped with a program to display tumor outlines on the scanogram (see Chapter 9, p. 113), then this information can be used to adjust therapy ports. One may perform two successive radiation treatment planning scans, the first with proposed ports and the second with modified ports based on the findings noted at the first scan.

SPECIAL STUDIES: LIMITED SCANS FOR FOLLOW-UP

Oral contrast:	Depends on the purpose of the scan.
Respiration:	Depends on the purpose of the scan.

Scanogram:	Depends on the purpose of the scan.
Slice factors:	10 mm contiguous; 10 slices or fewer.
Scan factors:	Comparable to the original scan.
Scan extent:	Through the index area of the previously identified abnormality.
Intravenous contrast:	Depends on the previous scan, but may not be necessary even if only contrast scans have been done before. For example, if the index area is a large retroperitoneal node well surrounded by fat, then contrast may not be needed. However, if the previous index lesion is a vague liver metastasis that has been scanned dynamically before, then contrast will help because it affects the detectability and apparent size of liver lesions.
Comments:	Even though only a few slices are obtained for a limited scan, they should be done in contiguous sections. The purpose of this scan is to follow the course of previously identified disease rather than scan to find new disease. If noncontiguous slices are done, it is often difficult to find slices exactly comparable to the previous examinations, and thus the purpose of the study is defeated. The examination is also designed to save money (we charge about half of what we do for a complete study) and therefore to make the CT more competitive with sonography, which may have serious limitations in following the size of some neoplastic lesions.

SPECIAL STUDIES: PERCUTANEOUS BIOPSY AND DRAINAGE

Comments:	CT-guided percutaneous biopsies and drainage procedures are thoroughly discussed in the radiologic literature. Many variations in techniques, needles, and drainage systems may be used. Although most lesions that can be biopsied or drained are initially detected or best characterized by CT, it is possible to perform the actual procedure under sonographic or fluoroscopic guidance in the majority of cases. The exceptions to this include periaortic and

pericaval lymph nodes and adrenal glands, which are usually biopsied under CT guidance. Both the premium on CT time and the greater ease in monitoring the progress of studies dictate the use of modalities other than CT for the actual biopsy procedure. However, although this is the consensus opinion at this institution, others feel equally strongly that CT is preferred for performing most percutaneous biopsies.

Although discussing the techniques of CT-guided biopsy is beyond the scope of this book, one technical point is worth discussing because it simplifies what is often a time-consuming and difficult procedure. After the biopsy needle is in place, it is a common technique to proceed directly with axial slices to localize the needle tip. This may require taking and sequentially viewing slices until the needle tip is found. If instead needle placement is followed immediately by a scanogram, the needle tip may be seen and a single slice prescribed from the scanogram at the needle tip. This step may save a great deal of time and patient discomfort.

SPECIAL STUDIES: ABDOMEN AND PELVIS FOR BLUNT TRAUMA

Oral contrast:	Depends on the clinical situation. If the patient is likely to have immediate surgery, oral contrast should be avoided. One may wish to avoid oral contrast also because the patients are often severely traumatized. This is usually acceptable because hemoperitoneum is still often detectable and major parenchymal injuries are still easily identifiable.
Respiration:	Suspended respirations if possible.
Scanogram:	Frontal abdomen.
Slice factors:	Contiguous 10-mm slices to below the liver and pancreas and kidneys; 10-mm slices at 20-mm intervals throughout the rest of the abdomen and pelvis to the pubic symphysis.

Scan factors: Faster scanning speeds are preferred. A special effort should be made to remove the arms and any tubes and devices from the scanning field.

Scan extent: Diaphragm to the pubic symphysis as noted above.

Intravenous contrast: Dynamic scanning is crucial. Injection technique should be identical to that for dynamic scanning of the liver and spleen (see Chapter 15, p. 228). The incremental dynamic scan is extended through the liver, and then routine scanning suffices for the remainder of the abdomen and pelvis.

Comments: CT is excellent for detecting intraabdominal injury and hemoperitoneum and to discriminate significant from insignificant injury. A small hemoperitoneum unaccompanied by significant parenchymal injury is often managed conservatively. Some splenic fractures may be managed conservatively. CT attenuation measurements of peritoneal fluid of greater than 45 in an acutely traumatized patient virtually always indicate hemoperitoneum. Be aware of whether the patient has had a peritoneal lavage, which may account for the presence of peritoneal fluid.

SPECIAL STUDIES: PELVIMETRY

Oral contrast: None.

Respiration: Suspended inspiration.

Scanogram: Frontal to include the fetus and the entire pelvis, and lateral of the pelvis.

Slice factors: Single 8-to 10-mm slice.

Scan factors: Very low mAs (perhaps 10% to 25% of the normal CT dose depending on the scanner).

Scan extent: One slice only at the level of the ischial spines.

Intravenous contrast: None.

Comments: Pelvimetry is indicated to help determine whether breech presentation fetuses should be delivered vaginally. The technique described here uses a much lower radiation dose than conventional pelvimetry (1), and is simple, quick, and accurate. Diagrams and details of positioning are indicated in the reference below.

Reference:

1. Federle, M. P., Cohen, H. A., Rosenwein, M. F., Brant-Zawadzki, M. N., and Cann, C. E. (1982): Pelvimetry by digital radiography: A low-dose examination. *Radiology* 143:733–735.

Glossary

This glossary attempts to clarify some of the confusion caused by the inconsistency throughout the radiological literature in the use of terminology pertinent to CT. However, the meanings of these terms will be best understood by reading the relevant sections in the text. These definitions are not meant to be all-inclusive, but rather as descriptions of the terms as they relate to CT.

afterglow An undesirable characteristic of scintillation crystals, afterglow is a short persistence of the flash of light after the crystals are struck by X-ray photons. Because data may be acquired rapidly in sequence before afterglow has ceased, the raw data values must be recalculated to compensate for this effect. Afterglow is not a significant problem with certain detector materials and scanner configurations.

air calibration (*see* calibration)

aliasing artifacts (*see* sampling artifacts)

analog-to-digital converter (ADC) A device that converts a continuous analog electrical voltage signal into a discrete digital signal, which can then be processed by a computer.

angular sampling The angle between which different data samples are obtained. Differs fundamentally between third- and fourth-generation scanners. On a third-generation scanner, the angular sampling rate is determined by the angular increment between successive views and can vary with scan time. On a fourth-generation scanner, the angular sampling rate is fixed and equals 360° divided by the number of detectors.

aperture (*see also* effective detector aperture) An opening. In CT, the circular opening in the gantry through which the patient passes (gantry aperture), or the face of the detector through which X-rays pass (detector aperture).

aperture grid A device placed over a fourth-generation scanner's detector array to partly shield the aperture of each individual detector. The grid reduces the effective detector aperture, improving spatial resolution capability but decreasing the capture efficiency of the detector array.

attenuation A decrease in the intensity of a beam or in the number of photons within the beam, caused by absorption and interaction with matter. Attenuation is an exponential process in which a given volume of tissue decreases the number of remaining photons within the beam by a specific percentage of the remaining photons at that point.

back projection A component of the reconstruction algorithm, back projection is the mathematical method of using raw data to create an image. The detector reading from each ray is averaged or "projected" across the line through which the ray passes in the field of view. All such superimposed ray projections are summed, averaged, and weighted to produce an individual attenuation number for each pixel. Spatial filtration of the raw data is performed before back projection to reduce artifacts.

beam hardening The process of filtration of a polychromatic beam by the preferential absorption of lower energy photons in tissue. This shifts the average photon keV upward.

beam hardening correction Weighting factors applied to CT data to correct for the beam hardening effect. These corrections may be first-order or second-order corrections. First-order corrections are applied to the data initially based on the presumed thickness of the tissue through which the X-rays pass. Second-order corrections utilize the data from the initial reconstruction to further refine the attenuation data.

beam shaping filter (bowtie filter) An X-ray beam filter composed of a material such as graphite, Teflon, or aluminum, which when placed at the X-ray tube more heavily attenuates peripheral portions of the X-ray beam, which pass through the thinner portions of the patient. The term *bowtie* refers to the shape of the filter.

bowtie filter (*see* beam shaping filter)

bulk film loading An option on some format cameras that permits the camera to be loaded with film by electronic rather than manual control from a cassette containing numerous films.

calibration This term has multiple meanings in CT. It may refer to the measurement of body size for the subsequent establishment of the scanned field of view. The term also describes the process used to achieve homogeneity within the field of view and maximize CT number accuracy. Calibration procedures include scanning air or solid test objects simulating water density at various technique factors.

clinically relevant detail Important clinical information in an image, which partly depends on spatial resolution, contrast resolution, and visual perception. This feature is somewhat subjective and difficult to measure. However, receiver operating characteristic (ROC) curves and other similar devices can be used to measure the ability of various observers to detect details in an image.

collimator A device that shields X-rays, shaping the beam into a desired pattern, such as a narrower beam for a thin CT section.

contrast control A control on a TV monitor that primarily affects the display of the white portion of the image. A low contrast setting darkens the white portions of the screen.

contrast resolution A measure of the ability to display structures of slightly differing density. This factor is measured with test objects containing homogeneous structures of slightly differing density. Contrast resolution depends on noise: the greater the noise, the poorer the contrast resolution.

convolution The process of applying a predesigned function curve (spatial filter) to acquire data to modify the depiction of detail. The process involves multiplication of overlapping portions of the filter function and the detector response curve selectively to produce a third function, which is used for image reconstruction.

convolution filter function (*see also* convolution) The specific function chosen that is applied to the data of each view.

data acquisition system (DAS) (*see also* detector channel) The assembly of components that gathers the raw data signals from all of the detectors.

detector A single element of a detector unit or array, which receives X-rays and responds by producing an electrical or light signal.

detector aperture The physical width of the face of a detector, which is sensitive to X-rays.

detector array The entire assembly of detectors including their interspace material.

detector channel The interconnected series of components from a single detector through its photodiode amplifier, analog-to-digital converter, offset and gain correction circuitry, and other components, to its point of entry into the computer.

dual-energy CT The use of two polychromatic X-ray beams of different kVp. Because of the predictable absorption characteristics of various elements at different X-ray energies, the elemental content of tissue can be more accurately calculated, tissue attenuation numbers are more accurate, and artifacts caused by beam hardening can be minimized. However, the calculation process increases image noise.

dual window A method of displaying CT images using two windows at different level and width settings. For example, use of a dual window may permit the display of a chest image that includes lungs viewed at an optimal setting for lungs and the mediastinum and chest wall at settings appropriate for soft tissue on the same image or the same frame.

dynamic range The range of X-ray intensities within which the detector channel produces a signal that is accurate and proportional to the received intensity.

dynamic scanning (*see also* single-level dynamic scanning *and* incremented dynamic scanning) A method of obtaining CT scans in rapid sequence. Also known as rapid-sequence scanning. Dynamic scanning is done either to follow the passage of contrast material through vessels or tissue or to decrease examination time. There is no rigid definition of the frequency with which scans must be obtained to be termed dynamic. However, a scan rate of greater than about 4 per min is a commonly accepted figure.

edge gradient artifact A streak artifact oriented tangentially to a flat surface having a high spatial frequency, such as a biopsy needle or a bone–soft-tissue interface.

effective detector aperture The width of the diverging X-ray beam at a point within the center of the patient as the beam passes from the X-ray tube focal spot to the edges of the face of a single detector. This is calculated as the physical detector aperture divided by the magnification factor.

electronic noise The portion of noise in an image that is introduced by electronic components and electrical interference within the DAS.

EMI unit A previously used unit for measuring attenuation values. One EMI unit equals 2 Hounsfield units. The EMI unit system has been completely abandoned.

environmental density artifact An artifact in which the attenuation value of a specific structure is modified by the density of the immediately surrounding tissue. This artifact is caused by beam hardening.

exposure time The time required to expose an image in a format camera. Increasing exposure time has an effect similar to increasing brightness.

filter (*see* convolution filter function *and* X-ray filter)

first generation The earliest CT scanner design, which used a pencil beam X-ray source and small detectors on the opposite side of the patient, passing simultaneously over the patient in a line. This source-detector assembly then rotated slightly, followed by numerous repetitions of this process. The first-generation scanner design was also termed a translate-rotate design.

first-order beam hardening correction (*see* beam hardening correction)

floppy disk A magnetic computer storage medium that contains a relatively small amount of information, enough only for several images. This medium is portable and convenient but limited in flexibility for CT use.

focal spot The point on the X-ray tube anode from which X-rays are emitted. The size of the focal spot helps determine spatial resolution.

format camera (*see also* multiformat camera) A camera capable of exposing multiple images on a single film. Generally, a single format such as 6-on-1 is possible.

fourth generation A scanner design in which a fan beam of X-rays encompasses the patient, and the tube rotates around the patient while exposing detectors, which are fixed in a 360° ring around the patient. This configuration may also be termed a rotate-only design, as is the third generation design, or a rotate-stationary design.

full scan A scan obtained from a 360° tube rotation around the patient.

gain corrections Compensations for slight variations in amplification of signals from amplifier to amplifier.

gantry aperture The physical opening in the CT scanner through which the patient is moved for the examination.

generation (*see also* first, second, third, and fourth generation) The fundamental geometrical design of a CT scanner. Generations are numbered from one to four in the chronological order in which they were designed. Not all designs are included within the generation terminology, although several types of scanners are variations on the fourth-generation (fixed detector array) design.

half scan (partial scan) A scan acquired when the tube rotates slightly more than 180° around the gantry aperture. The actual arc of tube travel is usually 180° plus the approximate angular width of the fan beam.

hard copy Any medium such as film or Polaroid prints on which CT images are recorded.

hard disk A magnetic storage medium that contains several magnetic platters capable of storing large quantities of computerized information for rapid recall.

high-pass filter A convolution filter or kernel that accentuates high spatial frequency areas such as bone edges, while suppressing differences between structures of low contrast.

Hounsfield unit (CT number) The generally accepted unit for attenuation values within pixels. Zero refers to the value of pure water and −1,000 to the value of air. All other attenuation values are based on these two reference points.

incremented dynamic scanning (IDS) A method of dynamic scanning in which the patient table is moved (incremented) between scans. The purpose is usually to permit maximum opacification of all structures during the injection of contrast material while surveying a specified body region. This technique requires a longer interscan delay than with single-level dynamic scanning because the table must be moved and other software preparations are required.

intensity Energy per unit area per unit time. The intensity of a single photon energy component is directly proportional to the number of photons having that energy.

interpolation A mathematical method of averaging or smoothing images that are being displayed on a larger number of pixels than that for which they were originally reconstructed. If the pixels themselves are magnified, their edges become more apparent and distracting. Interpolation reduces this effect and also permits displaying images at various fields of view on a fixed pixel matrix.

interscan delay The time during a dynamic or rapid-sequence scan between the completion of one scan and the beginning of the next.

kernel (*see* convolution filter function)

kiloelectron volt (keV) A small unit of energy used in radiology to measure the energy of X-ray photons.

kilovolt peak (kVp) The peak kilovoltage applied across an X-ray tube. The peak determines the highest keV photon that can be produced. The average photon energy is lower than the peak value, and the greatest number of photons (the highest intensity of photons) are also at a lower value.

latitude The range of tissue densities that may be displayed on a scanogram image. Certain types of convolution filters applied to scanograms permit a wide latitude of tissue density to be shown without changing window width and window level settings. For a film image, latitude is inversely related to contrast. When images with widely different tissue densities are displayed (a wide latitude), the image contrast between those tissues is low.

leakage radiation Radiation that leaks from the X-ray tube housing in a direction other than that of the primary beam.

linear partial volume artifact (*see* partial volume artifact)

localizer image (*see* scanogram)

low-pass filter A convolution filter or kernel that has the effect of suppressing structures with high spatial frequency and accentuating the display of areas with low spatial frequency or gradual changes in tissue density.

magnetic tape The most common form of long-term storage of computerized image information. Generally, several patient examinations can be stored on a single magnetic tape, which can be kept for up to several years.

matrix The array of rows and columns of pixels. Typical matrix sizes used are between 256 and 512 rows and columns of pixels.

milliAmperage (mA) (*see also* milliampere-seconds) A measure of electrical current through an X-ray tube filament, which is a measure of X-ray photon output per unit of time.

milliAmperseconds (mAs) The product of the current through an X-ray tube filament and the time of X-ray exposure. A measure of tube output for a single scan and therefore related to patient radiation exposure.

modulation A periodic variation indicated by a frequency or wavelength. In the context of the modulation transfer function, it refers to spatial frequency.

modulation transfer function (MTF) A curve plotting spatial frequency on the horizontal axis against a modulation transfer value on the vertical axis. This curve indicates how well an image represents the true spatial frequencies within an object at each spatial frequency. The maximum value for the modulation transfer is 1.0. This curve "function" indicates the degree of accuracy of "transfer" of the modulation (spatial frequency) from an object to the image at different spatial frequencies within the image.

multiformat camera (*see also* format camera) A camera with the capability of exposing various numbers of images on a single film. For example, such a camera may be able to expose either six or nine images on the film by reorienting and changing the size of each image.

multiplanar reformation (*see* reformatting)

noise A point-to-point variation in image density that does not contain useful information.

nonlinear partial volume artifact (*see* partial volume artifact)

nutation Wobbling in a circular motion. The motion of the detector ring in the Toshiba and old EMI 7000 scanners in which the detector ring angles out of the circular path of the X-ray tube.

Nyquist theorem There is a minimum frequency at which an object must be sampled to accurately represent its spatial frequency on an image. The

Nyquist theorem states that a structure must be sampled at least twice its spatial frequency.

offset corrections Compensation for the baseline amplifier current present when there is no X-ray exposure.

out-of-field artifact An artifact caused by the presence of tissue outside the scanned field of view. Such tissue may cause shading of the edges of the field, inaccurate CT numbers, and streaks within the field.

overscan A scan of greater than 360° rotation, usually 360° plus the approximate angular arc of the fan beam.

overshoot artifact (Gibbs phenomenon) The presence of an artifactually low density immediately adjacent to a structure of high density (such as the low-density edge seen inside the calvarium on older CT scanners). This artifact is caused by an error in design of the convolution filter (kernel).

partial volume artifact Sometimes the edge gradient effect is attributed to the partial volume artifact (although not in this text). Partial volume artifact here is synonymous with the volume averaging artifact. The linear partial volume artifact is the inaccuracy in CT attenuation number caused by the presence of a structure within only a part of the slice thickness. The nonlinear partial volume artifact is a streak artifact caused by inconsistency in ray projection data from objects of complex shape and high spatial frequency within a slice.

photon fluence (energy fluence) (*see also* photon flux) The total number of X-ray photons emitted from a tube and striking a unit area during a scan. Should be differentiated from photon flux.

photon flux The number of photons striking a specific area per unit time. Photon flux may remain constant while photon fluence changes with changes in scan time.

pixel A square picture element of a digital image display. Typically, displays consist of 256, 320, 360, or 512 rows and columns of pixels.

polarity In photography, the method chosen to display an image with either a black or a white background. A positive polarity creates a white background on a camera TV monitor, and a film exposed from this monitor thus has a black background. A negative polarity yields the inverse.

polychromatic Literally, "having multiple colors." With X-ray beams, the term indicates that the beam is composed of X-rays of varying frequencies or energies. This is important in CT because the beam is filtered, and therefore its average energy and overall composition are changed as it passes through the patient.

priority reconstruction (priority processing) The ability of CT software to select which slices will be reconstructed first by the computer, independently of the order in which they were acquired.

quantum noise Image noise related to the number of photons or quanta used to construct the image.

quarter offset (quarter-quarter offset) A geometrical feature of a third-generation CT scanner in which the tube and detector are shifted by one quarter of the effective detector aperture from the center of rotation of the field of view. This causes rays obtained at 180° from each other to represent slightly different projections, effectively increasing the number of samples that may be obtained through each point.

rapid-sequence scanning (*see* dynamic scanning)

raw data The values of X-ray detector response from all views and rays within a scan. These data are then convolved with the convolution filter function and back-projected to produce a CT image.

ray The thin beam of X-rays from the tube focal spot to a single detector within a detector array. This leads to a single detector reading. Each view or projection is composed of numerous rays.

ray sampling The angle or spacing between rays in a view. For a third generation unit, ray sampling is fixed by the fan angle, the tube detector geometry and the number of detectors encompassed by the fan. For a fourth-generation scanner, ray sampling is not fixed by geometry and can be increased by taking more data samples as the tube rotates.

reconstructed field of view The field of view actually reconstructed and displayed on the TV monitor. This may be a smaller field than would be possible from the scanned field of view. A synonymous term is *displayed field of view.*

reconstruction algorithm The mathematical method chosen to construct a CT image from the raw data consisting of all the detector readings from all the rays of all the views within a scan. Commercial manufacturers use a filtered back projection type of reconstruction and include other methods within the algorithm such as gain, offset, beam hardening, and scatter corrections.

reformatting (reformation) The process of recreating images in various body planes using a series of original slices. This should be distinguished from the process of reconstruction, which is the creation of an image from originally acquired raw data. Reformatted images are created using data that have already been reconstructed in original images.

region of interest (ROI) An area on a CT image defined by the operator. Usually used for average attenuation measurements, but may also be used to determine area or volume. The region of interest may be in the shape of a circle, an ellipse, a square, a rectangle, or an irregular area as allowed by the machine.

ring artifacts Circular artifacts, usually found in third-generation scanners, caused by faulty calibration or a defect in a detector channel.

sampling artifacts Artifacts caused by the acquisition of too few samples. The presence of sampling artifacts is related to the Nyquist theorem.

scan projection radiograph (*see* scanogram)

scanned field of view For some scanners, the field of view from which raw data are acquired for the reconstruction process.

scanogram An image obtained by moving the patient through the gantry aperture during an X-ray exposure while the X-ray tube remains stationary. The scan projection radiograph appears similar to a plain radiograph and is used primarily for localizing body regions for scanning. Synonymous terms are ScoutView™, Pilot scan™, Surview™, Topogram™, Scanoscope™, radiographic mode, and localizer image.

scatter A change in direction of X-ray photons caused by interaction with matter. Compton (incoherent) scattering is most common with diagnostic X-rays. Scatter leads to additional exposure of the X-ray detector without yielding useful information because the scatter is in a random pattern. The useful information reaching the detectors comes from X-rays that pass straight through the object without interacting with matter.

scatter suppression A decrease in the amount of scattered radiation striking the X-ray detectors. Scatter suppression is accomplished with beam collimation, grids at the level of the detector array, use of an air gap between the patient and the detectors, detector shape design, and use of a prepatient beam shaping filter.

second generation The second popular geometrical scanner configuration to be marketed, in which a limited fan beam of X-rays and a detector array with several detectors (rather than only two as in the first generation) was translated across the patient, followed by rotation and further translation in a repetitive fashion. This is termed a translate-rotate design, as with a first-generation scanner.

second-order beam hardening correction (*see* beam hardening correction)

segmented scans Scan images created from a portion of the data from a full or an overscan. Segmented scans are equivalent to partial scans in quality.

They are done to help follow changes over time such as the passage of contrast material through a blood vessel.

signal-to-noise ratio The ratio of the strength of the signal for information content in the image to the noise level (the standard deviation of the signal).

single-level dynamic scanning (SLDS) A method of dynamic scanning in which several scans are obtained in rapid sequence at a single anatomic level. This is done to follow the passage of contrast material through a specified structure such as the aorta or a suspected hemangioma. This permits a shorter interscan delay than with incremented dynamic scanning.

soft-tissue detail An image reconstruction technique that enhances the depiction of soft tissue of low spatial frequency by suppressing noise and slightly smoothing the image. This is used for target reconstructions or zoom reconstructions and has approximately the same spatial filtration effect as a standard reconstruction.

solarization The process used to create films for use in copying radiographs. Undeveloped films are exposed to high-intensity light. It is a property of the emulsion that, when further exposed to light, such as for a copy exposure, and then developed, the film will yield a positive rather than a standard photographic negative image.

spatial frequency A method to express tissue density changes in space. Abrupt changes in tissue density are represented by high spatial frequencies and gradual changes by low frequencies.

spatial resolution (*see also* modulation transfer function) A measurement of the ability to reproduce detail on an image. Measured by using a test object containing small structures with high contrast, such as small holes in a dense block. Spatial resolution is graphed on a modulation transfer function (MTF) curve.

stray radiation Radiation that is scattered into an area by interaction with matter such as the body of a patient. Considered a factor when determining the radiation dose to individuals near a scanner during operation.

structural noise Image noise related to superimposition of anatomic structures, which obscure the tissue of interest.

survey dynamic scanning (*see* incremented dynamic scanning)

table incrementation The movement of the patient couch to a different slice level during an examination, usually in the context of dynamic scanning for studies in which an entire body region is surveyed rapidly.

target reconstruction (*see* zoom reconstruction)

third generation A geometrical scan design in which a scan beam of X-rays encompasses the patient and is fixed in space to a detector array on the opposite side of the patient. The tube and the detector assembly rotate simultaneously. This is also termed a rotate-rotate or a rotate-only design.

underscan artifact An artifact found on half scans or full scans rather than on overscans. The lack of the additional overscan scan information tends to create artifactual streaks emanating from areas of motion, with the streaks oriented approximately parallel to ray projections that are obtained near the beginning and the end of a scan.

videodisk A magnetic storage medium that can record numerous frames of images for recall. The information is in video rather than computerized form, which eliminates the ability to adjust window widths and window levels subsequent to recording. This form of storage is more like videocassette recording than magnetic disk storage. The advantage of videodisk recording is the more flexible access to the desired images.

view A diverging set of nonintersecting ray samples encompassing a scanned field of view. Also termed a ray projection. These differ fundamentally between third- and fourth-generation scanners. On a third-generation unit a view is composed of all the rays from the X-ray tube that reach the array of individual detectors from a given point in time. On a fourth-generation unit, a view consists of the rays passing through the patient from the tube at different points in time during the scan, which are all projected on the same detector element.

view aliasing artifacts (*see* view sampling artifacts)

view sampling artifacts Fine, diverging streak artifacts in the periphery of an image caused by the acquisition of too few views for an image. Synonymous with view aliasing and view streak artifacts.

view streak artifacts (*see* view sampling artifacts)

viewing monitor A CRT monitor on which images are displayed for visual analysis.

volume averaging artifact (*see also* partial volume artifact) Artifacts caused by the partial projection of a structure into a scanned slice. Depending on the nature of the volume averaging, this may lead to the inappropriate reading of attenuation values or to streaks emanating from the structure in question.

voxel A volume element consisting of the square pixel plus an additional dimension of depth or slice thickness.

window level The CT attenuation number representing the center of a display window. Often simply termed *level.*

window width The range of CT numbers within which the entire gray scale is displayed. Often simply termed *window*.

X-ray filter (*see also* beam shaping filter) Substance used to attenuate and differentially absorb specific energy components of an X-ray beam.

X-ray magnification Enlargements of the projected image of tissue on the detector array. No magnification of the actual image occurs after the data are reconstructed. The magnification factor affects spatial resolution and radiation dose to the patient. This should be differentiated from image magnification, in which a portion of an already reconstructed image is made larger on the TV monitor.

zoom reconstruction Use of a smaller than maximal displayed field of view. This may be centered on the center of the field of view or placed off-center. Used to improve resolution by displaying a smaller amount of tissue over a larger number of pixels.

Subject Index